When Leadership and Spiritual Direction Meet

When Leadership and Spiritual Direction Meet

Stories and Reflections for Congregational Life

GIL W. STAFFORD

An Alban Institute Book

ROWMAN & LITTLEFIELD
Lanham • Boulder • New York • London

Published by Rowman & Littlefield
A wholly owned subsidiary of The Rowman & Littlefield Publishing Group, Inc.
4501 Forbes Boulevard, Suite 200, Lanham, Maryland 20706
www.rowman.com

16 Carlisle Street, London W1D 3BT, United Kingdom

British Library Cataloguing in Publication Information Available

Library of Congress Cataloging-in-Publication Data

Stafford, Gil W., 1953-
  When leadership and spiritual direction meet : reflections and stories for Congregational life / Gil W. Stafford.
    pages cm
  Includes bibliographical references.
  ISBN 978-1-56699-441-5 (cloth : alkaline paper) — ISBN 978-1-56699-441-5 (paperback : alkaline paper) — 978-1-56699-448-4 (electronic)
  1. Christian leadership. 2. Spiritual direction. I. Title.
  BV652.1.S665 2013
  253—dc23

                                                          2013020222

Printed in the United States of America

*To Dr. Catherine Ann Stafford,
my anam cara through over forty years of life together,
with gratitude for her love and perseverance*

Contents

Foreword

My mother used to take me to see my Aunt Bertha, who was a fine lady. The problem was that my mother always told me to kiss her when we got there. Well, as an 8 to 10-year-old kid, I never wanted to kiss anyone, especially an older aunt. When I protested, my mother would say: "Son, you may not want to do it, but you are going to kiss your Aunt Bertha." Don't get the wrong idea; Mama was a wonderful mother who loved me more than I loved myself. She just believed that when you greeted family, you kissed them. So, after she indicated clearly that I was to kiss Aunt Bertha, she would then instruct me on how I could do it to make it as painless as possible. She would say "Now, son, don't make a big deal out of it: just make sure your mouth is closed, your lips are dry, and then just kiss her quick."

The great German sociologist, Max Weber, could call that a means-end rational kiss, that is, if you want to perform a kiss in the most utilitarian way without detours of passion, affection, or just plain love, that is the way to do it. Think of means-end rationality as a straight line suggesting that if you are on the end of that line and that you want to pursue the means that will get you most directly to the other end, then you must move straight down the line to reach your goal without being diverted by other concerns.

Certainly we want some things to operate with this kind of rationality. When I take a shower, I want the hot water to operate in very utilitarian terms, that is, turn it on and very shortly it's hot. But the most important things in life do not operate in these means-end rational ways. For example, when I kiss my wife Peggy,

I do not desire a utilitarian kiss. Seeking the most direct means to get it done may mean that we do not kiss in all the ways that suggest how much we love each other, hold the other in affection, and convey the passion we have for each other. The problem with a means-end approach to kissing is that in a real kiss you want to take a lot of detours.

I think of kissing Aunt Bertha when I read books on church leadership. I often feel subjected to any number of utilitarian means for arriving at goals in the church. These means, however, seem to be extrinsic to the nature and mission of the church. Indeed, any number of these recommendations could turn church life into the flat affect of kissing Aunt Bertha over and over again. Pursuit of the deep things of faith cannot be found in the flat efficiencies of a utilitarian rationality.

But extrinsic, utilitarian approaches to church leadership are not the only problem. I think of authors who basically adapt the leadership discourses, practices, and concepts of corporate America as suitable for use in the church. You would think that the way some church books on leadership take on the language and approaches of corporate America that our capitalist enterprises are doing extraordinarily well and thus deserve imitation. This is strange indeed in a country where for the last forty years we have seen growing inequalities of wealth and income and a decline in the size of the middle class. It is strange when one looks back at the .com crisis, the housing crisis, the avoidance of corporate taxes, and the worst recession since the Great Depression. It is downright abhorrent when one examines how the flow of corporate campaign cash has diverted the U.S. Congress from a concern for the American people. I could also mention the kind of criminal shenanigans that occurred on Wall Street, for which no one has yet gone to jail. This is not an exhaustive list; other violations could be named. The point is that there is too much contradiction between the rapacious capitalism we have today and the Christian faith for the former to serve as models for church leadership.

All of this is by way of saying how much I appreciate this book by Gil Stafford. It is quite simply refreshing, not to speak of moving, to find a book on church leadership so thoroughly oriented around the spiritual practices that enable the community of faith to be an alternative to the culture in which we live. If you would be glad to live the rest of your life and not hear the word "entrepreneur" again, if your flesh crawls when church leaders describe themselves as CEOs, if you have "had it" up to your voice box with people who understand the Christian faith as a business to be conducted in rational, pragmatic ways, you want to read this book.

Tex Sample
Robert B. and Kathleen Rogers Professor Emeritus of Church and Society
Saint Paul School of Theology
Kansas City, MO

Acknowledgments

Leadership and spiritual direction are done in a community of concentric circles. The leader and the spiritual director live with their communities in the inner circle. At times both the leader and the spiritual director may feel isolated and alone as they offer their life and soul to the community. However, while they are doing their work in the inner circle, other individuals and communities in the surrounding circles support the leader and the spiritual director. My experience as a writer has been the same.

My parents Finis and Loretta Stafford were both strong leaders and devout people of faith. They have encouraged me in leadership, spirituality, and in my writing. Monsignor Michael O'Grady and the Rev. Dr. Scott Haasarud have nurtured and guided my soul in blessed spiritual-direction relationships. Over many years I have observed Monsignor O'Grady as the quintessential intersection of leadership and spiritual direction; without him, this book would not have an enfleshed model from which to draw. Down the many roads of my pilgrimage I have been privileged to work alongside some wonderful leaders from whom I have learned so much: my coaching partners, my college-administrator colleagues, and those who are my closest friends in the priesthood. The idea for this book would not have had legs without the many hours of conversations with my dear friend the Rev. Canon Mark Sutherland.

Without St. Brigid's Community and St. Augustine's Episcopal Parish, these ideas would have no life. Were it not for the young adults among whom I live, I would have no spirit. No man could be inspired more by his own children than mine, fierce leaders in the face of a tumultuous world. My thanks to Neil Seabern Stafford and his wife Jennifer Cole, and to Alicia Juliet-Ann Escobar and her husband Phil.

I am deeply indebted to the Alban Institute and their wonderful team for taking a chance on my writing this book and for working with me to its conclusion. No writer writes and survives to be published without an honest, forthright, and caring editor. I am forever grateful to Beth Gaede.

To you the readers, I am overwhelmed with gratitude and amazement, thankful and amazed you would think my writing worth reading. May the God of peace and grace shine the blessings of hope onto all your paths.

A Life of Leadership

Religious faith traditions "build communities, shape lives and tell stories that explain ourselves to ourselves. They frame the rituals that express our aspirations and identities [and they are] the compass of mankind."
—Jonathan Sacks, retired Chief Rabbi of Britain[1]

Sitting in the office of the Diocese of Arizona's assigned therapist was nerve-racking. This was one of the many hurdles I had to clear in the process of becoming a priest in the Episcopal Church. In my first visit to the doctor's office I had to endure a three-hour battery of psychological tests to which every aspiring priest is subjected. If I was not psychotic prior to the six-hundred-question test, asking me in thirty different ways if I had ever thought about murdering my mother (and a variety of other unthinkable acts), I might have been become a psychopath by having been forced to think about such heinous things.

"Should I call you *Doctor Stafford, Mr. Stafford,* or may I call you *Gil*," the therapist asked.

"Just Gil," I said, trying not to show my nervousness.

"I'm curious," she said. "How did you happen to make such a dramatic change in your career, moving from a coach, baseball was it," she asked, flipping through her notes, "to becoming the president of the university? That's a very unusual jump, is it not? And now you want to become a priest. This is very intriguing."

My first instinct was to say, "It's intriguing if you think going twenty-four rounds with Muhammad Ali would be an interesting way to spend an afternoon." However, I did not want to exacerbate any anger issues or other psychosis I had lurking in my shadow side. So I opted for a tamer answer, "Sure, I guess."

She raised her eyebrows. "Well now, maybe you could start from the beginning."

"Is the diocese paying for this session or am I?"

"Why do you ask?" she squinted her eyes slightly.

"Well, I was just wanting to know if I should give you the elevator version or the five-hundred-yard *Shawshank Redemption* version." The therapist gave me a quizzical look. "You know, the movie *Shawshank Redemption,* where Andy escapes from prison by crawling through a sewer pipe 500 yards long."

She said, "The diocese is paying, so why don't you tell me the entire story." So I started from the beginning, she listened patiently, offering healing, for me a cathartic experience.

At age 27, I became the head baseball coach at Grand Canyon University (GCU), a Southern Baptist college in Phoenix, Arizona. I had played five years of professional baseball, coached high-school baseball for three years and had a master's degree. My inexperience in college coaching was questioned in the newspaper. The president's hire, though, was quickly justified. We won the National Association of Intercollegiate Athletics (NAIA) World Series my first two years. By age 33, my teams had won three national championships. I was the head baseball coach and the director of athletics. I thought I had the world by the tail and I knew all the answers to all the questions.

My leadership style was plain, simple and direct. I had two rules for my team and those two rules pretty well extended to the other coaches in the athletics department. Number one, never be late. Number two, do whatever you are told without asking questions.

That system began to break down for several reasons. First, I assumed I held all knowledge. I did not. Second, I assumed everyone would either agree with me or just do what I said. They did not. Simply because I was a successful coach was not a guarantee I was a good leader.

While I deeply cared for my players and other coaches, my methods of leadership were ultimately ineffective because I only had one goal: to win, and a goal is not a vision. I was learning that people are neither sustained nor motivated for long periods of time simply by having achievable goals. People must see a vision connected to a larger cause in order to maintain the hard work necessary to build something worthwhile.

Conflict arose. Failures occurred. Questions set in. I had been coaching college baseball for nine years and was recognized by others as a success. We were winning. But there was a growing gap of disconnection between the team and me. I treated them as a team, motivated them as a team, and disciplined them as a team. The problem was that they were individuals and my once-successful methods were falling on deaf ears.

The pressure increased when GCU moved the baseball program to the National Collegiate Athletic Association (NCAA) Division I. The cost of winning increased exponentially. The baseball team was no longer a powerhouse. Overnight, we went from being a nationally recognized successful program to "Who are you?" Short-term goals needed to be replaced with a long-term vision.

Somewhere buried in the hundreds of leadership books I read was a study suggesting that in order for leaders to change their inherent leadership style, a crisis must occur. Then, if the leader survives the crisis, it would take seven years to adopt a new way of leading. And even then, under pressure, the leader would default to his old ways. Admittedly, this is a harsh and fatalistic view of changing leadership styles. However, there are some kernels of truth to be harvested. I believe leadership styles are, for the most part, learned. (A recent study indicates the genome rs4950 is a leadership indicator. However, while DNA has a role in determining some leadership qualities, the researchers still pointed out that learning how to lead was critical.[2]) Hopefully, in order to change we do not have to be crushed by crisis. But without some perceived need to change, what is the motivation? From my own experience, I think that taking on a new leadership style does require motivation, significant time, and committed hard work.

When the baseball program at GCU began to slip into obscurity, I undertook the hard work of reinventing my leadership style. I read books on leadership. Some of my reading was from successful coaches, but most was from the business sector. I also took courses on conflict management, consensus building, and organizational development. I attended workshops on leadership, and I consulted with respected leaders. Over the course of a few years, what emerged was a better educated and well-trained leader equipped with some new ideas about coaching, the dynamics of leadership, and institutional change.

The new "me" as a leader felt primed to implement the renaissance of my style. I had been a college coach and administrator for fifteen years. The winds of change started to blow. First, a new baseball player arrived at GCU: my son. My chemistry of coaching was about to change once again. The presence of my son presented the obvious realization that every one of the young men on the team could be my son. It changed how I looked at these 18- to 22-year-olds. My son was good enough to be a college player, but he was not an every-game starter, so he spent a lot of time on the bench. How I interacted with the team as a whole and the players as individuals began to shift. I had a good and loving relationship with my son, which had a distinctly positive influence on how I saw myself as coach and leader. Second, the university was going through a period of significant financial stress, which led to a leadership upheaval during the subsequent five years.

While maintaining my job as head baseball coach, I was thrust into a variety of high-level administrative roles within the university. The institution went through two downsizing reorganizations within a three-year period. In the first year, two jobs were morphed into one and I became the vice president of student affairs. The second year, three jobs were meshed into one and my new title was vice president for administration. The third year the institutional administration was reduced to the president, the provost (in charge of all academics), and me as executive vice-president (in charge of everything not academic). As I will mention later in this book, at this time in my life, religiously and spiritually I was moving away from being a Southern Baptist.

As a leader, I was being pressed upon from every angle. I was learning about the finances of higher education and facility management through a baptism of fire. Storms were brewing on every horizon from institutional trauma, donor demands, and church politics. I was working sixteen-hour days, seven days a week. Every night's sleep was a series of brief naps interrupted by waves of panic about the potential failure of the institution. I attended a Harvard summer institute of higher educational management, a program for grooming future college presidents. The leader as CEO was held up to me as the model to emulate. I was reinventing my leadership style once again.

A few months prior to my becoming the president, the university had lost its meager endowment in the collapse of the largest non-profit bankruptcy of the Baptist Foundation of Arizona (BFA), a subsidiary arm of the Arizona Southern Baptist Convention (ASBC). GCU was also a subsidiary of the ASBC.

On January 1, 2000, after serving twenty years at GCU, I became its ninth president. That particular day was supposed to be Y2K, the day of computer meltdowns. Some even predicted the end of the world. The day passed as just another "normal" New Year's Day with the only significance being that we had entered a new millennium. Personally, my inner being was trembling about the unknown world of my new job.

On January 14, 2000, the board of trustees of the university, under the advisement of legal counsel, separated from the ASBC to protect itself from anticipated ascending and descending liability due to the BFA bankruptcy. Also, under the advice of counsel, the board and I were instructed not to disclose the reason for this separation with the expectation of litigation.

Separating from the ASBC became a real estate transaction. Several years prior, the university was granted permission by the ASBC to sell any property it had received in donation. In 2000, the board used this bylaw as the means of selling itself to another entity, a newly created 501(c)3, Grand Canyon University, Inc., with the same board members and corporate officers as GCU. A Southern Baptist college once under the auspices of the ASBC was now an independent Christian university.

The ASBC called an emergency meeting to which I was summoned. Legal counsel instructed me not to answer any questions revealing the reason or method of the school's separation. Five hundred people showed up for the meeting held at North Phoenix Baptist Church (a megachurch of the Southern Baptist Convention). I was alone on the platform. None of the board members attended and our legal counsel stayed at the back of the room, incognito. There were two microphones made available for those who wished to speak. At first, the questioners were frustrated by my unwillingness to give them a plain and simple answer. Then many became angry and vented their angst at me.

As a professional baseball player, playing in small towns, in obscure leagues, I had learned to endure the insults of unruly and often drunk fans. As a college baseball coach I had stood on the baseball fields of Arizona State University, Texas Tech, and the University of Texas, and withstood comments from fans notorious for saying rude and unsavory things to coaches. Through my baseball years, though, I had not been subjected to anything as personally humiliating as the day I stood before the Arizona Southern Baptist Convention.

Now I was the president of a university whose constituents and alumni were confused and angry. I was the president of a university whose faculty was upset because they had to endure a "coach" as their president (whom they had no voice in selecting). I was the president of a student body that was distrustful of me. Rumors were swirling that I was not really a Southern Baptist, but instead, something dangerous, a Catholic.

I spent a lot of daily time praying and searching the scriptures for solace and direction. During those early days I was reading Bennett Sims's *Servanthood: Leadership for the Third Millennium*.[3] The image of Maundy Thursday and Jesus washing the feet of the disciples was dominating my thoughts. For my inauguration as president that spring, I asked the dean of each college to choose one student to represent them and also to choose one dean among themselves to represent the faculty. As a central part of the inauguration I washed the feet of those students and that dean; it was the image I wanted as the starting place of my leadership as president.

However, too much change, not enough time, very little constituent buy-in, and less financial backing, were all a recipe for failure. In 2003, Grand Canyon University, Inc. was near the point of filing for bankruptcy. On December 31, 2003, four years to the day after becoming president, I resigned. In the spring of 2004, GCU was sold again, this time to a for-profit corporation. (As I am writing this, GCU is thriving with 35,000 students and a beautifully remodeled campus.)

There was no golden parachute. There was no silver, bronze, or lead parachute. There was not a parachute. I was unemployed, broken, and hurt. I swore to myself that I would never again lead an institution. But my mother used to tell me never to say "never."

In December 2005, I was ordained an Episcopal priest.

A few months later I received an unexpected call from the Canon to the Ordinary, who provides counsel to the bishop. "Gil, the bishop wants to see you, immediately."

"I'm free most of tomorrow."

"He has an opening in an hour."

It was a hot, August Thursday in Phoenix, Arizona. Actually, every August day in the desert is hot, only now it seemed blistering.

I had been an ordained priest in the Episcopal Church less than six months, serving as the chaplain for the Episcopal Campus Ministry at Arizona State University (ASU). Now, I was scrolling my memory for what tragic miscue I had committed, warranting my summons within the hour.

The bishop's office is on the second floor of a historic house next to the Cathedral in downtown Phoenix. I was escorted into a conference room next to his office and sat on one side of a long, oak table for ten. I stood as he entered. We shook hands and he seated himself opposite me, across the imposing table.

"Well," he said, leaning back in his chair. "I have a no-brainer for you, Gil."

I felt like I was trapped in a packed elevator, stuck between the twelfth and fourteenth floors. Authority claustrophobia had arrested my breathing. Whatever the bishop said from this point on demanded I had to agree. If I disagreed, I thought, I was suggesting I was empty headed, or worse, he wasn't intelligent. I was not going down the latter road.

"It was obvious to me that your lifetime of work as a college baseball coach and college president has made you the natural person to be our chaplain at ASU."

I smiled in agreement. The ministry had been a good fit for me because I had been able to connect to students and faculty alike.

The bishop continued. "I have made some changes at Saint Augustine's in Tempe. The church used to be considered a university parish, being so close to ASU, but they have gotten away from their roots. It's time for a change. I want to combine your job as campus chaplain with being the vicar at the parish. Normally, I would ask you to prayerfully consider the position, but I need an answer right now. I want you at the parish Sunday morning."

I must have nodded affirmatively, or moved in the chair in such a way that the bishop saw what he wanted from me.

"Good," he said.

This part I remember with perfect clarity. "What advice can you give me?" I asked.

He said pastorally, "Just love the people."

"Just love the people" sounds like a pretty straightforward assignment. Surely I can do that, right? Just love the people, a good directive for a leader, the priest, for two communities, surely?

What I have discovered over my years of doing this work is that I do not wake up in the middle of the night worrying about how to love these people, though maybe I should. Instead, unfortunately, I find my sleepless nights are consumed by fretting about how to meet the financial demands of the parish, or wondering why more college students do not attend our Thursday night gathering, or struggling with how to ensure that the parish numbers continue to grow, or worst of all, agonizing over issues regarding the preschool.

Of course, I really find out what troubles me the most when I start to plan a vacation: Are the service bulletins ready? Will the supply priest get her check on time? Will the preschool director have a major meltdown? Will the junior warden remember to lock up after the third service, since he attends the second service? These are the "devil in the details," as a former senior warden used to tell me—and these are the distractions that keep me from living out my purpose of loving the people. This frustrates me into an anxious moment filled with private cursing.

What to do? I have searched for models, examples, and mentors to guide me. This book is the story of the search to stay focused on my purpose of loving the people and to be less distracted by my midnight demons of details and past failures at leadership. Once again, I found myself about the task of reinventing my way of being a leader.

Finding a model that describes how to bring together a tiny aging parish with a fledgling Episcopal campus ministry was virtually impossible. I talked to colleagues, searched the Internet and dug deep. Very little appeared.

My first inclination was to lead the two communities as separate congregations, parallel congregational development. They did not know each other, and their age difference was vast. The few members who attended the parish eight o'clock Sunday morning service were old enough to be great grandparents to the students in our ministry. The regulars at the ten o'clock service could have been the young adults' grandparents. The only bridge between the Sunday congregation and the campus ministry was my presence.

I learned quickly that the parish had been founded in the late 1940s by a few faculty, staff, and students who attended Arizona State University (then Arizona State Teachers College). The infant congregation met at a tiny chapel in the middle of the college campus. With hard work, sacrifice, and a grant from the Episcopal Church, the congregation bought property a few blocks south of campus and built the parish hall with volunteer labor. They worshipped in the parish hall for ten years while raising money to build the current sanctuary. The congregation's vision was to be a university parish, a church with its life in and among the ASU community.

The parish vision had fallen cold some years before I arrived. But a faithful remnant of those founding members still attended the eight o'clock service. They saw my arrival as the bishop's affirmation of their original concept. The parish began to breathe once again.

But I was still left with the task of discovering a game plan to combine two seemingly disparate ways of working. The first work was to create holy space for the caretaking of a generation in its last season of life, in other words to be a gentle "hospice-worker" priest. The second work was the pastoring of a generation of seekers and questioners; this is the role of a "mid-wife" priest. As much as I tried, I was unable to find a book describing how to lead such an institutional animal. Now after a few years of failures and some successes I am ready to share what I have learned.

I set out with the intention of writing this book without using the word *leader.* Surely, I thought, I can find a new or better term, because, frankly, I am exhausted from discussions about what makes good leaders and what kind of leaders we need for the future. I even had the notion that our scriptures, or at least Jesus, did not make any reference to a leader. Of course, I was wrong. John 10:3 set me straight: "The gatekeeper opens the gate for him, and the sheep hear his voice. He calls his own sheep by name and leads them out." The shepherd is the leader.

So, then, how does the shepherd lead? The sheep follow the shepherd because they know the voice of the leader. The shepherd has a distinctive voice and knows the name of every member of the flock. A relationship exists between the shepherd and the sheep. "I know my own and my own know me" (John 10:14).

Over time, I discovered that embedded in the craft of being a spiritual director were the skills I needed to be a shepherd, both as a hospice-worker and as a mid-wife pastor.

The four roles of the spiritual director I believe apply to pastoral leadership: the spiritual director as (1) steward of sacred safety, (2) holy listener, (3) the advocate of silence, and (4) wisdom teacher. Most of the work of spiritual directors can be understood through the lens of one or more of these roles. Because these roles of the spiritual director are fairly universal to the field, I am convinced that the church leader can express these roles through church business, pastoral counseling, the ministry of presence, preaching and teaching, and congregational discernment.

In chapter 1, "The Integration of Leadership and Spiritual Direction" by using my experience and research I will make the case that the reader should spend time with yet one more book on leadership, a book about the shift in how the congregational leader approaches every aspect of her work through the influence of spiritual direction.

Angela Reed's *Quest for Spiritual Community: Reclaiming Spiritual Guidance for Contemporary Congregations* gives evidence that the ministry of pastors is broadly affected when they are trained in spiritual guidance, the label she uses for spiritual direction. Practicing spiritual direction impacts the pastor's preaching, his casual interaction with parishioners, how he conducts business meetings and how often he refers people to counseling.[4]

In my years of leadership I have earned plenty of scars. However painful it may have been to acquire the scars, they are, at least, evidence of healing in my leadership trials. The mending is a sign of my willingness to imagine ways of reinventing effective leadership without acquiring any new "badges of honor."

My spiritual director guided me through this arduous process of reflection in order to reconnect with my original sense of purpose and calling as a way of going forward. He and several authors on spiritual direction have had a significant influence on my thinking about a leader's purpose and work.

Albert Camus (1913–1960), French Nobel Laureate, wrote, "A person's life purpose is nothing more than to rediscover, through the detours of art, or love, or passionate work, those one or two images in the presence of which his heart first opened." This is the work of a spiritual director: to spiritually walk alongside another person and to assist him in the rediscovery of the passions of his life.

Through my years of spiritual direction, both as directee and director, I have become convinced that spiritual direction can be a wellspring for congregational leaders. Those four roles of the spiritual director: as the steward of sacred safety, as holy listener, as the advocate of silence, and as wisdom teacher, deserve serious consideration because they are the foundation of subsequent chapters.

After the groundwork of the four roles of spiritual directors is established, subsequent chapters will draw upon the roles of the spiritual director for applications in the life of congregational leadership.

Ch 2

Chapter 2, "The Leader as the Steward of Sacred Safety," stresses the vital role of the leader, as in the relationship of spiritual director and directee, in providing a safe environment for the congregation. When a directee arrives at the office of the spiritual director, he expects her office to be a place of safety and confidentiality. Feeling safe is critical for the spiritually and emotionally wounded, as well as everyone else. The spiritual director and leader, while keeping to the tenets of her faith, is nonjudgmental, nonthreatening, and does not wield authority or power over the directee. People who gather in congregations also have the expectation of the church being a safe place. "The name of the Lord is a strong tower; the righteous run into it and are safe" (Prov. 18:10). The congregation has every right to demand that church leaders be the representatives of God. And the tower of the church must be a safe place to which church members can run. In too many unfortunate situations, trust in congregational leaders has been broken so that they must now work with extreme vigilance to restore what was lost. To regain trust, congregational leaders must provide children and adults a physically, emotionally, and spiritually safe environment in which to worship, learn, debate, explore, and play. With vigilance, every church leader can incubate physical, emotional, and spiritually safe communities. Leaders promoting safe practices in the parish will be, by example, encouraging parishioners to be participants in creating a "feel good" space. A community with a safe feeling is also one that is inviting and hospitable, contributing to the development of a flourishing community.

Ch 3

Listen 1st
& 187R

Chapter 3, "The Leader as Holy Listener," takes on the primary work of a leader guiding her congregation through spiritual direction. The best advice I received when starting a new job was to avoid making any changes for a year. Instead, I was told to spend my time listening to the people. After much listening, reflection, pondering, asking the "I wonder" question, and finally, given time, I could respond. Even parishioners who "are looking for a new direction" do not want change to be immediate. Congregations do not want a leader who "shoots from the hip" or gives "knee-jerk" responses. Instead, a leader who takes time listening will comfort the congregation. The work of the spiritual director can be a deep wellspring for the congregational leader who desires to improve his listening skills and practices.

Chapter 4, "The Leader as Advocate of Silence," considers the congregational leader who can be the advocate of silence in her parish. Silence will be the fertile ground for the transformative work of the Holy Spirit in the community. Various kinds of silence, instead of frightening, can actually be the leader's moments of creativity. My experience has been that this list could include the *metanoia* of silence, the milieu of silence, pregnant silence, vulnerable silence, paradox of silence, the ethics of silence, the ferment of silence, the crucible of silence, the stress of silence, and the disruptive ringing of silence. These different encounters with silence can be found in the natural rituals practiced in the worshipping community and in the not-so-comfortable task of conducting the business of God. The leader who is the advocate of silence will be an ear of the Holy Spirit in the life of the congregation.

Chapter 5, "The Leader as Wisdom Teacher," will explore the teaching and preaching practices of the leader. The leader who intentionally sets out to establish himself as the wise leader or sage is creating a dangerous recipe for failure or the creation of a cult. Positions of communal honor, like wisdom teacher, usually are placed upon the leader after a lifetime of service. The purpose of this chapter is to encourage the leader to emulate the spiritual director's role of wisdom teacher and storyteller, rather than to provide answers or solve problems. Storytellers can be wisdom teachers without ever offering advise or counsel. Sue Monk Kidd suggests that by our becoming storytellers, we will discover and shape our personal story, thereby "enriching God's universal story." Stories are the lifeblood of our reality. Stories move us through the extent of our emotional capacity. Stories let us escape and at the same time stories confront us with the existential pain of our existence. Without a story, we are without a life.

In chapter 6, "Leadership in the Discerning Community," the four roles of the spiritual director will coalesce as a wellspring for the congregational leader. There is a picture in my office of two men in a boat towing a house across a body of water. The picture was taken in the 1920s by an Anglican priest in Newfoundland.

The Canadian government had displaced his village. But instead of leaving their homes, the people moved every building across a strait between the mainland and Newfoundland. The priest, Father John, was the great uncle of my friend Kim. She gave the picture to me as an ordination gift. Her great uncle kept the picture in his office as a reminder that people are always in the process of making decisions and journeying. As a priest, his calling was to help in both circumstances. He was not called, he said, to make the decisions or do the work of the journey. That, he said, was the work of the people. Chapter 6 will offer some practical applications of Father John's truth. The "fetching," or calling, of assisting a people of faith in discernment (decision-making) and journeying, is the summation of the four roles of spiritual direction and will be the culmination of this book.

When Leadership Meets Spiritual Direction: Stories and Reflections for Congregational Life is not just another book about leadership. Nor is this a book about the leader being the spiritual director for an entire congregation. By following the example of a spiritual director, this book is simply making an offering of thoughts, reflections, stories, and experiences for the congregational leader.

Through my stumbling toward the ideal of leading as a spiritual director, I have become deeply indebted to my dear friend Mark Sutherland, Canon Pastor at Trinity Episcopal Cathedral in Phoenix, Arizona. He has been my conversation partner in this leadership pilgrimage and he has also introduced me to the work of Martin Thornton.

Thornton (1915–1986), an Anglican priest, theologian, and author of the late twentieth century, wrote of a pastoral theology that has begun to give me a language for this practice of leadership. Throughout this book I will refer to Thornton as well as others who have informed my ideas and praxis.

The purpose of this book is to outline the methods used by spiritual directors that can build the capacity of any leader. No leader can be the spiritual director for an entire congregation. But the spiritual leader can emulate the shepherding qualities of Jesus as seen through the practice of a spiritual director.

While on a pilgrimage across Ireland, those first few days of walking, while carrying my forty-pound backpack up and down the Wicklow Mountains, were a strain. There were times when I wished I were not carrying my pack. I thought often about how much farther I had to walk and when the long journey would be over. But after a few days I found my best daily rhythm and discovered a comfortable pace. I even realized my pack had become a part of me. When I set it down for a break, and then walked without it, I got dizzy. Without the forty pounds on my back, I lost my balance. Indeed, my body had incorporated the extra weight and I needed the pack for stability.

Taking on a new model of leadership will be difficult in the first leg of the pilgrimage—even to the point that it feels like a weight you might want to put down. But with time, your leadership "body" will find the "pack" filled with a new purpose that will be the stabilizing weight helping you find the rhythm and pace of your walk as a spiritual-director leader.

ONE

The Integration of Leadership and Spiritual Direction

The pilgrim is beginning to travel more by dark faith than by precise standards. And this can be frightening at times . . . serious pilgrims look for guidance from others. They seek out and listen to the help God makes available to them.
—Francis Kelly Nemeck and Marie Theresa Coombs[1]

"How did a college baseball coach become the president of a university?"

"Well," I say. "That's an interesting story. It is like a long-running soap opera, a series of episodes, sometimes connected, sometimes not."

The next question is usually, "How in the world did you make the leap from president of a Southern Baptist college to an Episcopal priest?"

"Well . . . ," I say laughingly. "Such a leap is a series of episodes, going from high expectations, to misunderstandings, to bad circumstances, to worse possibilities. And then it cycled back again, day after day, until I finally listened to the fetching voice of God instead of the voice in my head telling me to run far, far away."

Leadership is episodic, says Hugh O'Doherty of Harvard University.[2] Being a leader is also a series of failures, missteps, misfires, and, hopefully, enough successes to inspire. Having coached college baseball for twenty years, been the president of a small university for four years, and now a parish priest and college chaplain for seven years, I am convinced that leadership is indeed an episodic series of intense and critical moments of decision-making. At these junctures, hopefully the leader will be able to exhibit a personal capacity for holding tension. The leader will need the courage to risk her authority. Together, the leader and the people risk being vulnerable. Leadership requires the inner strength to walk across the abyss of uncertainty, time and time again, and to lead a group of people into a new garden of possibility, which is sometimes found in the desert.

Leadership also requires a deeply felt belief in, and connection to, a sense of personal purpose. Someone might say the purpose of a college baseball coach is to win games. Or the purpose of the university president is to raise money. Of course, the parish priest's purpose is to grow the church numerically. However, these are mere functions of the job, not a purpose. Frankly, the same person doing these three different jobs, at different points in time, may well have the same personal purpose across each scene of life, for purpose is found in the integration of spirit, soul, mind, and body. And while leadership may be episodic, what stabilizes the chaos of the stress is the non-anxious spirit of the leader, which is tethered to a well-tested and formed purpose.

As the head baseball coach at Grand Canyon University, I had experienced the height of success and the depth of failure. Three times we won the National Association of Intercollegiate Athletics (NAIA) National Championship. With my leadership the university transitioned from the NAIA to the NCAA Division I. At one point my team finished with the worst won-loss record (14–42) in the NCAA Division I. However, the following year we qualified for the Western Athletic Conference Championship and were awarded the turn-around team of the year. Was it a mistake to leave the NAIA for NCAA Division I? The answer depends on whom you ask.

During the first few days of my tenure as president of GCU, the board of trustees voted to separate the university from its owner, the Arizona Southern Baptist Convention (ASBC). Five years later the university board voted to sell the university to a for-profit company in order to avoid bankruptcy. Was either action a success or a failure? The answer to that question is debatable.

If the purpose of the coach is to win games and the purpose of the university president is to raise money, then moving from the NAIA to NCAA Division I was a failure, and separating the university from the ASBC and the eventual selling of the university was also a mistake. Of course, if you believe the purposes of the coach and president are the obvious (winning games and raising money), then to suggest otherwise is simply an attempt to make a case for the deflection of responsibility or the transference of blame. If you believe that, you should probably stop reading at this point.

Through years of spiritual direction, Jungian therapy, and the eye-opening three-year experience of the Clergy Leadership Project, I came to recognize my purpose as a coach was not to win games, nor as a university president to raise money—and my purpose as a parish priest is not church growth. When I fall into the mode of wanting to take full responsibility for the perceived destruction of Grand Canyon University, my Jungian therapist always asks me to look at my hands for the signs of any nail prints. A messiah-complex is not a purpose—it is a neurosis, or at the least a dangerous hearing of the "calling" of the Holy Spirit, for there was, is, and ever will be only one Jesus who is called the Christ.

Purpose is what sustains the leader in the face of a weary soul, moves the leader forward when encountering seemingly insurmountable obstacles, and grounds the leader when the waves of chaos deem to throw her out of the boat. Purpose is not a vision statement or a mission statement and definitely not a strategic plan. A purpose is not a goal. A purpose may not be achievable in a lifetime. Purpose is not a big hairy audacious goal. Purpose is holy and sacred and could be as mysterious as a sacrament. Purpose is how one "lives, moves, and has his being" in the world. Purpose may not be definable, but it is observable. To use Anglican author and priest Martin Thornton's words, those without the eyes to see may miss the obviousness of the leader's purpose, while those in the inner concentric circle, those who are a part of the remnant group, those who feel the force of the purpose, will, without a doubt, experience it.

Purpose is like the calling of a lover that fetches the leader to climb again the sheer face of a mountain from which they have just fallen. Purpose is the core essence of the leader's soul motivation. And more often than not, purpose will be found in the leader's dark night of the soul. Purpose will be the golden thread woven through the heart of every episode of the leader's lifetime of shepherding the flock.

The leader's purpose must also be intertwined with her personal work. The leader's personal work must be differentiated from the functions or tasks of her job. My purpose is to be present in my spirit to God, who is present in my work and me. My work, then, is to be a window for others to see the same potentiality and possibility of connection with God in their lives. My job as vicar of the parish and chaplain for campus ministry includes countless functions and tasks, including leading meetings, budget preparation, countless reports, and endless paperwork.

The ideal is when my purpose and my work become one with my way of being. I become an integrated, non-dualistic soul, living my life in God, who is in me. In other words, when I am in the flow, every part of my work and every function have their proper place and priority. My work is the actualization of my purpose in a palpable reality that will be experienced by others. Writing is my work. Spiritual direction is my work. Praying is my work. Living into the life of a mystical Christian is my work.

Functions, however, are the immediate tasks that are part of our daily responsibility. There is nothing inherently wrong with the functions we are obligated to engage in. A function, however, will need an appropriate response, dictated not by the loudness with which it screams, but instead by its value relationship to my purpose and work. This may often be determined by the whispering of those souls who need tending, shepherding, or care, along with the concomitant stilling of the screaming function. This prioritization of decisions should be made in the process of silent reflection and prayer, not in the guilt of demand or the expectation of others.

Integration of purpose and work in the life of the Christian leader looks like this: two lovers gazing eye-to-eye in the intimate stare, hands locked, fingers interlaced, palm-to-palm—as if nothing in the world can come in between this moment of intimacy. Time stands still. God and me, face to face, my consciousness connected at the unconscious level to the very consciousness of God—deep intimacy—pure contemplation. Nothing can come between us. My purpose and work are in rhythm with the Holy.

But, alas, it seems something is trying to pry our hands apart. Is it evil? No. Worse, it's something insidious—it is the well-meaning, the good, the mundane, and the immediate, which is the most seductive, something convincing me the sacrifice of my soul's energy is worth the cost—it could be the "anything" of doing good deeds. The well-meaning function will break my contemplation of the true fetching of God to my specific purpose and work in life. Dealing with the functions of life requires prayerful attention in relationship to my purpose and work in order not to get sucked into the dryness of the mundane.

This pilgrimage of leading out of my purpose, committed to my true work, is a leading through the lens of spiritual direction. The way of leading by spiritual direction is a difficult journey. This way asks us to walk slowly, allowing the integration of our being into the Being of God, our collective souls living in the soul of God, who is in each of our souls. It is a holy pilgrimage.

A portion of leadership is artistry. Much of spiritual direction is a charism. The artistry and the charism meet in the transept of the creative work of the heart. The work of the heart is the "seeing through the third eye of the heart," the mysterious place of the new and the now, the seen and the unseen, where the possibility of the divine within the community can emerge. Leadership influenced by spiritual direction is the seeing into the soul of the community, the soul of the communion of saints. The leader sees into the soul of the community as a way of being diligent and attentive to the ongoing restoration of the community—the restoration into the irrevocable fetching of being in union with God.

Spiritual direction is typically thought of as a one-on-one relationship between two individuals. In some instances, spiritual direction may be conducted as a group activity, still relying on a mode of "what's best for the individual." However, leadership as the art of spiritual direction is a medium of the collective, seeking to discern the will of God for the community. In congregational life, the leader guides, using spiritual direction, incorporating the methods of preaching and of teaching spiritual direction in every aspect of life together. This includes the obvious situations of pastoral care and counseling and, just as important, leading meetings, and making organizational and business decisions. The pastor will see responding to e-mail, and even casual conversation, as a time for offering spiritual direction. The leader will live out the calling, or fetching, of being in the mode of mentoring leadership development through spiritual direction at every opportunity. Practicing spiritual direction impacts the pastor's preaching, casual interaction with parishioners, how he conducts business meetings, and how often he refers people to counseling.

My own experience of being in spiritual direction has afforded me the privilege of witnessing and learning from some wise and experienced folks who have lived life as if they were offering spiritual direction to every person they meet. A thirty-second exchange with the coffee barista can turn into a two-minute spiritual direction moment.

Martin Thornton, the Anglican priest, wrote about the practical leadership of the parish through spiritual direction in several works from the 1960s until his death in 1986. In his books, *Feed My Lambs: Essays in Pastoral Reconstruction,*[3] *Spiritual Direction,*[4] and *The Heart of the Parish: A Theology of the Remnant,*[5] he outlines the setting for spirituality and direction in the life of the congregation.

Thornton's ideas on individual, small group, and congregational spiritual direction incorporate the artistry and praxis of coaching athletes. However, he differentiates the goal of spiritual direction from the goal of coaching. In *Feed My Lambs*, he writes, "The ultimate Christian goal is not purity of heart [the perfectly trained athlete] but the vision of God."[6]

The vision of God is experienced ontologically in the intimacy of the heart and the integrated soul, in conjunction with the Spirit.

Spiritual direction is the action of the guide (coach) listening to the needs of the individual, assisting the soul in ascertaining its place in the mystical body, and equipping the soul in its navigation and the negotiation of its relationship between the community and the world. The pilgrimage of the soul travels toward a life of the spirit with the Spirit, sacramental in practice, and integrated (non-dualistic) in worldview.

Thornton states in *The Heart of the Parish* that the health of the integrated soul and the clarity of the vision of God will depend upon "the health of prayer [individually and corporately] which in turn depends upon its adequacy of the conception of God."[7] The capacity of the conception of God is expanded then through the existential experience of the sacramental life (Mass, corporate worship, and the Daily Office).

The work of the leader and the congregation, says Thornton, is to develop the maturation process of "soul-making." Soul-making, he writes, is the spiritual progression of a life of discernment, strengthening the courage to choose in the face of the risks of decision-making. This maturely developed capacity of soul decision-making is based upon the Christological theology of the self-forgetful risk-taking of God in the incarnational act. In *Prayer: A New Encounter*, Thornton writes, "Risk and make your soul . . . for [this] way of decision [making] requires greater responsibility and more developed powers of discernment than ever before."[8]

Leadership is episodic while spiritual direction is a way of life. Decision-making, the risk of soul-making, then, is the intersection of leadership and spiritual direction. It is in this crucible that I would like to explore the potential alchemy where leadership and spiritual direction meet. But, before exploring the junction of spiritual direction and leadership, we must first understand the nature of the spiritual director.

"Why do I need a spiritual director?" my young friend asked.

"Did you walk the five-hundred miles of Camino de Santiago in Spain, alone?" I asked.

"Yes," she answered.

"You didn't walk with anyone else on that long journey?"

"Well, yeah, I did, actually, most every day," she said.

"Did you ever stop and ask for directions?"

She laughed, "Okay, so a spiritual director is going to tell me which road to take when I'm lost?"

"No," I said. "The spiritual director will ask you which road you feel attracted to. Then he will ask you why you feel this is the way to travel. If you ask him, he might share some story about a similar time when he came to a fork in the road. But you have to decide which way to travel. It's your pilgrimage. The spiritual director is there to pray and ask the questions so that you may open the way for the Holy Spirit to be your guide."

Spiritual direction is the willingness to walk alongside my young friend in the pilgrimage of her life. The director cannot carry her pack. Nor can he tell her the way to walk. He can only share his experience of the pilgrimage. She may choose to hear his stories, adjust her course, and look for the roadside markers. Or she may decide to ignore the director. Spiritual direction is an offering to walk with someone, nothing more.

On December 6, 1995, I wrote in my journal about having breakfast with my good friend and pastor of the Southern Baptist church I was attending. I had been a lifelong Southern Baptist and was working at a Southern Baptist college. The preceding five years had been a spiritual struggle. I was wrestling with God and the conservative theology I had grown up with. I had deconstructed my theology to the point of agnosticism. Yet, strangely, I still ached for a personal experience of God. My study of the scriptures and my theological reading had left me empty and without a language to express the disconnect between my intellectual agnosticism and the longing of my heart.

My pastor, a wise and gentle soul, suggested it was time I consider spiritual direction. He told me he personally did not know how to give me such guidance but recommended I read Thomas Merton's *Spiritual Direction and Meditation*.[9]

I stopped at the local bookstore on my way to work and bought a copy. Later in the week a friend at work was in my office and saw the book on my desk. She remarked about having read Merton's work. Tentatively, I told her the short version of my spiritual angst. "You need to meet Father Mike," she said. I asked for his number. Instead she picked up the phone on my desk and began to dial. When the person on the other end of the phone answered, she said, "Father Mike, I'm sitting here with my good friend Gil Stafford. That's right, he's Canyon's baseball coach. I really think it would be great if you could meet with him. Sure, I'll put him on." She handed me the phone.

Father Mike has been my spiritual director ever since that day. His soft Irish accent and brilliant blue eyes are the reflection of his loving soul. I told him I wanted to give up on God and he said, "I know," and then asked me to pray Psalm 103 for a season. I told him I needed to "really experience" the God I was praying to and he said, "I know." With his cup of coffee and muffin he began to explain the holy eucharistic meal. I told him I wanted to become a Roman Catholic and he said, "I know," and suggested I slow down. Father Mike walked by my side during the final years of my college coaching career and through the tumultuous times of being a college president. He continued to pray with me and for me as I left the college and my career and stepped off into unemployment. He encouraged me through the discernment process of becoming an Episcopal priest.

Spiritual direction is the experience of a patient, prayerful relationship where two people trust each other to work together with God, at the soul level, on the most important matters of life. The Irish call this spiritual companionship the relationship of the *anam cara*, the soul friend. The *anam cara* is the one who walks with your soul in the pilgrimage of life.

Spiritual director Thomas Dubay writes, "What then is spiritual direction? It is the guiding of a person into life truly under the dominion of the Holy Spirit . . . assisting to advance on the path of prayer—the road to union with God. Given the sublimity of this task, it is easy to see why in the tradition it has been called the *ars artium*, the art of arts."[10]

Spiritual direction endeavors to integrate the whole person in her relationship with God, with others, and with herself. The artful work of the spiritual director will engage the questions of prayer, the study of scripture, spiritual reading, journaling, fasting, as well as dreams, visions, vocation, occupation, personal relationships, the practice of social justice, self-care, and other topics of spiritual growth and formation. The list will depend upon the pilgrim, the directee, and the skills of the spiritual director. This delicate work with individuals must be conducted with the full expectation of confidentiality, both from the director and the directee. With the exception of legal requirements, both parties in the relationship must be able to rely on the sacred safety of confidential conversations. If confidentiality is violated, trust will be broken. When the relationship is honored in a healthy manner, the realm of spiritual conversations will open to a broader horizon of spiritual growth. Richard Foster in *Celebration of Discipline: The Path to Spiritual Growth* writes, "Spiritual direction is concerned with the whole person and the interrelationship of all of life. . . . Spiritual direction takes up the concrete daily experiences of our lives and gives them sacramental significance."[11]

The sacramental significance of which Foster writes is the work of the Spirit of God spiritually forming the individual soul. Spiritual direction is the participation of the directee with the Holy Spirit, assisted by the director. Being spiritually formed is yielding to the molding hands of God in our life. "Yet, O Lord, you are our Father; we are the clay, and you are our potter; we are all the work of your hand" (Isa. 64:8).

A friend of mine is a ceramist. I love to watch her work at the potter's wheel. She controls the speed of the wheel with a pedal at her foot. With one hand inside the clay, the other on the outside, she forms the clay into a piece of art. It takes pressure on both sides, she says, to shape the pottery. I have also watched her stop the wheel and throw the clay back onto her table, to begin again. "The clay isn't cooperating with me," she tells me. There are multiple stages when the clay is in control, she says; in the formation, how it takes the color, and in the firing. "You just never know," she says. That's the mystery of the work.

This is also the mystery of the work of the spiritual director, the risky work of the ancient art. The spiritual director is not the "Holy Spirit, Junior." The Holy Spirit of God is the potter. The directee is the clay. The spiritual director is the wheel, spinning at the guidance of the Spirit. The clay can choose to cooperate with the Spirit or not. The director is simply assisting with the formation.

The potter's wheel will be spun at various speeds with the expectation of creating a variety of artistic effects. The spiritual director will need to be in tune with the moving and work of the Spirit in order to adjust to the formation that is taking place within the soul of the directee and the director's soul as well. Participating with God in the formation process of another's soul can be exhilarating, exhausting, troublesome, and frightening, but done under the care of the Spirit, it is a most holy experience. To do such meaningful work, the director must constantly be attuned to the subtle and shifting roles she must play in soul formation.

Let's look more closely at the four roles of the spiritual director. While this is not exhaustive, it is representative of the comprehensive work of the director. These roles are intended to be the path we will walk throughout this book. It has been my experience that these roles can be used as a wellspring from which the congregational leader could draw.

The Spiritual Director as the Steward of Sacred Safety

"So, you're not going to tell me which road to travel?" he asked.

"No," I said.

"Well, what if you know I'm going to take a dangerous road? What about that?" he asked.

"My responsibility is to be the steward of sacred safety," I said.

"What does that mean?"

"It means that I am bound as a spiritual director to honor your dignity by respecting your values and your choices. I am a steward of your trust. In order for you to make appropriate decisions, I think you need to feel safe in this office. I must work so that you trust I am a safe person for you to be with. By my maintaining appropriate boundaries, by never taking advantage of you in any way—physically, emotionally, or spiritually—I can build an environment of safety for you. At that point you can be able to make the best choices for yourself. In other words, your safety is a sacred trust for which I am a steward."

"You're not going to let me walk down the wrong road, are you?" he asked.

"Hopefully, I will ask you enough questions about the dangerous road, before you make a decision. But the choice is still yours. I can only shine a light down the path as far as my spiritual flashlight will shine."

The spiritual director cannot expect the directee to trust him in the first meeting. As a spiritual director I cannot rely on my reputation. I must build trust with each new person. I must earn the directee's trust. I have to continually hold sacred the responsibility of maintaining a safe space for the directee.

One way to build trust is by establishing reasonable boundaries. The director might be old enough to be the directee's father, but he is not his father. And clearly, the director should not be the directee's "best friend," but instead a spiritual friend. The spiritual director is there to provide prayer and counsel. These appropriate roles and boundaries can help establish a trusting and safe relationship.

The spiritual director cannot depend on her position of authority as a sign that she is a safe and trustworthy person. She must continually be vigilant, working to establish reliable and dependable markers that she is indeed the keeper of the directee's sacred safety. She must provide spiritual direction only in appropriate venues. All conversations within spiritual direction are held in confidence (abiding by the requirements of the law and the church, of course). The director is careful to hug or touch only a directee who offers the hug first, and in the manner the directee chooses. Common sense should be the director's guide. But even that seems to fail at times.

In these post-9/11 times, our society lives in a state of fear. Those who come to spiritual direction hope the director's office will be a safe place. The spiritual director must do everything in her power to respect the dignity of every person and to keep the directee safe while in her care.

We know that some leaders have violated that expected trust and that countless numbers of people have felt the loss of that trust. We have witnessed the devastating effects of sexual misconduct in many churches, among college coaches who have violated young boys, and among teachers who have had inappropriate contact with students. Yet every spiritual director, clergy person, school teacher, and administrator, and every other person entrusted with someone's dignity, considers himself the keeper of sacred safety. Nevertheless, we still read of this trust being broken again and again. The point here is to reiterate and reinforce the sacred responsibility of the leader to respect the dignity of every human being.[12] Sometimes our generational background, gender bias, and cultural preferences need to be reeducated and retrained.

In the Episcopal Church all lay and clerical leaders, including spiritual directors, must take regular courses in *Safeguarding God's Children*, as well as classes in anti-racism and workplace ethics. Like most classes concerning appropriate behavior, anti-racism, and ethics, what we learn from them is a matter of common courtesy. However, the church leader cannot take it for granted that every other leader in the church completely understands his or her hidden bias, prejudice, or generational frame of mind.

The spiritual director must be circumspect when it comes to the spiritual, emotional, psychological, and physical safety of all of her directees. No sexual harassment, inappropriate conduct, or misbehavior can be tolerated from the spiritual director or from leaders of the church. The safety of God's people is the sacred trust of the leader.

A safe environment will be the seedbed of spiritual growth in the life of the individual who is in spiritual direction. The same could be said for the community that exists in a safe environment. When parishioners know the church leadership will work to gain trust and keep confidentiality, the people then can begin to build trust with each other. A community where the feeling of safety exists will be inviting and hospitable to the newcomer. The first-time visitor will often remark, "This place feels like home." The church and all its agencies are a significant part of God's home and every parishioner and newcomer should expect and feel God's home is a safe and sacred place.

THE SPIRITUAL DIRECTOR AS HOLY LISTENER

Prior to a directee's arriving at my office, I work and pray to create a safe place for him so he might better process the story of his life and work on his decisions through discernment. In order for him to progress, I must listen.

From scripture we hear good counsel for the spiritual director: "Let everyone be quick to listen, slow to speak" (James 1:19). And from the Apocrypha (Sirach 11:8): "Do not answer before you listen, and do not interrupt when another is speaking." Holy listening means adopting the value that truly listening to another's words is more important than a verbal response.

"Maggie, tell me your story," was how I began our first session. She talked almost without breathing for an hour, as if she had not been listened to in years. Finally, she stopped, stared at me, and gave an enormous sigh. We sat in silence and she began to cry. "Let it out," I said. Eventually the crying ceased, then it was time to let her rest, relax, and recover.

Listening may be the most important of the four roles of spiritual direction. After the directee feels safe, she can begin to open up in the presence of the quiet listening of the director. Listening is a gift of hospitality. It is also exhausting work. Listening with full attention is draining because it requires all the senses, psyche, emotion, and intellect to be focused on another person. I set aside my thoughts in order to focus on the speaker. I do not think about what I am going to say next until I am asked a question. I have to take time to process my response. During emotional and spiritual conversations of this kind, holy listening will necessitate moments of silence for reflection.

As the spiritual director, I have relinquished my thoughts for an hour in order to make room for Maggie's words. In listening to her, my body feels her abandonment. In listening to her, I smell her loneliness. In listening to her, my eyes absorb the sadness of her tears.

After listening to Maggie, and letting her finish completely, I try to repeat key phrases of her story in order to assure her that I have indeed heard her. Then I will follow up with open-ended questions about her story. "Maggie, you told me you haven't spoken to your mother for seven months because your last conversation with her was an angry one. And then you phoned your mother at Thanksgiving. But she never returned the call and that really hurt you. Why do imagine your mother didn't call back?"

Holy listening can evoke further opportunities for reflection on Maggie's part. If she can hear her story repeated back to her, given some time to ponder, she can then construct her response to the issue at hand. Maggie may not know for certain why her mother did not return the call, but her speculations will help her sort out her feelings and determine what she wants to do next.

To become a better listener, I take time to imagine God listening to me. We hear in the scripture that God listens to us by self-emptying in order to make room for the words of our hearts. My words are poured into God's chalice, mixing my thoughts with God's holy wine. God drinks in my words, allowing those words to become a part of God's being. God feels the tears in my eyes of grief. God carries me, feeling the weight of my burdens. God hears me at the depth of my core and God settles there with me. When I imagine this, I feel God is listening.

God is the epitome of patient, holy listening. God hears me at the deepest levels in spite of the irregularity of my prayers, my prayers in an emergency, and my prayers of desperation. God listens to me and to everyone else at those moments. When I make hospital visits, I am graphically reminded of the infinite capacity of God to listen to a universe of prayers. God is forever mixing the prayers of the universe into heaven's sacramental wine so that God might taste all the grief, pain, and anguish of our collective words.

Can I listen like God? Not with the depth and intensity of God. But can I be the listening ear of God for the person who has come to me for spiritual direction? Can I listen with intensity to the person who follows Maggie's appointment? This is the calling of the spiritual director, to be the listening ear of God to every person who seeks spiritual direction. With practice, the capacity to listen grows within the spiritual director, even to the point where the hospitality of listening can be extended in other conversations outside the office. By practicing holy listening I have been moved to regard every encounter as an opportunity to provide spiritual direction, every phone conversation, every e-mail, and every casual conversation in the hallway; even every moment of saying good morning is a moment to listen with holy ears. The spiritual director learns to be a holy listener, making internal space to hear what is being said, as well as what goes unspoken.

While holy listening requires a tremendous amount of personal energy in one-on-one settings, the demands on the leader intensify within group settings. The idea of group spiritual direction is to afford people the opportunity to share personal experiences of God with others. By sharing in a small group, facilitated by a trained spiritual director, the individuals may discover new and unfamiliar ways in which God speaks to people. Directors who lead these types of small groups require specialized training, due in part to the skills needed for listening to six or eight people process individualized concerns in a group context.

Group rules for speaking and responding are necessary. In some groups I conduct, we use a figurine, typically a "Weeping Buddha," with the rule that you may only speak when you are holding the Buddha. The figurine is passed around the circle allowing for silence between the speakers. The second rule is that you may not respond directly to what the previous person said; you may only tell your own story or ask an open-ended, wondering question of the previous storyteller. Hopefully, this prevents the next person from the temptation to "fix" another person or provide a "better way of thinking." Using these simple rules, the director, without taking notes, will better be able to repeat individual story lines and ask personal questions for clarification. I have found in my groups that if my body language mirrors the speaker, my hearing is more profound and my recall is sharper. In these situations the spiritual director is modeling effective listening skills. Individuals, in small groups like these, have often commented how they have learned to practice listening skills and subsequently used these skills in their relationships with a spouse, partner, or work colleague.

Holy listening can be learned and improved with practice. Whether listening to a person in a one-on-one conversation or listening to a group, the spiritual director will use the practices described above. And these techniques can be adopted and used by leaders in relationship to individuals and congregations.

THE SPIRITUAL DIRECTOR AS THE ADVOCATE OF SILENCE

I showed up on time for my regular session of spiritual direction. There was a lot on my mind and as soon as my spiritual director asked how I was feeling, I spewed a stream of words for thirty minutes. I stopped to breathe. My spiritual director sat there, looking at me, smiling, and saying nothing. I wanted to break the silence. I looked at the floor. I shifted in the chair. I looked up at my spiritual director and he was still smiling at me.

"If I didn't say something, how long would we sit in silence?" I asked.

"Until you are ready to speak," he said. "I'm holding the silence, the tension of the silence, for you, for us, for God. If I hold the tension of the silence, then we can hear what God is saying. We need the silence and the tension."

"I don't understand what you mean by the tension of the silence, is that the same as being uncomfortable because I don't like the quiet?" I asked.

"We need to move beyond describing a situation as something I like or don't like. The question is why do you feel tension in the silence? What makes you uncomfortable in the silence? Where is the dis-ease coming from? What in your interior is resisting the quiet and instead making room for the chatter in your head and in your heart? You want to break the silence, why? Do you want to get up and leave, why? Are you considering not coming back for another appointment, why? Do you think the questions I am asking are creating tension? Or is the silence creating the tension? Which is it?"

I remained silent, acknowledging to my interior that I was filled with tension, dis-ease, and discomfort.

"By why the tension?" I spoke again. "Wouldn't it be better if I were comfortable in the silence?" I asked.

"The tension is anticipatory. If you're comfortable with the silence, you might go to sleep," he chuckled. "Most people are unwilling to remain in the silence because they don't want to deal with their thoughts, conscious emotions, and physical feelings, much less what might arise from the unconscious. If the air is filled with noise, then there is something to distract me from listening to you and God. I am holding the tension created by the silence. You evidently want to disturb the silence. Therefore, I will keep silence. I will hold the silence for both of us. For if I hold the tension of the silence, I can anticipate that God is going to speak to us. How much better might we hear if we both held the anticipatory tension in the silence? That's why I'm an advocate for silence."

Hugh O'Doherty can hold silence better than anyone I have met. He is a professor at Harvard and faculty member of the Clergy Leadership Project (CLP) of which I was a participant. Our CLP class consisted of twenty-five experienced Episcopal clergy. We gathered for workshops on leadership at the beautiful Trinity Conference Center in West Cornwall, Connecticut.

We met each morning in a lovely conference room with a low ceiling and a fireplace in the corner, giving the space a homey feeling. The eight-foot tables were placed in an oblong egg-shape with an opening at each end. At the "head of the circle" were the typical podium, projector, and other electronic equipment we have become used to seeing in any classroom. Our group had come to expect whoever was facilitating the day would begin by standing near the podium and giving an introduction for the session. Because I have come to expect every conference and workshop to start this way, the familiarity is comforting and kept me at ease.

Hugh O'Doherty is a gentle Irishman. He has spent thirty years working on peace and reconciliation issues with paramilitary groups in Northern Ireland. Hugh is of average height, fit build, with shocking silver hair and crystal blue eyes. His accent is pleasant and enticing. He has a fetching charisma about him.

On the second morning of classes with Hugh, he stood where every other teacher had begun the daily session, the same place he had stood the day before. However, this day he stood with his hands behind his back. Saying nothing, Hugh looked slowly around the room, making and holding eye contact with each of us. As his eyes finished circling the room he maintained his silence. Again, only moving his head, the fetching of his crystal blue eyes captured our silent attention. Time stood still. The room was silent. The birds stopped singing. I could not hear my neighbor's breathing. I could feel the tension rise within my interior.

The monkey in my mind was asking, "What was he doing? Was he waiting for one of us to break the silence? What if I asked a question? Would I be reprimanded and asked to remain silent?"

After about ten minutes of silence, my inner monkey mind began to calm, but it was replaced by the tension of the unknown. If I kept silent, what would happen? How long could I remain in the silence Hugh was holding?

Timidly, after about fifteen minutes, one of my classmates broke the silence and asked an innocuous question.

But Hugh would not be distracted by a question he thought would let us "off the hook." He responded with his own questions. "How did the silence make you feel? Was the silence moving you to do anything?"

Someone asked in a mild retort, "Was it the silence moving me to do something or was it my response to silence that would move me?"

Hugh asked, "What power is there in the tension created by, and in, silence?"

Hugh told us he was holding the tension in the room. He knew his purpose was to mobilize us to do our work, the work of being church leaders. He felt the best way to fulfill his purpose and for us to access our work was for him to hold silence. By holding silence, he was anticipating that we would begin to ask our personal interior questions and then we could ask intimate and meaningful questions of the group. Before we could work as a group, he said, we needed to experience the tension of silence as a group. While he was there to facilitate, model, instruct, guide, and mentor, he was not in the room to tell us how to lead. Hugh was there to assist us in the discovery of our leadership abilities and then, to use a Ronald Heifetz metaphor, he "stepped on the balcony" to observe us doing our work. O'Doherty had moved from the role of teacher into the role of group spiritual director. I have participated in dozens of spiritual direction groups and have led even more, but have yet to experience the confidence and skill of holding group silence as well as Hugh did with our CLP class.

A spiritual director who can hold the tension of a group created in silence can then draw the community into the presence of God. For that is where the people of God can meet the Creator. In silence and tension is where the people can be co-creators with God, doing the work of the community.

As a spiritual director, I ask myself, how long can I hold silence? Can I keep silence privately for one minute, three minutes, ten minutes, or an hour? How long can I hold a group in silence? If I tell them we are going into a period of silence, how long will they tolerate the quiet? More importantly, how long can I hold a group in silence without announcing my intention?

For the spiritual director there are times she will have to let the directee talk himself out, say everything that needs to be said and then move to the point of exhaustion. It is hard for a directee to listen when his soul is full of words, needing to be expressed. Over time, through the skillful work of the director holding the silence, the soul pilgrim will learn the important place of silence in his life. However, both the director and the directee require patience.

Even more patience is necessary of the spiritual director who has the courage to practice holding the silence for a group. Groups rarely weary of the noise of talking. How often have you experienced a group willing to maintain silence without being asked?

O'Doherty told our CLP class about his work with paramilitary groups in Northern Ireland. He found the way to hold silence for people who mistrusted and hated one another to the point of murder.

I asked Hugh for some tips on how to practice holding such silence. He gave me a one-word answer: meditation. My spiritual director uses the practice of centering prayer. For the spiritual director to be keeper of the tension of silence, she must have the spiritual discipline of silence in her own life. O'Doherty and my spiritual director both believe that if they can maintain their own inner silence in the face of a person or group resisting silence, their personal silence will invite the individual and even the group into a still place, the place where God speaks.

Christianity and most other religions have natural moments for silence within the prayer and practice of the individual's life and of the community's life together. Meditation, centering prayer, contemplative prayer, praying with beads, and *lectio divina* are some forms commonly used. The spiritual director, who practices silence in his own life, can then capture the communal moments as opportunities to guide small groups into the practice of silence. He becomes the holder of the tension of silence for the group.

Through the personal discipline and practice of silence the spiritual director is able to provide a non-anxious presence in the face of conflict, chaos, and uncertainty. The director can pause for more than a few moments, then ask an open-ended question, holding the silence of the group while they mull a response. In times of emotion-filled conversation the spiritual director may ask for a moment of silent prayer or a time of reflection, or ask the group to stand or sit in silence for another moment of silent prayer.

Forced or imposed silence is oppressive and punitive and does nothing to quiet the monkey mind much less enhance the growth of the soul. However, silence held by the spiritual director invites others to willingly give into the tension found in collective silence and that experience then births power, creativity, and healing, giving a new voice to the previously marginalized or voiceless among the group.

Silence allows the individual and the group to recognize the primacy of the voice of God in hearing the still small voice of the Holy Spirit. Hearing the voice of the Spirit then liberates the voice of the one and the many to join in with the voice of God. The role of the spiritual director is to be an advocate of silence, inviting God to speak.

THE SPIRITUAL DIRECTOR AS WISDOM TEACHER

"Who is wise and understanding among you? Show by your good life that your works are done with gentleness born of wisdom. . . . [T]he wisdom from above is first pure, then peaceable, gentle, willing to yield, full of mercy and good fruits, without a trace of partiality or hypocrisy" (James 3:13, 17).

I have had the privilege of meeting some experienced and well-respected spiritual directors. None of them would refer to themselves as wisdom teachers. Yet without fail, when I have asked one of their directees to describe his or her spiritual director, they use the word "wise." The spiritual director is wise in spiritual matters with regard to insight, discernment, foresight, discretion, and judgment. Her wisdom will come from experience, theological training, and ongoing training and education.

In *Spiritual Direction and Meditation*, Thomas Merton makes it very clear, though, that the director's wisdom does not come from her own intelligence or work but instead, as James states, "from above." "[The spiritual director is] only God's usher, and must lead souls in God's way, and not [her] own."[13]

Knowing God's way and having wisdom is the product of a deepened prayer life, says Thomas Dubay. He writes in *Seeking Spiritual Direction*, "The experience often mentioned as needed in spiritual directors includes both wisdom . . . and a feel for the things of God which accompany a deepening prayer life."[14]

Indeed wisdom encompasses a wide spectrum across the complexities of life. Morton Kelsey quotes from a spiritual director of the Middle Ages in *The Other Side of Silence: Meditation for the Twenty-First Century*, "In the sixteenth century, Benedict Pererius, a Jesuit priest, suggested that to find the interpreter of dreams [spiritual director] we should look for a person with plenty of experience in the world and the affairs of humanity, with a wide interest in everything human, and with an openness to the voice of God. This is a good summary of what one is looking for in a spiritual director."[15]

Wisdom is the ability to share personal experience gently, discreetly, and sparingly. This is the sign of an experienced spiritual director. Those who follow the school of Carl Jung would also add, "and only when asked."

"I hate my job," Henry said. The loathing for his job was a reoccurring theme in our direction sessions.

"I know," I said.

"I've prayed that God would open the door for another job. I just wish someone would call me, you know, with another opportunity."

"Are you anticipating hearing a response from some job applications you've made?"

"No, I haven't applied to any place. I was just hoping something would open up, a friend maybe, anything. I just need for something to happen."

"Why haven't you made any applications?"

After a brief silence Henry said, "I'm really bogged down right now."

"Bogged down, how?"

"Well, when I start thinking about applying for another job, I worry that the next job could be worse than this one. Then I don't want to think about that, so I find something else to do so I don't have to think about how I hate my job so much."

"What about your current job makes you hate it so much?"

"To be honest, it's not so much what I do, but it's my boss I hate."

"What is it about your boss that you hate?" I asked.

"He's always pressuring me to do things I didn't sign on for."

"What do you mean, 'things you didn't sign on for'?"

"You know, things that aren't really a part of the job description. It's not so much that those things are bad. I just don't like it because he assumes I should just do it because I work for him and I need the job. So I feel like he's taking advantage of me."

"Have you talked to your boss about how you feel about being taken advantage of?"

"No," he started to shut down.

"Okay, so why?"

There was a long period of silence.

"I don't like being taken advantage of," he said quietly, almost to himself.

"What does it feel like when someone takes advantage of you?"

"It feels like they don't respect me. No, worse than that; it feels like they are cheating me, yeah, and they are stealing my integrity, because they don't respect who I am, you know, my talents and skills. When they take advantage of me they take away my dignity, that's what it feels like."

"Henry, why can't you talk to your boss about how he makes you feel when he takes advantage of you?"

"I'm afraid," he said.

"Afraid of what?"

"You know, of being fired, or written up, or something. I don't know."

"So, what are your options?" I asked.

"I can't think," he said.

"I understand. Maybe if we wrote your options on a piece of paper, that would help clear some space in your mind to continue thinking, like thawing out. So, what is one option?"

"I can quit."

I wrote that on a piece of paper. "That's a start. What is another option?"

"I could tell off my boss," he said with some enthusiasm.

I wrote that on the paper. "Okay, what else?"

"I could look for another job, seriously look."

I wrote that down. "Keep going, other options?"

"I guess I could talk to my boss instead of telling him off. You know, that would be a risk."

Again, I wrote what Henry said. "Anything else?"

"I think I'm tapped out. You got any ideas?"

I offered a space of silence for my own reflection.

"You have a good list here. Between now and when we meet next week, would you take the list I have written for you and put it in a special place where you can look at it each day, maybe on your fridge? And would you pray Ps. 37:1–9 each day? And after you pray the psalm, look at your list again and see if anything else comes to you. Can you do that?"

I took out my Bible and read Ps. 37:1–9. "Do not fret because of the wicked; do not be envious of wrongdoers, for they will soon fade like the grass, and wither like the green herb. Trust in the Lord, and do good; so you will live in the land, and enjoy security. Take delight in the Lord, and he will give you the desires of your heart. Commit your way to the Lord; trust in him, and he will act. He will make your vindication shine like the light, and the justice of your cause like the noonday. Be still before the Lord, and wait patiently for him; do not fret over those who prosper in their way, over those who carry out evil devices. Refrain from anger, and forsake wrath. Do not fret—it leads only to evil. For the wicked shall be cut off, but those who wait for the Lord shall inherit the land."

I said, "Henry, I pray by asking God to place the desires of God's heart into my heart. Even when I don't feel like I can pray, I can let the psalmist pray for me. Over time, new images begin to emerge. I can see myself doing something creative. It's in those moments I am creative, when I feel closest to God."

Henry committed to giving the list and the prayer of the psalm a try.

The spiritual director as wisdom teacher will listen to what is spoken with attention to the details of the story of the directee, to what is subtly said and what goes unspoken. The director will ask questions intended to open the directee into new discoveries about himself and what probably already resides within his soul. The director then, when asked, can provide wisdom from the scriptures, spiritual writers, and from the director's insights of life, and through personal stories and reading.

Martin Thornton, the twentieth-century Anglican priest, wrote in his book *Spiritual Direction* that the spiritual director (1) is a physician of the soul, (2) is a spiritual coach, and (3) offers familial love. He describes the director as a mystical theologian who is a research expert that combines an ancient theological tradition with contemporary spiritual work.[16] Later he provides some practical guidelines for the director: (1) to listen rather than talk, (2) that direction will be a long continuous process,

(3) the director is a guest and not an authoritarian figure, and (4) the director and the directee share a mutual love of God.[17] These descriptors and guidelines are necessary for the director to be able to offer wisdom teaching. If the director is not a "research expert" always mining spiritual texts, novels, and short stories for examples to share, then the director's wisdom relies solely on his personal experience. Conversely, if the director is well educated and erudite, yet he cannot relate his learning to life, then the "coaching" will be dry and without relevance for the directee. As Thornton wisely says, the spiritual director is a mystical theologian, which I have called the wisdom teacher, who indeed must combine ancient theological tradition with a contemporary expression.

Michael O'Grady, a Roman Catholic priest and my spiritual director, is a wisdom teacher. When he reads this he will blush, laugh nervously, and in his Irish way dismiss the statement as silly. Father Mike has walked with me during some of the most trying times of my leadership life. Rarely has he made any suggestions about how I might solve problems or deal with frightening situations. However, he is quick with a personal story, Irish tale, or a quoted poem. Typically, at the time he tells me his subtly laden story, I cannot make the connection. Usually, it takes several days of marinating for the meaning to rise in my consciousness. Through stories there is an unconscious learning always at work in the psyche. Psychologist and author Joyce Mills calls this unconscious learning the therapeutic power of the parabolic metaphor.[18]

A few months after I took over as president of Grand Canyon University, Father Mike invited me to a presentation on Celtic spirituality featuring poet and author John O'Donohue. I had devoured O'Donohue's two books: *Anam Cara: A Book of Celtic Wisdom*[19] and *Eternal Echoes: Celtic Reflections on Our Yearning to Belong.*[20]

My wife and I sat with Father Mike just a few rows from the front. His lyrical voice was hypnotizing. He rarely looked at the audience. Most of the time he kept his eyes closed or stared off into the face of the unknown. Hearing O'Donohue recite his poetry and read from his book was like listening in on his private conversation with God. I felt as if I was in heaven, sitting next to the wisest man I knew, listening to the wisest writer I had ever read.

At the break, Mike excused himself to go chat with a few friends. I stood, stretched, and looked around the room. As I turned to the back of the room I found myself staring into the face of the university's banker. Prior to this moment our relationship was strained, to say the least. The bank was uncertain about the financial stability of the university and that caused for many conversations through clenched teeth. At the O'Donohue gathering, we shook hands and exchanged polite greetings.

"Surprised to see you here," the banker said. "Didn't think a Southern Baptist would have any interest in an Irish mystic."

I told him I loved O'Donohue.

"Are you with Father Mike?" he asked.

"Yes," I offered. I noticed his posture was beginning to soften and a wry smile was creeping over his face.

"How do you know him?" he asked.

"Well, to be honest, he's my spiritual director; has been for four years."

"Interesting," the banker said. "Mike's my priest. He's the pastor of the church my family attends."

"Small world," I said.

He laughed.

Later I told Mike about the random meeting. He smiled and said, "Imagine that." My relationship with the banker took a 180-degree turn. I am not sure the banker and I began to move closer together because of our respect for Father Mike or because we found faith as a common ground. We have even maintained friendly contact after my leaving the university. It has always been my banker's and my suspicion that Mike knew we would meet at the O'Donohue gathering. Father Mike's wisdom has a mystical quality, much like O'Donohue's. Saint Francis is quoted as saying, "Preach always and when necessary, use words." The saying could apply to wisdom teachers as well.

There is much to be gained from the practice of someone who lives the life of a spiritual director, especially leaders. Spiritual directors are stewards of safety, holy listeners, advocates of silence, and wisdom teachers. Indeed, spiritual directors offer a wellspring of knowledge and practice for any congregational leader.

The purpose of this book is not to suggest that the leader be the spiritual director of every individual of the congregation, which is neither possible nor wise. It is also not the intent of this book to propose that the leader act as the spiritual director of the congregation at large.

Rather, the objective of this book is to suggest that the roles of the spiritual director, and her methods, can be adopted by the church leader and put into practice in her leadership of the congregation. The following chapters will provide the specific means of incorporating the methods of the spiritual director into the life of congregational leadership.

Two

The Leader as the Steward of Sacred Safety

> What happens when we offer hospitality? We invite someone into a space that offers safety and shelter and put our own needs aside, as everything is focused on the comfort and refreshment of the guest.
>
> —Margaret Guenther[1]

The Redemptorist Renewal Center at Picture Rocks is a sunbaked spiritual hideaway in the Sonoran Desert. The center is perched in the southwestern foothills, overlooking Tucson, Arizona. There is a labyrinth on the property, made by volunteers with hundreds of hand-sized stones gathered from the nearby wash. The labyrinth is modeled after the one on the floor of the Cathedral of Notre Dame de Chartres. It is round, depicting the circle of life, about thirty feet in diameter. Around the edge of the circle are 128 half-moons representing the lunar cycle. The labyrinth is divided into quarters, marking the seasons of life. Even though on first observation the labyrinth may look like a maze, it is not, for there is no getting lost in a labyrinth. The walk does take a serpentine path to the center, the womb, representing our physical and spiritual birth. As we leave the womb we enter the winding path of life until we reach the end of the circle, death, and pass into the next life.

On the most pleasant of February afternoons in the desert, I began to walk and pray the labyrinth. My prayer was, "God, speak. I will listen." The sound of my steps on the coarse sand

and pebbles caused me to slow my pace and go deeper into my prayer. My footprints joined those of thousands who have worn this path. The stones lining the path have been in this area for millions of years before they were called into place as a labyrinth, as if it were the vocation of the stones to mark this way of prayer. The stones will be here for an untold time after this retreat center has long been forgotten. The stones, created by God, are held in the memory of God, just as each of us, formed by God, is also held.

I walked and prayed. A few turns into my prayers I began to recognize that the stones of the labyrinth represented the people I have encountered in my life as spiritual director, pastor, and priest. God has created each stone and each person. Some stones were grey, some reddish, some green, some blue, some white, some flat, and some rounder than others. Time and weather must have etched on some of the stones stars, moons, and night-crawling creatures. Some stones were smooth, and some were jagged, varied as the individuals I see daily. I walked the labyrinth carefully, acknowledging each stone but careful not to disturb its place.

At some points, especially at the turns in the path, a fellow pilgrim walker, I assume, making a corner too sharp, has disturbed a stone. I am called to stop. I sense the need to speak to the stone. I ask the stone if it wants to be returned to its place on the path. This particular stone acknowledged my presence and affirmed its desire to be in its original position. Gently, carefully, not lifting the stone, I nudged it back into its intended place. This is my role as a leader and spiritual director in the community I serve. I walk in prayer with the people. And, if given permission, I attempt to help the individual find her place, a safe place, where she can live out how she hears God calling into her vocation.

As I prepared to leave the labyrinth, the appointed psalm for the week was fresh on my lips. "For God alone my soul waits in silence. . . . He alone is my rock and my salvation" (Ps. 62). Here in the silence among the stones I have met the presence of God. I turned to face the path of stones, made the sign of the cross, bowed, and offered the salutation, *Namaste,* the God in me recognizes the God in you.

I had every intention of returning to my room after the walk, but as I turned to leave the area I noticed a very large sign perched on the hill overlooking the labyrinth. "Stay Off the Rocks!" It made me laugh. Okay, I said. I hadn't thought about climbing on the rocks until then. Then I saw a smaller sign warning me that, were I to deface any of the petroglyphs, my action would result in prosecution and heavy fines. I walked a few yards around the base of the hill, and not on the rocks, as instructed. It was there that I saw the petroglyphs, about twenty feet above my head. I learned later from some materials provided by the retreat center that these petroglyphs are carvings, most likely the work of the Hohokam people about 1100 ce.

A few drawings depicted animals and birds of the desert. One showed a human figure holding the head of an animal. The person depicted may have been a shaman or a healer connecting with his or her spirit animal. The dominant etching, a large spiral, was on the largest flat surface in the center of the hill facing the western sun. The spiral reminded me of similar spiral carvings that encircle the burial mounds of Newgrange in Ireland, carved over 5,000 years ago. Similar to the site in Newgrange, the spiral petroglyph of the Hohokam is designed to be in sync with the solstice-equinox movement of the sun. At the site of the Hohokams there is a large pointed rock positioned above the spiral petroglyph. As the sun strikes the sharp rock above the spiral it produces a "sunsword," or pointer. The point of the sun-sword is at the center of the spiral, creating what was possibly a seasonal calendar used by the Hohokam people.

Encircling the spiral is a drawing of people holding hands. One person—most likely the tribe's leader, priest, or shaman—holds a staff. It appears that the people may be dancing and performing a ritual around the spiral. The stone of the spiral, worn at the center much more than at its edges, suggests that as the people danced past the spiral they would rub the stone with their hands as part of the ritual.

My spirit was caught up in the near simultaneous experience of praying the labyrinth and then witnessing the history of prayers being offered by an ancient people. In my prayers in the labyrinth, I envisioned the faces of the people I encounter daily. I saw their faces on the same stones that the Hohokam people walked across and prayed among, at least a thousand years before. I felt our prayers wafting together in a cosmic milieu of the labyrinth and the spiral. As I left the holy sight, I bowed as I had done leaving the labyrinth saying, "The God in me recognizes the God in you."

I asked several of the staff at the retreat center if the labyrinth was intentionally built close to the spiral petroglyphs. No one knew. The best guess was that it was built in its location simply to be close to the lodges and because the ground was fairly flat. Surely, though, cosmic synchronicity of the collective unconscious was at work. Tens of thousands of prayers—prayers offered by the Hohokam people and prayers offered on the labyrinth by hundreds of spiritual pilgrims—have been said around this site for at least a thousand years. The stones on the hills, where the petroglyphs are carved, stand as ancient hierophants keeping the vow of confidentiality and protectors of the arcane secrets of faith. Today's spiritual directors and spiritual leaders stand with these ancient holy leaders, responsible for maintaining the people's safety in prayer and ritual practice.

As a spiritual director and a leader, I am charged with the physical safety of everyone who comes into my care. The trust of safety is heightened when I acknowledge her creation by God, the presence of God within her, and her arrival in my life at a specific time and place. When I notice she is out of place, I ask her, and when she gives me permission, I may gently attempt to nudge her back into her sacred space through my faithful commitment to prayer and ritual. I must acknowledge she was present before I arrived and will remain after I am forgotten. She is in the memory of God, at one with God, and I must care for her soul and her safety. The practice of the spiritual leader caring for his people is an ancient responsibility.

This experience of praying the labyrinth near the ancient petroglyphs has given more depth to my theological reflection about those for whom I provide spiritual direction and those whom I lead. Each new experience and subsequent theological reflection has an influence on my next experience and theological reflection. I feel as if I am writing the story of my experience of God. I have no idea what will emerge next, but I am often surprised by what God brings my way. God provides a new experience, and I write the story, awaiting the next opportunity, which will change the direction, flow, and rhythm of my story. The theological plot thickens as God continues to do the work of formation in my life, which in turn will have an impact upon those I lead.

Just as when I read a novel, I love to be surprised by the twists and turns of my story. My wife and I have been married for over forty years. We have two adult children who are both happily married. For differing reasons, it appeared that neither of our children would have their own children. My wife and I handled our personal disappointment privately. We accepted the decisions of our adult children, but in not having grandchildren, a grief, a void, arose in our life.

Then one beautiful summer day, our son, who had been married eight years, surprised us with the glorious news that he and our daughter-in-law were expecting a child. Our grief was replaced with glorious, but at the same time, anxious excitement. We knew all too well the health risks my thirty-something daughter-in-law and her expected child would face in the months ahead.

As my wife and I awaited the birth of our first grandchild, friends who have grandchildren repeatedly told me being a grandfather would change my life. I believed them, but I was unsure how the relationship with my grandson would affect me. I received lots of unsolicited advice, all well-meaning. Some of my friends offered me the much repeated adage, "You can spoil your grandchild and then send him home with his parents." Until our grandson was born, however, I could only mentally store the information awaiting his arrival. A close friend simply said, "Wait until you hold him." In the last few months before our grandson's birth, I lovingly began to refer to him as the holy grandchild, reflecting my sense of the mystery of what was happening.

Hours after our grandson was born, my son slipped the most beautiful child I had ever seen into my arms. My grandson glowed. He was peaceful. Innocence radiated from the tiny bundle. I was in love like I had never experienced. In that moment, I felt like I was holding holiness, purity, and the divine love of God in my arms. Indeed, my life was changing. And this change was going to play itself out in how I would see and encounter other people.

With the birth of my grandson, I felt like my beliefs had a new face. Represented in my grandson, this new face has been shining a warm light on a constantly growing love, a kind of love that I had not known existed. But it had always been there, deep within my being, in my subconscious. Through the experience of holding my grandson for the first time, love was now emerging and expressing itself in a brand new way. I was beginning to discover an invigorated language for a newfound emotional stirring, which was visibly surfacing from the depth of my fresh experience of God. In holding my grandson, I felt I was holding God. This experience caused a rising sense of my responsibility to provide for the safety of my grandson. And I recognized this sense was having an impact on how I saw my responsibility in providing safety for others.

Several young families attend our church with their numerous children, and I have worked hard to build a healthy relationship with these children. I listen to their stories. Laugh at their cute jokes. Admire their art. And encourage them in their budding relationships with God. I love these children of God. Through the experience of holding my grandson, my love has deepened for each of these children. My new experience of God and then my theological reflection has made me aware of the image of God residing within each of these children and every other person I encounter.

As humans, we are more than the creation of God. We are God's beloved children, heirs, sons, and daughters. We are carrying the genetic imprint of God upon our life. The experience of holding my grandchild continues to blow the breath of the Holy Spirit across the embers of my theology, creating now a roaring fire. My responsibility for the safety of the children and the adults of our church has always been a top priority in my ministry. As my experience of God and my theology continue to evolve, however, my passion for the safety of our parishioners continues to intensify. I see our parishioners with my eyes and I believe in my heart that I am beholding the very presence of God within everyone who comes through the doors of our church. The responsibility of caring for the safety of those in my community has moved from my mind into every molecule in my being.

I don't think everyone needs to have a grandchild in order to see the presence of God in every person he encounters. Like the spiritual director, who has been trained to access his experiences of God as a way of finding meaning and language for his theology, we leaders also have our own experiences that can deepen our theology and thereby re-enforce our commitment to ensure the safety of everyone in our parish.

Foundational to a theology of safety is one's understanding of the "person." Recognizing that holding my grandson was a spiritual experience has further enriched my theology of the human being, the person as a whole, complete in mind, body, and spirit.

Our "completeness," the totality of who we are as human beings, is powerfully and lovingly found in our being created in the image of God. The image of God or the characteristics of God—mind, body, and spirit—are our connection to the unseen God. God breathed God's image into humans. God spoke to humans. The human creature is unique among God's creation. Therefore humanity is set aside both to serve as and to be the stewards of the rest of God's creation. This stewardship is carried out on behalf of God and includes the care of other human beings, as well as the rest of God's creation.

The Genesis story is the root of our theological understanding of the person and our stewardship of God's creation and one another. "Then God said, 'Let us make humankind in our image, according to our likeness. . . .' So God created humankind in his image, in the image of God he created them; male and female he created them" (Gen. 1:26a, 27). Then again in Gen. 5:1, "When God created humankind he made them in the likeness of God." God also gave humanity dominion over the rest of creation (Gen. 1:26). Dominion is not a matter of having absolute freedom to reign over creation and its resources without regard for its welfare. God did not create the heavens and the earth; light and darkness; sky, water, and dry land; plants; sun, moon, and stars; and living creatures in the sea and on the land for the benefit of humanity. God formed humanity from the dust of the ground for the benefit of God's creation. Humanity and the rest of God's creation must live in harmony, and humans must live in unity and peace with one another.

German theologian and martyr Dietrich Bonhoeffer (1906–1945) wrote specifically about God's intention for humanity's relationship to God's creation and to other human beings. "In man God creates his image on earth. This means that man is like the Creator in that he is free."[2] Bonhoeffer goes on to explain that the person is free by "being free for others," as "God does not will to be free for himself but for man. God in Christ is free for man."[3] Bonhoeffer is saying we are more than simply God's creation. We are the very likeness of God, created in the image of God for the sake of the other person. According to Bonhoeffer, God chooses to be free, not for the sake of God, but instead for the sake of God's human creation. Our freedom, the same as the freedom of God, is found in our relationship with the other. Therefore, we, bearing the image of God, enact our responsibility of freedom by caring for the image of God in the other person.

Bonhoeffer is saying that God acted freely, without coercion, to create humanity, and God self-limited God's freedom in the act of creation for our benefit. And in the same self-limiting way, with the pure motive of love, God freely loves us (Gen. 2:18) by coming into the world in human form, in Jesus for our sake (John 3:16). Therefore, as human beings, just as God freely cares for us and loves us, we, created in the image of God, have the same self-limited freedom to act as God's responsible stewards in caring for all creation.

This image of God created within each person is a gift of God. The gift, the imprint of God upon the human being, encompasses the whole being—mind, body, and soul. In other words, the image of God within me loves the image of God within you. To view our caring for one another as if we are caring for the image of God elevates the leader's level of responsibility for each person in her community beyond the standard set by the laws of our land.

German Catholic scholar Henricus Renckens expounds upon the Hebrew theology of the created image of God within each person:

> When . . . the author of Genesis 1 says that man is the image of God, he is indeed truly saying something unheard of. He is attempting to express a truly overwhelming mystery, a mystery which for the Israelite is the source of holy awe of himself and his fellow man, and which reveals to him that he owes everything that he is and has more to Jahweh than to himself and that in this life he has a task to fulfill and a responsibility to bear. . . . "Covenant" and "image of God" are parallel realities for both express God's nearness. Just as Jahweh commits himself to his people Israel, so the Creator commits himself to the human race.[4]

The late professor emeritus at Fuller Theological Seminary Ray S. Anderson (1925–2009) studied under Thomas F. Torrance, a student of Karl Barth, and taught courses on Barth and Bonhoeffer. In Anderson's understanding, the significance of the image of God imprinted within the human being is so profound that the hatred of the other is hatred of the image of God within the other. He goes further to say that murder of another person is an "affront to the *imago Dei* which is present as embodied humanity."[5] When I encounter another person I am encountering God. I must care for the safety of the other because I am, literally, caring for the safety of God. Any affront I commit against the other affronts the God within the other.

It seems clear this theology was active in Jesus's life and ministry as well. Jesus said:

> For I was hungry and you gave me food, I was thirsty and you gave me something to drink, I was a stranger and you welcomed me, I was naked and you gave me clothing, I was sick and you took care of me, I was in prison and you visited me. . . . Truly I tell you, just as you did it to one of the least of these who are members of my family, you did it to me (Matt. 25:35–36, 40).

A theology of safety will include the idea that "the very image of God" is created within each of us and that, therefore, the way we treat God is also the way we treat others. Jesus, incarnate of God, himself the image of God, teaches his disciples that when I treat another person with love and respect, I am treating Jesus himself with love and respect. And when I am not respecting the dignity of another person, I am showing a lack of respect for Jesus. Our understanding that the image of God is created within each person moves us from an intellectual acknowledgement of our responsibility to care for the other to a deeper, mystical, impassioned fervor for the care of the presence of God and Jesus in the everyday encounter with every person. "Deeper" means I recognize that when I harm the God in the other, I harm the God in myself. If I harm the other, I am not loving my neighbor as myself. "Mystical" means that while it is easy for me to see God in my grandson, the work of the God within me is transforming me, enabling me to see God—the same God in my grandson—in every human being I encounter. God's transformation blazes within me. I am being formed in such a way that my actions are as free as the actions of God loving others. As God is free to be God, so I am created in the image of God to love others freely—not out of requirement, obligation, or legislation. The free love of God is the reciprocal love of the Trinity, happening in and through each person.

The theological perspective that as human beings we are created in and carry the image of God, and that in our experience we encounter God in the other, heightens the leader's responsibility for the safety of those within his care. Leaders of the church have a high calling and a deep motivation to ensure the safety of everyone within the congregation. Leaders, like spiritual directors, are responsible for the care of the mind, body, and soul of each person. The responsibility to care for each person, built upon a theology of safety, will cause the leader to respect and care for each person she encounters as if she were responsible for the very image of God. Because I care for each person in my parish, my grandson included, as if we are all created in the image of God, I must ensure each one's physical, emotional, and spiritual safety.

Providing safety for each individual, and the congregation collectively, in all three aspects can be a daunting task, a task seemingly impossible at times when we feel caught in the clutches
of the unpredictable world in which we live. Tragically, Sydney
Browning, a friend of mine, was among those shot to death by a
suicidal gunman while she sat on a sofa near the front door of the
Wedgwood Baptist Church, Fort Worth, Texas. While her church
took the normal precautions for the safety of its parishioners, they
could not protect her and six others from the acts of a psychotic
individual.[6]

The tragedy at Wedgwood may be an extreme example of our
vulnerability, but the fallout from rare events often exacerbates the
fear of members in other congregations, causing them to lose sight
of the mission of the church. Sydney was an alumnus of Grand
Canyon University in Phoenix, a thousand miles from where she
was murdered. Some churches in her home state of Arizona considered posting armed guards at the doorway. The intent of these
churches was probably well-meant, but could they achieve complete safety with such drastic measures? Maybe. But a perpetrator
might have even caught a guard unaware. Even when I feel safe, I
may not be.

Just as we cannot ensure every person's physical safety, so we
cannot guarantee everyone will feel emotionally safe in every setting. A lesbian, gay, bisexual, transgender, or queer (LGBTQ) person could feel unsafe in a church she perceives to be anti-gay. She
may feel vulnerable to ridicule or judgment. She may think she
will not be accepted for who she is. These feelings are real for her
and cause her to feel emotionally threatened. Likewise, someone
opposed to the inclusion of LGBTQ persons in a faith community, for whatever reason, may feel at risk in a radically inclusive
setting. This person may feel emotionally unsafe because he finds
himself in the minority opinion.

Faith communities, by their very nature, have a tendency to
offer a place for like-minded people to gather. The assumption
that everyone at my church has the same beliefs can be spiritually intimidating to someone who may question a commonly held
viewpoint. If I attended your church and questioned, for example,

the Virgin Birth (or any other credal statement), what response would I receive? A spiritual seeker will have many questions and doubts. How the church leaders react to the seeker's questions and doubts will communicate the level of spiritual safety within the faith community.

My own experience with many young adults is that they do not feel safe asking questions in church and this becomes a serious deterrent to church attendance. My observation is confirmed by research presented in Christian Smith and Patricia Snell's book, *Souls in Transition: The Religious and Spiritual Lives of Emerging Adults.*[7] Smith and Snell's research points out that young adults expect to have the autonomy of choice in determining their core religious beliefs. Emerging young adults question traditionally held beliefs as a matter of gaining understanding and then deciding what they think is right for them. If a particular person or religion is too rigid, according to the research, most young adults consider that religious group to be "too into it" and threatening. Most young adults, say Smith and Snell, "think that too many religious people are negative, angry, and judgmental, and nearly half say that mainstream religion is irrelevant to people their age."[8]

A faith community closed to questions is likely to be perceived as spiritually threatening not only by young people but also by adults, as pointed out in Robert Fuller's work, *Spiritual, But Not Religious.*[9] In his research Fuller takes a systematic and historical look at the growing phenomena of adults who are seeking spiritual fulfillment outside the traditional church. He suggests people who may be spiritually mature but not affiliated with a traditional religion are looking for a spirituality that is heuristic and flexible and that views life as a pilgrimage. Religious organizations that are not open to their spiritual search are considered unwelcoming. He observes, "Many [seekers] feel they have been emotionally victimized or belittled by the church due to their gender, curiosity, or simple unwillingness to conform for conformity's sake."[10]

Each aspect of safety—physical, emotional, and spiritual—requires our dedicated attention in order to develop strategies and put them into practice in our congregations and faith communities. As hard as we try, though, it may be impossible to create an environment that is always physically, emotionally, and spiritually safe for every person. As impossible as it might be to create safety for everyone, the faith community still has a responsibility to provide as safe a space as possible. An environment that feels physically safe may lower the anxiety of the worried parent, afraid to let her child out of sight. It could reduce the tension of the wary visitor who is venturing a risk to give church "one last chance" after years of absence. Safe space could encourage a troubled soul to seek counsel from the pastor, in spite of his fear of rejection or judgment. As leaders, our efforts to nurture safe space will prove worth the cost when that one person, in desperate need, comes to feel the loving embrace of God.

I have chosen these three aspects of safety realizing they are broad strokes and do not include every facet of congregational safety. Nor do the categories adequately capture the effects of any failure to provide safety for an individual. Any violation of a person's safety causes harm to his or her entire being. Physical abuse, for example, also affects the person's emotional and spiritual well-being. In a similar way, if a person's emotional safety is not maintained, that abuse will also affect the person's physical and spiritual health. And if a person's spiritual safety is dishonored, his or her physical and emotional wellness are also violated. We are holistic beings, and any trauma to one aspect of our being will affect the rest of our life.

The human being can never be understood as a collection of parts and bits. Therefore, I recognize there is some significant overlap in most areas in the pages that follow and so I proceed with gentleness and sensitivity into an exploration of these three broad-stroke areas of congregational safety.

PHYSICAL SAFETY

Whenever I go to the airport, I am reminded how prevalent physical safety is in the mind of the American traveler. On my most recent trip, after I removed my shoes, belt, cellphone, and sundry other items, I was subjected to an X-ray and a pat-down search, and the security personnel rummaged through my bag. Other people in line went through the same routine search. I expect no less the next time I go to the airport. In our world today, this type of airport security is a matter-of-fact, done for the sake of physical safety. We are not surprised anymore when we encounter a similar search at the courthouse, at a major athletic event, and even at our school. Physical safety is a dominant issue in most of the world, and this concern for physical safety extends to our churches as well. Of course, we probably would be appalled if we had to go through a metal detector at church. Still, we expect the same care for our safety.

Providing physical safety for the congregation is complicated. Most churches understand the importance of abiding by building codes and laws governing ease of access for the physically handicapped. Ensuring the safety of our facilities is especially trying when we are dealing with aging buildings. In spite of the difficulties, however, we are still responsible for providing as safe a physical space as possible for our worshipping community.

There are several ways of ensuring the safest space possible. Of course, leaders must ensure the space is clean and free from harmful chemicals and anything that could lead to an accident. A good way to start your planning is to ask your insurance company to do a physical audit of your campus. The insurance company will provide an excellent review as well as resources to improve the church site. Some churches are regularly inspected by the fire marshal. If yours is not, contacting the local fire service and requesting such an inspection could assist the church in preventing fire hazards. These routine inspections may also reveal other issues of facility safety that need attention.

Safe and accessible facilities, whether under required compliance of the American Disabilities Act or not, are matters of concern for the church. A church that is not easily and safely accessible by those with handicaps is not a welcoming church. Expert consultants in the areas of disabilities are available to meet with congregational leaders and assist the church in developing plans for a facility that is inviting to all people.

While the faith community assesses the facility, clergy and lay leaders (employees and volunteers alike), should be trained in the procedures of providing a safe church campus and appropriate ways to handle emergencies. Ushers should be trained in how to evacuate the building in case of fire and other types of emergencies. They should know where medical emergency equipment is located and be trained to use it. They should be coached to spot potential issues before trouble arises and to respond appropriately so they are prepared to assist people with disabilities, support those looking for financial assistance or food, and handle anyone who might be a possible danger to the congregation.

Volunteers and staff who use the kitchen should be trained in food handling and kitchen safety. All volunteers should know where the fire extinguishers are located and how to use them. Bright colored signs or posters should be visible near doors and light switches with information about emergency procedures and contact phone numbers.

Protecting the church property from vandalism is also a matter of physical safety. My parish had a history of break-ins before I arrived, and subsequently they put bars on the windows and built wrought iron fences to deter future trouble. Improved building security, anecdotally, has made parishioners feel safer. The down side, though, has manifested itself in a resistance from some parishioners to open the church campus at various times for guests to enter the space for prayer and contemplation. To reduce fears, we have conducted several group conversations where people can express concerns and talk about ways to alleviate worries.

A well-trained leadership team and congregation can prevent many unsafe situations before they happen. When the parishioners know the leaders practice safety, they will feel safer. When leaders involve the congregation in safety preparedness, the quality of physical safety will improve and members will feel safer.

Sexual Abuse

Another area of safety that is sometimes mistakenly included under the category of physical safety concerns is sexual abuse. Sexual abuse violates every aspect of the person as it is a violation of physical, emotional, and spiritual well-being.

Sexual abuse of any person is not acceptable in any situation. We would hope sexual abuse would not be tolerated within the church. Unfortunately, history has proved that church leaders and congregants cannot make this assumption. Every church must be proactive in protecting its people from abuse of any kind. Leaders must be vigilant to protect children from predators. In the office the leader must strive to create a safe work place for all employees. Beyond reproach, the leader absolutely must never violate or abuse any person. The radar of the collective community is appropriately and extremely high in our society. To this end, and for good reason, leaders sometimes choose to fall on the side of super-vigilance and develop a personal code of "no touching."

Few Christian denominations could boast of being free from the evils of sexual abuse among its leaders. However, the Roman Catholic Church's sexual abuse scandal has been well documented. One outcome of this horrific tragedy has been some beneficial research conducted on behalf of the Catholic Church. The conclusions of this research, if properly put into place, could help prevent further abuse by clergy and church leaders in every denomination.

Katarina Schuth holds the Endowed Chair for the Social Scientific Study of Religion at the Saint Paul Seminary School of Divinity at the University of St. Thomas in St. Paul, Minnesota, and has served as a consultant for the research studies on sexual abuse by priests and deacons prepared for the U.S. Conference of Catholic Bishops by the John Jay College of Criminal Justice of the City University of New York. In an article in *America* summarizing the research, Schuth provides some insightful reflections and recommendations for both Catholic and Protestant seminaries preparing future church leaders. The studies revealed that seminaries using psychological screening for admissions were less likely to graduate a clergy person who subsequently was an abuser. The study also indicated that seminaries engaging in specific and intense formation programs addressing the issues surrounding abuse had fewer graduates who later abused others. Her conclusion is helpful:

> Seminarians need to cultivate moral virtues like integrity, justice and prudence, to grow in self-knowledge and self-discipline and

to forgo a sense of entitlement. . . . Priests will benefit from ongoing education about the dangers and pitfalls of a lifestyle that increases vulnerability to abusive behavior. Those who understand that their lives are to be modeled after Jesus Christ and oriented toward humble service in ministry are much less likely to engage in sexual abuse of any kind.[11]

There are no easy solutions for the problem of clergy sexual abuse. However, every person in the church must give his or her full attention to protecting God's people from abuse. There are programs offered by some denominations that can be a resource in providing training for and increasing sensitivity among clergy and lay leaders.

All adults leading and supervising children's activities should be trained in how to protect children. The Episcopal Church uses a training program entitled *Safeguarding God's Children.* The training is offered in small groups or online, making it convenient for church leaders. Every person in leadership within the Episcopal Church and all leaders of any group with children are required by the canons of the church to complete *Safeguarding God's Children.* Training, once again, is critically important in protecting the safety of the congregation.

Because of the damage inflicted upon victims of sexual abuse, the church should have resources ready to support anyone who has been abused, including physicians and mental-health professionals who can assist the victim over long periods of time. In the circumstances of abuse, leaders must be prepared to offer a safe and healing environment for victims of abuse for years following the personal violation. As church leaders, we cannot take our responsibility to protect our parishioners from abuse too seriously or place too high a priority on the measures we enact to protect them.

PROTECTING PEOPLE DURING RITUALS

There are times when the leader must touch a person, in the name of the church, for ritual expression and sacramental rites.

A theology of safety, acknowledging the image of God present in each person, can create an experience that safely and appropriately communicates to the parishioner, "The God in me is touching the God in you."

My ministry includes baptism, anointing, the rite of reconciliation, healing prayer, healing touch, and at rare times, prayers to release spirits (or demons). All of these rituals require that I touch a person in the name of the church and of God. To ensure a safe environment, below are the guidelines I follow as spiritual director and parish leader.

When possible, I have a third person present. When it is not appropriate for the third person to be in the immediate room, I make every attempt to ensure there is someone in the next room, doors slightly ajar, and window coverings open. I do not feel safe unless the physical space is open enough to be transparent while providing the privacy needed. As a leader I also have to feel safe. If I do not feel safe, I cannot expect another person to feel safe. When performing a sacramental rite or pastoral office, I wear the appropriate vestments, symbolically recognizing God's presence and the sanctity of the moment. For some rites, like that of reconciliation, I might take my stole off and place it over the shoulder of the person seeking absolution, drawing him or her deeper into the presence of God. When reasonable, before I touch a person to anoint or to bless, I ask first. There are some circumstances in the hospital, in hospice care, or other similar situation, when the person cannot respond. But I still ask the question, reminding myself of the sacred trust involved, and then I proceed with pastoral care. Sometimes, in a sacramental moment of prayer, instead of holding a hand, I ask the person to take hold of one end of my rosary, while I hold the other end in prayer. We are then held together in "holy communion" without physically touching.

Ritual and sacramental ministry is a vital part of ministry, which happens often in the most vulnerable moments of life. It is possible to offer privacy, a beautiful ritual, and to be fully present to an individual while maintaining a physically safe environment. But it requires vigilance and careful planning. When the parishioner feels physically free of harm and protected from abuse, the leader has begun to develop an emotionally safe environment for the congregation.

Emotional Safety

The work of the leader is to ensure the emotional safety of the congregation in one-on-one situations, in small groups, and in the congregation as a whole. The emotional safety of the entire congregation is a work in progress. Leaders must be constantly testing the felt safety within the community. Listening to overt comments is an obvious way of determining what the congregation is feeling about safety. But also listening for subtle undertones provides clues about how members and constituents of the congregation are feeling about their emotional safety. Wise leaders keep in mind that when someone is experiencing stress at home or work, he might react to something insignificant or unrelated in a meeting or other setting as a way to vent pressure he cannot release with a spouse or boss. The leader who listens well can anticipate and be sensitive to such behavior. Anger or other inappropriate or intense public expressions of emotions may also be symptoms of issues not addressed in the congregation as a whole.

Leaders can draw on the skills of spiritual directors in their work with individuals, first recognizing that emotional safety can be most difficult to achieve. If a person has been abandoned, hurt, or violated in any way, he will experience a feeling of emptiness, loss, or grief about a problem he once felt he had but is now gone. The feelings that caused the hurt can be consciously expressed in a wide range of physical emotions. Loss and loneliness can precipitate tears. Fear can provoke physical trembling. Uncertainty can be displayed in anxious behaviors, such as bouncing feet, a twitching face, or the wringing of hands. The spiritual director, faced with these emotional expressions, will recognize them to be what they are: manifestations of the underlying current of dis-ease. As a leader, it is very easy to get "sucked in" to others' emotions. Leaders can learn to be attuned to the swirling that goes on underneath the display of emotions and can thus avoid becoming intertwined in the outward storm.

The spiritual director's and the leader's reaction to emotion will send a message to the parishioner. Maintaining a non-anxious presence is paramount. Silence, stillness, slow breathing, eyes softly resting on the other's eyes are evidence of being able to hold the emotions of another person without falling into "fix-it" mode. The leader who understands he cannot fix a situation will translate emotional safety by remaining present in prayer-filled silence.

My mentor and director of Clinical Pastoral Education (a program for training clergy to do pastoral care, often through hospital chaplaincy) was Sat Kartar Khalsa-Ramey, who was ordained in the Sikh tradition. Early in my chaplaincy training, she escorted me on rounds in the hospital. On one particular evening, the cardiac unit paged me. When I arrived at the unit an anxious nurse met us. She explained that a man had been brought in from the local prison with an irregular heartbeat.

Before entering the room, Sat Kartar told me to "lean in" to the patient—to be as spiritually present as I could. "Create a safe confessional," she said. Sat Kartar wanted me to be as close as I could to the patient without violating his personal space. Too close and he would turn away; too far away and he would sense a barrier between us. She suggested, while staying back physically, that I could lean in with my spirit, so my empathy could reach across the space between the patient and me. Walking through the door, I saw he was in a black and white striped prison jumper. His feet were chained to the foot of the bed.

I pulled up a chair and asked him if I could sit down. He didn't say no, so I sat my chair at the head of the bed with my knees against the edge of the frame. "How are you feeling?" He stared at the ceiling. I waited in silence for several minutes. Then I leaned a tiny bit closer. "What are you feeling right now?" He did not move, but turned his eyes, looking into mine. "Why are you here?" I whispered. We held our positions for an hour. Slowly, he told his story, shed a few private tears, and finally, when he was finished, raised his hand to shake mine and said, "Thanks."

In a hidden hospital alcove, Sat Kartar assisted me in unpacking the experience. She asked me what I was feeling, what emotions came to the surface, and what his story had evoked in my story? I told her I felt trusted. "He trusted you because you trusted him. You leaned in to him, you got as spiritually and physically close as you could while maintaining his safety, you were vulnerable and you relinquished your position of power. He needed a safe space and you gave it to him."

Creating emotionally safe space demands non-judgmental acceptance. The spiritual director, like the leader, does this by relinquishing the position of power. When I as the leader let down my defenses and communicate my own vulnerability, the other person perceives my transparency as spiritually leaning into his space, a place where he is in control, where he feels safe. Obviously, invading someone's personal space is inappropriate. The point of spiritually leaning into a person's space while maintaining appropriate physical boundaries is not to gain power over a person, but instead to relinquish power.

In Jesus, God is born into the world as a helpless child. In the act of human birth, God leans into the human story, thereby self-limiting God's power. Jesus's human experience is the sign of God's leaning into the human experience through identifying with human weakness. Jesus experienced hunger, thirst, fatigue, being misunderstood, rejection, physical pain, and the emotional trauma of feeling abandoned. In the experiences of Jesus, God leaned into the human experience. God became intimately close to humanity. God, through Jesus, models the value of spiritually and physically "leaning in" to create a safe space for the individual.

Benjy showed up to my office unannounced. A friend told him I was a safe person to confide in. He was a handsome twenty-something, near the end of his undergraduate degree. His hair was neatly styled. He wore tight new jeans, low at the hip. His soft blue sweater was worn over a pressed white collared shirt. His low-top Converse tennis shoes matched his sweater. When he crossed his legs, he revealed a tattoo on his calf of what I surmised was a dragon's tail.

"How can I help you?" I asked.

"I need to talk, to sort some things out, with someone who will keep confidence. I assume you do that?" pointing to his neck, indicating the fact that I was wearing a clerical collar.

"Benjy, as long as you haven't molested a child or murdered someone, I will keep absolute confidence. If you are considering suicide, I will ask you to seek psychological help. Have I touched on anything you want to talk about?"

"Not yet, but that's all good to know." He didn't smile and neither did I.

"What do you want to sort out?" I asked.

"I'm bi." He sat with legs tightly crossed and his arms folded, closely pressed around his chest. I sat with my hands lightly held in my lap, trying to communicate openness.

"Bisexual," he said. I nodded to affirm I understood but did not judge. "I haven't been that sexually active. And I always use a condom. Except a month ago. I went to this party with some friends. I had a few drinks. Popped an X. I danced with a few different guys. But this one gorgeous man paid special attention to me. He's older, big, athletic, you know what I mean?"

I gave a slight nod. Then he was quiet. We sat in silence. I waited for him to continue. At one point he shifted in his chair. He appeared to be uncomfortable. He started to get up. I had the feeling he was going to leave. I maintained silence. He must have reconsidered and lowered himself into the chair. He stared at the floor for a bit and then turned to look me in the eye.

"I got tested last week . . . There was something about that guy . . . I just knew it . . . The one time . . . I'm HIV positive. Now what?"

Benjy was not asking me the question. He might have been asking himself. Or maybe he was asking God.

"So, what do you think is next?" I asked.

The question opened the door to begin a safe relationship between us that continues today. The relationship is based on emotionally safe, non-judgmental conversation with honest, uncomfortable questions, intended to allow Benjy to find a way forward in his relationship with himself, God, and others.

Months before I was ordained I was experiencing a lot of uncertainty about my "worthiness" for the priesthood. I confessed to one of my priest mentors that my greatest fear was being in a situation in which I had no idea how to help a grieving parent. He responded, "In that moment, you will realize God is present. And you will accept the fact that without God, you can do nothing." Like probably every clergyperson, I would learn what he meant.

A young man in our community committed suicide. I met with his parents, estranged from each other and their troubled son. In a two-hour period, they filled the room with stifled tears, moments of sobbing, anger, laughter, and storytelling, then waves of regret and instances of horror. I did not judge their son or them. I did not try to provide answers, which would have been trivial. Nor did I offer pious platitudes, like "He's in a better place now." It appeared this young man took his own life because he felt abandoned by God, his family, and his friends. In his final note he wrote he was exhausted, too weary to go on.

In between the oscillating crushes of emotional expression, we sat in awkward silence, waiting for the next storm to erupt. Finally, the parents reached a point of emotional exhaustion. It was time to pray. I had absorbed the stories of their son. My prayer repeated their story with the words only God could provide.

This emotionally charged moment appeared to be the beginning of a healing process that will never be completed. Because of our time together, the parents had become somewhat comfortable sitting in stillness at the funeral. When the father lost emotional control and then when the mother could not hold her flood of tears, God provided my silence, and the Spirit of God gave me a non-anxious presence. As a leader, I was sustained by God's presence of peace when every fiber of the parents' emotions was raw and when I knew I did not have the strength they needed.

Of course, in the situations I described above, church leaders anticipate an array of emotions to be displayed. However, the more difficult circumstances are when outbursts arise unexpectedly. How does the leader respond when two congregants express harsh words over seemingly trivial circumstances? What is the leader's reaction when board members exchange heated words over the budget? Providing emotional safety for one person under stress is challenging enough. Ensuring emotional safety in a communal setting can be like walking a tightrope.

Congregational leaders confronted with conflict in groups can incorporate the same techniques relied upon by spiritual directors in one-on-one sessions. The leader who desires to create emotional safety will, first, operate out of a theology of safety, regarding every person in the situation as bearing the sacred image of God.

Second, the leader will lean into the situation, not avoiding, denying, or neglecting the conflict, no matter how uncomfortable. This means, for example, that when a vestry member gets angry and expresses his anger toward the leader, or worse, toward other vestry members, the leader must protect anyone being attacked. If the leader does not protect the group, she cannot lead.

To defuse the anger, the leader must make it perfectly clear that everyone's safety is at risk. The leader can tell the angry person that she does not feel safe. If the assault continues, the leader can ask for a season of silence and then lead prayer, asking the Holy Spirit to bring peace into the situation. If the anger continues, the leader should call for an end to the meeting and ask the angry person to remain in order to discuss the situation with the leader. At times, leaders must lean in with all the strength the Holy Spirit of God can provide.

Third, the leader will be open about her feelings in the situation. While maintaining a non-anxious and non-judgmental presence, the leader must exemplify how the group will work forward through the conflict. In moments of intense conflict, the leader who expresses her feelings will allow other members of the group to share how they are feeling in the meeting. The leader must model the capacity to express how he is feeling without being overwhelmed by the outward expression of emotions in the group. As the leader, I may feel anger, and I may say someone's behavior angers me, but I do not have to use angry words or express angry behavior, thereby setting an example. If, however, anyone in the group continues to express anger or abusive behavior, the leader must be direct in setting the parameters for safe group dynamics.

Fourth, the leader must create a safe alcove for group members to tell each other short personal stories. When I can tell you my first grandchild was born this week, you may have a better understanding as to why I feel so good about life. Or if I tell you my mom is near death, you may express sympathy for my weepy behavior. A good way to start meetings is with a "check-in." The leader can start the session with two or three sentences about how he is feeling or what might be happening in his life outside the church setting. Then ask each member to go around the circle and share briefly. This gives folks the opportunity to share good news or concerns in their lives. This is also an opportunity for the leader to "check the temperature" in the room. If anyone is suffering extraordinary stress, the leader and other group members are made aware and can anticipate the stress being played out in the meeting. After each person has had time to share during the check-in, the leader can offer prayer, weaving each person's story into one picture instead of isolated images, and allowing individuals to recognize that they are part of the holy tapestry of God.

The most important time for us to listen to a congregational check-in is when shaking hands with the people as they leave the church. Facial expressions, body language, and eye contact are important ways people communicate. After the congregation has worshipped, people will usually communicate a collective "feel" to the leaders. Every congregation will translate their feelings differently. Some of these differences will depend upon the denomination, the church season, the season of the year, and particular stresses of the congregation, like the recent loss of a beloved member or a leadership transition.

As difficult as it may be to sense the collectively felt emotional tenor of the community, the leadership as a whole must work hard to get a read on the climate in order to determine, for example, when to introduce new initiatives or how to work through congregational conflict. If the leader and the leadership team are feeling uncertain about how the congregation is feeling collectively, it may be a good time to bring in an outside consultant or judicatory officer. Often an experienced outside resource can quickly read the congregation by observing worship, interviewing leadership groups, as well as casually conversing with people at the coffee hour.

Bringing in someone from the outside may feel intimidating or feel threatening to the leaders of the congregation. However, consulting with others is a common practice among spiritual directors. Spiritual directors do not operate in isolation. A competent director will have her own supervisor to consult about the progress of her directees. In difficult cases, the director may ask the supervisor to sit in on a session or two. When the emotional safety of an individual, a group, or a congregation is in question, it is wise to seek counsel to develop the best plan forward.

Unfortunately, the work of creating and developing an emotionally safe environment for the church community is never finished. Each facet of safety has its own unique twists and requires attention. However, the leader must always keep the larger picture of congregational safety in mind. This means our work continues.

SPIRITUAL SAFETY

Providing spiritual safety for our congregants should be a given for the leadership of the faith community. And creating a church environment for people to rely upon for emotional safety is a part of our pastoral concern for our members. However, in some instances spiritual safety is overlooked. If the leader makes the assumption that everyone in his community shares the same beliefs, then it is likely some people will feel threatened if they share doubts and questions about faith and religion.

Since the terrorist attacks of September 11, 2001, spiritual safety has been a priority conversation among interfaith groups, especially when Christians and Muslims are in the same meeting. In March 2010, I was invited with Ahmad Shqeirat, imam at the Islamic Cultural Center in Tempe, Arizona, to attend an interreligious conference at Virginia Theological Seminary (VTS). The conference organizers, funded by a grant from the Henry Luce Foundation, invited twenty Anglican (Episcopal) and twenty Muslim global leaders to discuss a peaceful response to the tenth anniversary of 9/11. Ahmad and I had been invited because we had been leaders of a gathering on September 11, 2009, in Tempe, held in response to the threatened burning of the Holy Koran by Terry Jones, pastor of the Dove World Outreach Center in Gainesville, Florida.

The VTS conference consisted of three twelve-hour days packed with listening to intense stories like Ahmad's. On November 20, 2006, he and five other imams had been escorted off of US Airways Flight 300 bound for Phoenix out of the Minneapolis-St. Paul International Airport. They were alleged to have said prayers and made comments to each other in Arabic, apparently making some passengers on the flight uncomfortable. Ahmad told the conference that one imam was blind. All six were handcuffed, escorted off the plane, forced to walk unassisted down a ramp, placed in separate police cars and taken to a detention center for interrogation. After hours of questioning, a federal agent determined the arrest was unwarranted and the six were returned to the airport. US Airways refused to issue them new tickets or let them board another flight. The imams had to purchase new tickets from another airline. A year later, US Airways reached an out-of-court settlement with the six imams. Ahmad and a few others shared their stories to the entire group.

Then facilitators divided the forty participants into small groups. We were asked to share a moment in our life when we experienced spiritual pain, whether from prejudice, mistreatment, or being misunderstood. We also were able to ask one another questions about how our different faith beliefs informed our response to mistreatment and pain. We learned that Christianity and Islam have similar views about how we as human beings are supposed to treat each other, about loving God and loving one's neighbor.

Learning about the commonality of our two traditions made me feel a deeper connection with my friend Ahmad and the others at the conference. However, developing a deeper friendship heightened the discomfort I experienced of sitting in a room with twenty Episcopalians and revealing to our Muslim counterparts that though we were Episcopalians and a part of the worldwide Anglican Communion, we Anglicans did not share a common interpretation of scripture, prayer book, and social practice, especially with regard to the ordination of women, gays, and lesbians. Even greater diversity was revealed between the American Episcopalians and international Anglican clergy. We discussed our differences openly in front of our Muslim counterparts even to the point that some of the dialogue became very tense.

With what appeared to be the same discomfort, our Muslim brothers and sisters also revealed their lack of uniformity in their beliefs about Islam and their approaches to global diplomacy. I do believe the experience of the Muslims watching us Episcopalians wrestle among ourselves and then we Episcopalians watching a similar conversation among the Muslims, raised the level of commonality among the conference participants, in spite of the dis-ease it caused. The conference experience raised the level of resolve of both the Episcopalians and the Muslims attending the conference to work together to develop peaceful responses to the tenth anniversary of 9/11 in our own communities.

Forty people from around the globe were able to listen to one another's varied stories because we were in a spiritually safe environment, facilitated by a professional team. The leaders of the conference were experienced in creating small interactive groups of Christians and Muslims. Throughout the three days the facilitators constantly changed the makeup of the small groups based on faith, region, and gender. The questions before each small group were focused with the intent of allowing each individual the appropriate time to tell his or her story and then for others to ask questions. At the conclusion of each small-group session, we were brought back into the large group to share our reflections on the time together. We ate as a community. Time was allotted for Christian prayer, for Muslim prayer, and the invitation to share in one another's experience. We also had the opportunity to pray together, with people of two different religions, birthed out of the Abrahamic tradition, praying as one.

The facilitators acted as spiritual guides throughout the VTS conference. Their role was to create opportunities for conversation among people of two different religious traditions, as well as to explore the less than subtle nuanced differences within the two traditions. At times the conversations were tender, other times intense, and many times emotional. But the facilitators gave the participants some tools to work with inside our small groups. These tools can be used by anyone who might not be as well trained as the VTS facilitators.

When we take time to listen to one another's story of spiritual pain, we begin to recognize that each of us has suffered and that life is a fragile experience. Spiritual direction is an experience of mutuality. The directee obviously is in the relationship to share her stories with the director in the hope of gaining insight into her spiritual journey. The relationship has to be transparent for the directee to feel safe; therefore, the director must also share some personal stories with the directee. The congregational leader can follow this pattern and create storytelling events with the purpose of allowing people to share their stories of suffered spiritual pain in a non-threatening environment.

The storytelling event can be planned around a special day in the life of the parish, like a special anniversary of the church, a celebration, or remembrance of a special occasion, such as 9/11. Small-group leaders can be trained before the gathering. The leader can begin the event by sharing a personal story. He will be modeling how to tell a story. Then the leader can distribute guidelines for sharing and the larger group can be broken into groups of five, including the small-group leaders.

Guidelines for small-group sharing should include the following instructions:

1. Each story should be no longer than six minutes, giving everyone in the group time to share. The small-group leader is given permission to be the timekeeper.
2. Group members should listen to the story without interruption. Follow-up remarks and questions are to be held until everyone has had an opportunity to share his or her story.
3. The group leader will close with a prayer.

When each small group has finished, the congregational leader will then pull everyone back together. At this point the leader can ask the small-group leaders to share (1) common themes found within the stories, and (2) surprises heard or new things learned. The congregational leader can write these items on newsprint or a white board for everyone to see. Sharing stories about common experiences will bring people to a greater empathy for one another.

Once congregation members have shared such an experience, the congregational leader can expand storytelling events to include participants from a neighboring church of a different Christian tradition, a synagogue, a mosque, or an interfaith gathering of all three faith traditions. Sharing spiritual stories brings communities together.

Also attending the VTS conference was Dorothy Saucedo, ordained deacon in the Diocese of Navajoland, who serves at the same parish I do. She was invited because she was the Christian storyteller at the 2009 interfaith event in Tempe. Dorothy brought not only her Christian perspective but also her Navajo tradition and spirituality to the VTS conference.

Dorothy leads the Diocese of Arizona in Native Urban Ministry by developing outreach programs bringing native peoples and Anglos of Arizona together for education and dialogue. Our parish is host to her work and some of these events. Vivian Winter Chaser, a Lakota and deacon of the Diocese of Arizona, and also a member of our parish, partners with Dorothy in this work. Together these women help foster an air of interreligious sensitivity in our parish, teaching us that each First Peoples Nation has its own specific religion and perspective on Christianity.

Dorothy and Vivian are excellent storytellers. Each brings together her native spirituality with her understanding of Christianity. These women are honest about the injustices they suffered under the hands of Anglo teachers in the reservation schools. Both were denied the right to speak their native language. And both were refused the opportunity to learn the spirituality of their people. Only as they became adults were they able to regain a lost language and religion. Now both are deacons in the Episcopal Church. The power of Dorothy's and Vivian's stories is moving.

Dorothy and Vivian are loving, authentic, honest, and inviting. These characteristics invite others to tell their own faith tradition stories. Because Dorothy and Vivian have shared their stories of personal struggle and the recovery of their tradition, they create a safe space for others to share openly and to listen to new stories.

Spiritual safety is possible in spiritual direction because the director is open to theological and intellectual diversity. That does not mean the spiritual director is a practitioner or believer in every faith tradition he encounters. When Thomas Merton was preparing to write *Mystics and Zen Masters,* and then travel to Asia for what would be the last journey of his life, he was asked if he was going to become a Buddhist. He said he wasn't, that he was a Catholic and that Catholicism was his home. He said he could learn a great deal, however, from those who had practiced meditation for thousands of generations, and that from these Buddhist monks he could bring much to his own understanding and practice of the Christian tradition of meditation and prayer.[12] Merton was open to the presence of God within all people.

Sometimes the best spiritual-direction relationship exists between two people of different Christian denominations or even different faith traditions. Acceptance of a variety of spiritual thought does not weaken the spiritual director's mooring. Rather, the director learns practices that enrich her own spiritual life, while at the same she learns to relate to the faith of other traditions.

One of the most helpful practices the leader can engage in is spiritual direction. Leaders who receive spiritual direction will be better equipped to lead, using techniques learned under the guidance of a spiritual director. And the spiritual director will be a resource for experiencing new practices. Whether or not the leader incorporates any of these practices into his personal spiritual routine, being familiar with a variety of spiritual practices can in turn be a resource for others.

Whenever someone comes to me with the question about whether I have tried a certain practice, it is helpful if I have some experience with the practice in order to counsel the person about the suitability of that practice. Some of the helpful practices I have experienced are yoga, meditation, chanting, and the use of prayer beads.

I learned the most about meditation from Sat Kartar. She taught me that during meditation I should "attach" myself to the

Ground of Being (the mystery of the essence of the divine Creator). Because I am making this attachment, my mind is free and my body is relaxed, and I can then go deeper into God as a part of the meditation. She explained that attachment is like dropping an anchor. When the anchor is attached to the bottom of the sea, the boat is free to simply float without the fear of wandering into dangerous waters. So if I anchor myself to the Ground of Being, I am liberated to float in the meditation, free of worry that I might wander into spiritual waters I did not intend. The effect of Sat Kartar's teaching about meditation has created softness, gentleness, and more openness in my relationship with God and with others who are exploring our church community for the first time.

The church leader can incorporate the spiritual director's gentle manner of openness in order to create safe space for spiritual seekers he encounters in his ministry. Gentle openness is the willingness to metaphorically place our stone, our spiritual beliefs, in God's flowing brook. By placing our stone in the gently running water, we know that over time we will be made smooth. Or we may be like the Hohokam's spiral-etched stone, rubbed by the dancing people so often that the image of the spiral became smudged by the pressure and oils of centuries of hands. Spiritual formation is a process requiring the gentle openness of being formed by the active agency of God being used by the spiritual director.

When the leader is willing to be open to new spiritual ideas, he will at times have to revisit some of his personal beliefs in order to maintain a surefooted theological grounding. While Sat Kartar was willing to teach me a few of the methods of Sikh meditation, she insisted these methods only be used to enhance my Christian spiritual practice. Physical exercise uses resistance to strengthen the muscles, and the spiritual muscles are also made stronger through the leader's practice of periodically questioning long-held beliefs, the practice of resistance against tradition. This practice is not intended to deconstruct his faith or reject tradition, but instead, to strengthen faith.

In the same manner, the community will be strengthened when a diversity of practice is experienced that creates softness, gentleness, and openness towards those in our community and those in different faith traditions.

Our young adults gather every Thursday night for St. Brigid's Community, a time of worship, dinner, and conversation. Regularly, an older outside observer will ask if he can join us. His motive is typically to see what we are doing in order to take some ideas back to his home parish. Visitors are always welcome, but I have learned to ask these observers to simply watch and listen and to hold any questions until after the gathering. My work in these young adult conversations is patterned after group spiritual direction sessions.

The conversations typically start with a question about the scriptural text or the homily I offered during the worship. The structure is free flowing. We only have one rule: that we keep each other safe. All questions are welcomed, even the question, "God?" I rarely respond to any comments, though I may ask more questions. My experience has taught me to also expect follow-up questions later from the young adults in a private setting.

Invariably, after the gathering, the observer will want to know why I did not set "straight" incorrect biblical references or theological statements. My intent for St. Brigid's Community is for the participants to be willing to return time and again, leaving their tea bag to steep in the spiritual climate. Over time, if the young adult knows she will never be put down or corrected and she is safe to express her opinions, she will stay engaged in the community. Being continually connected, she will hear the scripture, be surrounded by the liturgy, and remain in conversation with me and the other folks in the community. The patience of the Holy Spirit is the teacher. My responsibility is to provide a spiritually safe environment where the formative work of the Spirit is palpable.

A leader relying upon the wellspring of the spiritual director's techniques may need to remind congregants that he is not necessarily accepting the views of another tradition, but instead creating a safe environment allowing all persons to participate in the community. Admittedly, this is a difficult, if not impossible undertaking in some religious climates. But as a leader in our community,

I continue to discover ways to create spiritual safety for everyone who comes into our community.

In our congregation, we have been able to bring together significant partners in dialogue about critical communal issues. I have had conversations with other young adult leaders—Christian, Jew, and Muslim—listening for the practices or rituals that might be helpful in developing spiritual depth within our community. And then I bring these practices or rituals back to our group, praying that some of our members will find them meaningful in their experience of God.

Spiritual directors also depend upon the power of prayer and ritual to call upon God to be present to ensure spiritual safety. I had the privilege to visit Canterbury Cathedral in England. It happened to be noon and I was at one of the tiny undercroft chapels. A voice came over the intercom asking everyone to stop for a few moments and offer the Lord's Prayer in his or her own language. I knelt at the rail in front of the small altar and prayed. There were no cushions at the kneeling rail, only stone, worn over the centuries by the thousands who had prayed at the millennium-old chapel. I entered into personal contemplation of a story that included the saints, kings, queens, and noblemen buried just a few feet away. In the story, I envisioned these ancient ones praying at this same rail. Surely Thomas Aquinas, Augustine of Canterbury, popes, and archbishops (most likely including Rowan Williams, archbishop of Canterbury) prayed here. Their prayers and my humble recitation of Jesus's prayer were lifted at this safe rail. But I would not have had the epiphany of my humble prayers being woven into the prayers of the communion of saints were it not for the daily ritual in the safety of the Cathedral. The liturgy of prayer drew me into its safe, sacred space. As leaders, we have the privilege of creating hospitable opportunities for revelatory experiences by providing a safe spiritual space through ritual, prayer, and liturgy. My parish is not Canterbury Cathedral; it does not have to be. It must, though, be as safe and as hospitable as possible, allowing visitors to experience God.

Providing for church safety is much easier if the threatening force is visible and identifiable. As I have written above, we leaders can work to improve safety when we can see the problem, like a cracked sidewalk, or when we see the need to protect children, or to reach out in love to provide a safe place for a family to grieve when they have suffered the loss of a loved one. Our community is committed to providing a safe space for all people to enter in prayer and the peace of God. We are not perfect. There is a cost. We fail sometimes. And then we ask forgiveness—and we remain in the presence of God and one another. To walk apart from our sisters and brothers who bear the image of God is not an option.

When Spiritual Safety Is Compromised by the Demonic

Given the responsibility of leaders to provide safety for the congregation, they should be sensitive to the possibility that demonic forces will try to interfere with healthy congregations. The safety of the church can be invaded from the world of the unseen, the demonic. In these instances leaders can draw upon the practices of some spiritual directors to invoke ritual and liturgy to protect the space and the people, as I did several years ago.

On a hot July day in Tempe, someone broke into the outdoor columbarium in our parish courtyard and stole the ashes from two niches. The police had never heard of such a thing. They took a report, looked for fingerprints, and suggested we contact some local mortuaries for advice. Parishioners, who needed a logical explanation for such a heinous crime, surmised the thieves took the ashes for the copper they believed the urns were made from. I did nothing to dispel the idea, though I knew the urns did not contain any copper. To say the least, our parishioners were alarmed and spiritually upset.

At the time, my experience with such an unusual occurrence was limited. I contacted Phil Jackson, a colleague and friend in our diocese, for counsel. He had a quiet reputation for being a priest who knew what to do in such circumstances. Phil spent an afternoon asking me about the history of the parish, my personal story, and a reading of the recent spiritual thermometer of our parish.

I told Phil that dozens of years prior to my arrival a priest at the church had violated clerical ethics in a serious misconduct in his role as pastor. Rumors about the reasons for the pastor's indiscretions were numerous, but the consistency of the painful and strange stories always caused me to cringe. Upon discovery of the violations, the priest was immediately removed. The parishioners responded with an exodus from the pews. By the time I arrived decades and several priests later, a church that at one time had had an average Sunday attendance of six hundred had declined to fifty.

Over time, God continued to work the healing of many old wounds. In the first two years of my ministry, we experienced a slow but steady growth both numerically and spiritually. Just months prior to the theft of the ashes, a founder and elder saint of the church, George Morrell, died a gentle death. His family wanted to honor his lifetime of commitment to the church by commissioning a new altar and financing the refurbishing of the chancel. Remodeling began, and at about the same time we began to tear out the floor on which the old altar rested, the ashes were stolen from the columbarium.

After listening to my account of the history of the parish, Phil recommended we offer special prayers to cleanse and ritually re-bless and consecrate the space around the perimeter of the church, the desecrated columbarium, the ancillary buildings, the sanctuary, and particularly the chancel. Phil said these prayers were necessary in case any unseen demonic forces had ever been present in the parish, especially considering the reported inappropriate acts of a priest from years past.

At this point we decided that the old altar would be taken out of the building sooner than planned, deconsecrated and ground into sawdust. The old carpet immediately under and around the altar was burned. I gathered a few parishioners, known to have an active prayer life. Together, offering prayers for cleansing, walking with incense, we spread salt and holy water around the perimeter of the property. Every room was blessed with sacramental water and incense. Every door was blessed with oil. Salt was spread across every threshold. Prayers for cleansing and protection were offered throughout the church buildings.

The rituals I used in this experience are those used by generations of holy leaders and spiritual directors. Water, which is blessed in preparation for baptism, provides the cleansing force of the sacramental presence of God. Baptismal water strewn in a room will drive any demon from the space. Incense used to represent the presence of the Holy Spirit would further purge any evil force. Holy oil blessed by the bishop will provide a protective portal for a room. Salt, necessary to sustain life, is repugnant to any spirit threatening human life. Jesus said that when two or three are gathered together our prayers are heard. The number-one agency in battling the demonic is the power of prayer. The prayers offered over the water, incense, salt, and oil combined with the prayers said by those gathered ensure God's hearing of our desire to drive out any unwanted presence.

As we entered the sanctuary, our prayers intensified. More water, salt, incense, and oil were used in the worship space. When we stepped into the chancel, we offered prayers written especially for the cleansing and protection of this space. Months later, when the remodeling had been completed and the new altar was ready, we wrote a liturgy for the service. Our bishop presided over the worship and offered his special blessing of the new altar and chancel.

For months following, many of our people remarked about how much "lighter" the space felt. Our parish continued to grow. During the next two years, though, someone would occasionally mention experiencing an "odd sensation," typically in the sanctuary. Immediately I would offer prayers, and sprinkle water, salt, and incense throughout the worship space. Spiritual leaders can enact these same rituals and liturgies today when they sense or feel that the demonic is present or attacking the community or the life of an individual.

After the break-in of the columbarium, I had promised the people we would not inter any more ashes in it until we could either secure the space or move it to a safer location. A year after the remodeling was finished, George's wife, Patti, passed away. The family wanted to contribute to the purchase and installation of a new columbarium in the confines of the sanctuary. With an additional estate gift, the parish was able to complete the project four years after the theft of the ashes. We blessed the new columbarium with water, salt, oil and incense. Then I interred the cremains of several individuals that had been awaiting the new sacred space, including those of George and Patti. At the final moment of the special service of dedication, I felt a wind blowing everything unsafe out of the building. A breath of fresh fragrant air blew into the church. A cleansing and a settling had taken place.

Without any visible reason, our parish experienced a quick surge of energy and new growth. I cannot explain it. It was a mystery. But I am convinced that the completion of the columbarium and the settling of disturbed souls contributed greatly to the feeling of a new sense of spiritual safety in our parish. Our desire and mission to be hospitable was set free.

A congregational leader may serve a lifetime of ministry and never encounter the demonic. Maybe he will need these rituals only once in a career. But the leader may be a person like my colleague Phil, who is called upon frequently to share his knowledge with other leaders.

In these mysterious circumstances, precautions must be observed. A leader should never enter into work against the demonic alone. An experienced mentor must be available to support the leader with her presence and to pray for him. Devout congregants should be enlisted as a prayer team. The forces of the demonic should never be taken lightly and never be confronted without careful preparation.

My experience has been that once a leader encounters the demonic and then calls upon God to cast the force of evil away from the church or a person, that leader will become ever more sensitive to the existence and activity of the demonic. I do not look for people seeking help to cast out forces from their homes, hospital rooms, or their lives, but, instead, these people seek me out to do this work. I admit that being always on the lookout for the demonic is a mysterious way of seeing life.

The Leader's Stewardship
of Congregational Safety
Is a Mysterious Work

The life of a leader in a spiritual community who chooses to draw from the wellspring of the spiritual director will indeed begin seeing life in a mysterious way, one that sharpens the leader's lenses, so she might see how best to protect her congregation from physical, emotional, and spiritual harm.

Scholar and Presbyterian pastor Annemarie S. Kidder wrote the following in the introduction to Catholic theologian Karl Rahner's book *The Mystical Way in Everyday Life*: "In the mystical way of seeing, ordinary life and everyday events are interpreted in light of the extra-ordinary, the natural from the perspective of the supernatural, the concrete from the position of the transcendent, the human from the view of the divine."[13] A different way of seeing is necessary for the leader to be able to give his intellect, wisdom, and energy to ensure the safety of every individual within his care. Creating safe space can be the most demanding work of the spiritual director, church leader, or leader of any organization. Vigilance, constancy, never being satisfied with "safe enough"—these are the characteristics of those who faithfully keep the people safe. As the shepherd keeps watch over the flock, the work is done out of love for the people. Just love the people, my bishop told me. Indeed, love for the people is the best motivator for such a daunting responsibility.

THREE

The Leader as Holy Listener

You no hear me.

—Dinah Stafford

Contemplative listening, then, means bringing a full-bodied, loving presence to the person before you, as well as to what is said and what as yet remains unsaid.

—Elizabeth Liebert[1]

I began learning the value of listening as an eight-year-old boy. Our family was visiting my aunt and uncle for a holiday. The rain was pouring down in Los Angeles that Friday of Thanksgiving weekend. My dad and his brother had left the house for the afternoon. My teenage cousins were gone for the day with friends. My younger sister was taking a long nap. I had my mother and aunt to myself. The two women were close but did not get to see each other very often. They were craving time for a deep conversation.

I was a chatty child, or needed attention, or was just being an annoying eight-year-old boy that particular day. Whatever the reason, my mom and aunt evidently could not enjoy the afternoon. My aunt left the room. She reappeared holding a silver dollar. She told me if I could be quiet for one hour the coin was mine. She laid it on the table. I remember distinctly: the shiny silver dollar was motivation enough.

I found a book and a corner to sit in at the end of the room. Soon I was looking at the rain playing on the window, imagining that I was running through the yard. It was quiet, except for the rain and the hushed tones of conversation. I could hear my mother's trembling voice, telling her sister-in-law about the trials of being a parent of a handicapped child (my sister). My mother's words began to sink into my mind and my heart. I had not realized my parents' life was so different. The color of my world was changing. The shape of my life was being altered.

I have no idea how long I sat there, listening, thinking, and being formed. Lost in my eight-year-old thoughts, without my noticing her arrival, I became aware that my loving aunt was sitting beside me on the floor, putting the silver dollar in my hand, asking me if I wanted to play our favorite game, Yahtzee. I still have that silver dollar close at hand. And I still hold firmly in my soul my first lesson of listening.

Listening is a learned skill. Even a child can learn to listen. Listening at a deep level is hearing in such a way that the speaker feels heard and the listener is transformed by the act of listening. Anyone who desires to hear deeply can learn the skills needed to be a good listener.

But as leaders in a Christian community I believe we are called to go beyond the realm of being good listeners. We must become holy listeners. The leader, who listens at the deepest level of holy listening, must be present like Jesus, listening as if she is the very ear of God, taking in every sound and word being spoken and unspoken by the one in need.

We think of Jesus being a proclaimer, but he was a listener as well. He listened to:

the Spirit of God (John 4:34)
the teachers of the cultural and religious past (Luke 2:46)
children (Luke 18:15–17)
those in pain (Mark 1:40)
strangers in a foreign land (John 4:7–29)
the grieving (John 11:1–37)
the criminal (Luke 23:39–43)
the perplexed and the confused (Luke 24:13–35)
his critics (Luke 20:1–8)

He heard his followers at a compassionate level. And because he listened to them, he was able to minister to their needs and effectively lead the flock.

He also implored his disciples, who would be leaders, to be listeners (Mark 4:9 and Matt. 11:5). A leader who is being like Jesus will recognize the importance of his place as a holy listener and will be fully present, so the hearer can feel in her heart that she is heard, as if by God. When she tells her story and the leader of her community really listens and takes in her words, hopefully she will know that God truly hears the inner words of her heart. A leader who fails to listen, then, to hear at the deepest level, to understand, to know intimately, is not leading the people but instead is simply giving orders. People who do not feel they are being heard will not tolerate a non-listening leader for very long. Members of a congregation who do not feel heard will vote with their feet; they will either leave the church or revolt against the leader.

Martin Thornton offers four practical guidelines for effective listening by spiritual directors that can easily be applied in the work of the congregational leader. First, the spiritual director listens rather than talks. Second, the spiritual director exercises extreme patience and focus, recognizing that spiritual direction will be a long continuous process. Third, the spiritual director is a guest who listens and is not an authority figure. And fourth, because the love of Christ is equally shared between the spiritual director and the directee, both are listening to what the Spirit is saying.[2] The leader, then, as a guest of the congregation, will be constantly listening.

To learn the skills of listening, one must often spend time with a mentor or take continuing education classes. Good listening skills are not easily acquired, but practicing in a safe laboratory setting, like a classroom, prevents us as listeners from having to learn "in the field" at the expense of parishioners. As spiritual director Pierette Stokes has so eloquently written, holy listening requires the hearer to be open to the vast array of ways in which individuals are able to hear the Divine and one another. Holy listening is tuning into the varied channels through which God speaks to us.

Spiritual directees listen for how the Holy breaks into the material reality—through prayer, meditation, holy text, ritual, dreams, art, music, literature, nature, mature love relationships, creation, crisis, thoughts, feelings, deep desires, weaknesses and struggles, and the shadow side of self and society. They want to understand and be in relationship with the beloved Soul more intimately.[3]

Spiritual directors are trained to listen to the Divine speaking into their reality. The spiritual director actively models holy listening by being present simultaneously to the directee and to the voice of God. The director desires for the directee to learn how to listen to the Divine at an intimate level.

A church leader, then, guides her people in ways of hearing what the Spirit of the Divine is saying to the congregation. The leader must know how to listen to the Spirit of God and to parishioners, in order to teach congregants how to listen to the Spirit themselves. By dipping into the spiritual director's wellspring of effective listening techniques, the leader can learn both how to listen and how to teach others to listen.

There are at least three dimensions of holy listening: listening to the Spirit, listening to the other, and listening to the self (to both the conscious and the unconscious). I believe that within each of the three facets of listening there are techniques used by the spiritual director that a leader can also develop to improve her listening skills.

LISTENING TO THE SPIRIT

In the Episcopal tradition, as well as in other churches, following the reading of scripture, the reader says, "The Word of the Lord," and the people respond, "Thanks be to God." After an uplifting reading, the response from the people is usually heard as a resounding affirmation. However, following a difficult or strange reading, the response is often muffled. What I sense the people would like to say is, "Really?" As Episcopalians, we have the option of using another call and response, which we have incorporated into the liturgy in our parish. The reader says, "Hear what the Spirit is saying," followed by silence, a time for us as the congregation to listen and reflect. To listen does not mean to give approval. Instead, listening is paying attention to every nuance of the text.

God, the Living One, desires to be in a dynamic relationship with us. Listening is a reciprocal and a spiritually mature activity, involving the speaker, which in this case is God, and the listener. I listen. The Spirit is heard. The Spirit listens. I am heard. The congregation has a right to expect the leader to be attuned to the whispers of the Spirit, especially in regard to the path of the flock. As a leader, I may hear the Spirit, the word of God, but the question is, "Am I listening?" To listen is to swallow the word of the Lord into the depth of my soul, where the words begin to shape and form my inner being, to transform me into the leader God is calling me to become. In order to be a spiritual leader, like the Good Shepherd, I must be listening to the Spirit at the deep, holy, and interior level, causing a visible change in my life.

How, then, does the leader listen to the Spirit at the intimate and sacred depth? The Spirit may be heard at the holy level in various ways, and the congregation will want to know how their leader is listening to the Spirit. People also want to know how to hear and listen to the Spirit of God in their personal lives. I believe they can best learn these methods of spiritual listening when the leader models how she listens to the Spirit. The only way the congregation can know how the leader hears the Spirit is for her to openly, and with vulnerability, talk to her congregation about the varied ways she listens to the Spirit. While we can listen to the Spirit in many ways, I believe there are at least three specific places we can hear God: in solitude, in consultation, and in community.

Jesus found a haven in listening to God in solitude. Repeatedly we hear stories in the gospels of Jesus slipping away from his followers in the early morning to pray, to talk and to listen to God, in solitude. It was his lifetime practice and especially in the final moments of his days on earth. Jesus's communication with God sustained him. Our daily practice of prayer, talking and listening to God, can mirror Jesus's spiritual practice in solitude and shore us up both in life's mundane moments and in the crises of living and dying.

Prolific author and lecturer Glenn Hinson[4] is a dear and gentle saint of the gospel. However, his life has not been without pain. Born deaf, he had a difficult path to become a respected scholar in the Southern Baptist realm. Much of his early scholarly work was born out of his relationship with a monk who lived nearby, Thomas Merton. Hinson's life is the testimony of a person who could not hear, but did listen at the deepest level. Unfortunately, his life is also an example of the damage caused by leaders who are unwilling to listen. Hinson was caught in the Southern Baptist war of fundamentalism, eventually losing his faculty position at Southern Seminary in Louisville because he engaged in listening to the Spirit through his interaction with the Roman Catholic Merton. Ever resilient, Hinson moved on to the Baptist Theological Seminary in Richmond, where his ecumenical work was supported. It has been my privilege to get to know Glenn. He has a mature and developed spiritual life, but the one practice he relies upon most is his daily one-hour walk. He describes the time on his daily journey walking through his neighborhood as a conversation with God, like two lovers might have on a stroll down the beach. The communication is intimate and deeply meaningful. These times alone with God have been a haven for Glenn.

It had long been my habit to walk every morning. But after hearing Glenn's wise words, my morning monologue, which had been trapped in my head, was transformed into a dialogue with God, whom I love. Spending time alone with God, talking and listening in solitude, however we find that solitude—on a walk, in a closet, on the pond with rod and reel in hand, whether we chant the office, pray the psalms, clear our mind in centering prayer, or have a free flowing chat with God—will open our soul to the presence of God and to hearing what the Spirit is saying.

When I can be alone with God in a safe place, I feel my intimate relationship with the lover God. I feel enriched by the God who continually is fetching my soul, like a sweet lover, into the presence of the Triune Divine. To hear what God has to say, I must be alone in God's presence, a holy place unlike any other. While I share inner secrets with my wife, my lover, that no one else knows, my relationship with God is even more intensely intimate. I crave time to speak to God with the assurance that God will hear my cries. In my leadership role, it is critical that I can discuss with God the concerns of the people and how God would desire me to respond to the congregation's needs. I cannot prepare a sermon, teach a class, offer spiritual direction, lead a meeting, or make decisions without having time alone with the Holy One. I must be able to hear what the Spirit is saying to me as a leader, and that hearing requires solitude.

Once I find comfort in hearing God in solitude, then I can gain confidence in listening to the Spirit while in consultation with others. Jesus consulted with wise mentors in the story of the Transfiguration. There on the mount, Jesus sought the counsel of Elijah and Moses. Little wonder these were the two saints Jesus consulted as his ministry was gaining steam. Moses, who would be God's leader, heard God in a burning bush, battled against the oppression of Pharaoh, and led the people out of bondage, following God through the wilderness. Elijah heard God in the sheer silence. He was a wonder worker, courageous prophet, and priest, and he was also a valiant leader, even a savior, of the people of Israel. These two men of God could surely mentor Jesus.

We too, must have those trusted mentors who provide a haven in which we can hear what the Spirit is saying. These mentors can hold us accountable in our prayer life, and they will offer us a listening ear, so that we may discern what the Spirit is saying. If I listen only in solitude without the consultation of a trusted mentor, I may not be listening fully to the Spirit. A spiritual director must have her own spiritual director, someone whom she can consult on a regular basis regarding her spiritual life and practice. An effective leader must have a confidant, a trusted colleague, coach, or mentor whom she can consult regularly regarding leadership issues, the primary concern being what the leader is hearing from the Spirit.

The third place for holy listening is the most complex of the three and at times may not feel like a haven of safety. Hopefully, in most situations the leader and the people together are hearing what the Spirit is saying, and they agree and can accomplish a great deal of good for the kingdom of God. Unfortunately, there will be times when listening to the Spirit in community causes conflict to arise between the leader and the people, because they disagree on what they are hearing. Sometimes the leader may hear the Spirit but the people do not, and there can be periods when the people are hearing the Spirit clearly but the leader is not listening or is missing the message. Hopefully, the leader and the congregation love each other enough in the Spirit of God that they can remain in a healthy relationship in order to hear the Spirit together in community, carrying out what God has spoken for them to do.

Dietrich Bonhoeffer writes in *Life Together* that the Christian leader's service to the community is to listen to the people. "We do God's work for our brothers and sisters when we learn to listen to them. . . . We should listen with the ears of God, so that we can speak the Word of God."[5] Bonhoeffer is describing holy listening as God's work. He is also saying that listening to the people in turn affords the leader a better platform when it comes time to speak the prophetic word of God. That prophetic word may be uncomfortable for the people to hear. But when the people know their pastor has heard them, they may be able to trust what he has to say. In trust, the congregation can listen to the Spirit through the words of the preacher. Bonhoeffer warns that Christians who fail to listen to one another will "soon no longer be listening to God either."[6] If as the leader, I cannot listen to the people at a holy level, I am denying the holy residing with the congregation. By dismissing the congregation, not listening to them, I deny the presence of God created within them. In this lack of listening, I am also denying that God may be speaking to the people. Any lack of willingness to listen to the people could well be a sign that I am not humble before God and not listening to the Spirit of God. The same can be said about the congregation when they collectively do not listen to their spiritual leaders.

Jesus listened while in community. The story of the Canaanite woman in Matt. 15:21–26 is a vivid example of Jesus hearing the Spirit even while he was in the company of his disciples, who disagreed with him even though they loved him deeply. When Jesus first heard the cries of the Canaanite woman, he ignored her. Jesus may have turned away from her because of his belief that salvation was only for the people of Israel. Jesus may also have been exhibiting cultural bias here by stating, "It is not fair to take the children's food and throw it to the dogs." Yet she would not be denied. Instead she increased her pleading, begging Jesus to heal her daughter. The disciples cautioned Jesus against listening to a woman from the evil district of Tyre and Sidon and encouraged him to send her away. Jesus gave into his disciples and shamed the woman, maybe hoping she would give up. The woman, undeterred, threw herself at Jesus's feet. In a great act of faith, she humbled herself. Jesus, finally listening to the agonizing desperation of a mother's breaking heart, healed her daughter.

I believe that because Jesus listened, he changed his mind about what he thought about the Canaanite woman. Initially he heard what his community was saying. He understood them. In the beginning he agreed with them. Then something clicked. Jesus, listening to the Spirit through the Canaanite woman's pleas, responded to her needs. Theologian Miguel De La Torre writes, "Her remarks shocked Jesus into realizing that faith was not contingent on a person's ethnicity. In fact, Jesus had to admit that this was a woman of great faith."[7] Jesus, in community, heard the Spirit and included the Gentile woman, a social and racial outsider, into the kingdom of God. Deep, holy listening changes our way of thinking and believing and allows the leader to guide others into the process of personal transformation.

Jesus responded to the pleas of the woman with the compassion of God, while offering a glimpse of the love of God to his disciples. Listening to the Spirit in community, especially if the leader changes his mind, comes at the risk of losing authority over the group. Jesus took that risk and gained more authority by doing so. We have to hope the disciples learned a valuable lesson as well. From their prospective they may have felt Jesus did not listen. He disagreed with them and did not heed their counsel. Yet, one of them must have learned the lesson, for the story was retold, maybe at his or her peril of being ultimately rejected like Jesus was.

One of the many reasons that leading a religious community can be so challenging is that those seeking to be heard by the leader have competing agendas. It takes fortitude from the leader to hear the Spirit when those with different agendas are raising the volume of their dissenting voices in an attempt to drown out the leader.

Kirk Smith, bishop of the Episcopal Diocese of Arizona, has listened in community. The issue of immigration has caused divisions in the state, even among churches within the diocese. Smith has listened to many sides of the controversy. He has also listened to the Spirit. Not without risk, he has supported migrants in the state and diocese. He has visited the border on many occasions, praying in vigil at the wall. He has also financially supported the ministries of those providing water, supplies, and spiritual encouragement for those who have crossed the border. Kirk Smith has listened in community and responded to the call of the Spirit, even at his own risk, without neglecting the spiritual needs of the community.

Smith also maintained community by listening to those who have a much different opinion. He listened when he visited his many parishes and was present to those who disagreed with him. Even with different viewpoints, the bishop and the people of the diocese could still gather in worship to hear the scripture, celebrate the sacraments, and participate in ministries of justice other than those on the border, like rebuilding Haiti and supporting the Millennium Development Goals, eight international goals established by the United Nations in 2000 in order to improve the lives of the world's poor and underserved. Bonhoeffer wrote, "Leadership in the church community is unfaithful to the Spirit if this intimacy is not fostered in Word, sacrament, and action for justice."[8] The bishop risked his authority while still being able to lead.

The hard work of listening to the Spirit in solitude, collaboration, and community creates a softening of our heart, preparing us to be more receptive hearers, and readying us to listen to other people as well as to our inner self.

LISTENING TO THE OTHER

As a leader in a spiritual community, I listen to individuals every day in a variety of settings. The opportunities for individual conversation seem endless: the person who makes an appointment for spiritual direction, the drop-in who wants to talk about a problem, the homeless person who needs to tell me his story before asking for money, the intern who is sorting out his next sermon, the caller who needs just a minute of my time, the writer who sends an e-mail seeking "just a little advice," the person in the hospital bed, the nurse who stops to ask an informal personal question, the barista who says, "Can I ask you a question?" Every person I encounter wants more than to be heard; they want me to listen to them at a deep level, a holy level.

The title of this chapter is borrowed from Margaret Guenther's book *Holy Listening: The Art of Spiritual Direction*, referred to above. Guenther is an Episcopal priest and professor of ascetical theology and director of the Center for Christian Spirituality at the General Theological Seminary in New York City. Guenther's work is applicable not only to the spiritual director, but also to the Christian leader, as well as those working in secular settings. Guenther defines "holy listening" as being fully present to the person in front of me. Listening is an action of being attentive to the speaker with my ears, my senses, and my soul.[9] Holy listening is being present to the person I am listening to as if I were listening to the Spirit of God. Guenther suggests listening begins with the listener doing the inner work of self-preparation in order to welcome the stranger.[10] In spiritual direction, the "stranger" is the soul of the directee while the spiritual director is the midwife of a maturing relationship between the directee and God.[11]

Listening involves some specific skills that can be learned and improved upon with practice. Even an experienced and skilled listener can deepen her listening competence. These skills involve listening to both nonverbal cues and to the words spoken. Listening to what is communicated through the nonverbal includes understanding body language, eye movement, and facial expression, and intuiting what has been left unsaid. Listening to what is spoken entails the skills of fully comprehending and having empathy with what is being communicated verbally, through words.

A leader can model good listening by being aware of her own body language, ensuring she is communicating to the speaker that she is fully present, aware at the deepest level, with all her senses. The listener should reflect a calm spirit—by sitting still, breathing slowly, looking at the other person, and adopting a warm and a friendly facial expression. While the other person is talking, a nod, smile, or frown at the appropriate time communicates to the speaker that she is being intently listened to. The leader's initial objective is to present nonverbal cues that communicate that he is listening but that are not distracting to the person talking. When the listener exhibits good listening practices with nonverbal communication, the speaker will often feel heard and can safely and comfortably reveal more of her thoughts and feelings to the listener.

Good listeners will also pick up on the speaker's nonverbal cues. For example, the listener recognizes that the speaker who is unwilling to face or look at the listener and sits with his arms and legs folded tightly is usually unsure, apprehensive, or unwilling to reveal his inner thoughts. Someone who is anxious or doubtful will have a tendency to wrap her arms around herself or pull her hands inside the long sleeves of her sweater. However, some forms of body language can relay varying messages, so the listener must avoid making assumptions about what the speaker is communicating. A person may tuck her legs underneath her when sitting. Her position could be a sign of withdrawal, or it could simply indicate her legs are too short for the chair. Though the speaker is sitting in a manner that seems to say, "I will not be open to you," the listener keeps in mind that he might actually be embarrassed. A man may slouch in the chair, not necessarily out of disrespect, but because he is feeling depressed. The listener is constantly gathering information from all of the speaker's nonverbal signals. The effective listener is attuned to the contextual clues and astutely determines what is being communicated. This takes experience.

The listener notices when the speaker's physical clues change during the course of conversation. The conversation may begin with the speaker facing the listener, sitting straight up in the chair with legs comfortably crossed. Then, at a pensive moment, he might lean forward with his elbows on his knees. And from this reflective position, he may shift into a self-protective mode when uncertainty arises. The more animated the speaker is, the easier it will be for the listener to perceive the nonverbal clues. The more subtle the gestures and movements of the speaker, the harder the listener will have to work to "hear" the speaker's body language.

Some adults in today's culture also present us with a unique opportunity to hear the stories they wear on their bodies. A person with multiple visible tattoos is inviting us to hear the story behind the skin art. A young woman told me "My skin is my journal." Her tattoos were nonverbal messages begging for an oral interpretation. If I can hear what her tattoos are telling me, I can better connect with her story. I have found people very willing to tell me the story behind their tattoos. Many adults of all ages also communicate their feelings by the music they listen to. It can be helpful to ask people to burn a CD of the music they have been listening to the past month. Listening to their music helps me hear the moods the person is experiencing.

Hearing someone's nonverbal communications helps the listener fill in the words left unspoken. If I can hear what he is not saying, I can better listen to what he is saying. Effectively listening to his story takes as much skill as telling a beautiful story. The art of listening is like a spiral. When I hear with compassion, I allow the words to travel deep into my inner being. Taking someone's story into my interior builds a bigger capacity within me for holy listening. Like sea creatures in the nautilus family that build next year's chamber in a logarithmic spiral as they grow, so deep, holy listening creates ever-expanding spaces in my soul to carry the story of the other.

One of the best gifts as a listener that I can offer to the storyteller is to elicit her story so that she can hear it for herself. As a leader relying on the model of holy listening, I listen to what is told on the surface as well as below the surface. If a person comes to me and the story has a natural flow, a beginning, middle, and end, it usually means I am hearing a story that the storyteller is excited to tell, something wonderful, or good, or curious that has happened in his life. Of course, there is always a backstory, so an effective listener notices gaps or pieces of the story that need more explanation and asks clarifying questions.

However, if the story is disjointed, taking unconnected trails, I consider the possibility that I may be hearing the results of a painful inner struggle with a personal conflict, perhaps even one that defies a solution because the problem is related to depression or some other mental health concern. This may not always be the case. Indeed, the person may be healthy and just now beginning to sort out the story. In either case, with a fractured story, there can be so much backstory that I may never hear it all. However, the best way for the storyteller to solve her problem is to hear herself tell her own story, so I try to be fully present to the speaker, encouraging her to tell as much of the story as she can, for what lies within must be exposed in order for the deeper significance to be discovered.

To draw out the story, I use verbal cues to communicate while I am listening. These cues are subtle and require good timing. A simple "hmm" tells the speaker I am listening. "Go on" helps the person talking to know that I, as the listener, am still engaged and willing to hear the entire story. The question, "Can you tell me more about that?" tells the person that I am listening, that I am curious and eager to hear the story in detail.

If I ask a question or make a comment and the other person later says he can't remember where he was in the story, I then know that I broke his train of thought and spoke at the wrong time. It is always best for me as the listener to wait until the speaker has stopped talking for a few moments before I speak. It is best if I wait, even risk an awkward silence, so the storyteller may continue the story before I ask her a question. When I as the listener am asked a question, I know the speaker is ready to listen. If I wait through the awkward silence, I can trust the speaker has finished his story and is waiting for me to ask the next question of him. As a listener, I would rather err on the side of too much silence than too much talking.

When it is time for me to speak, I can ask a question by repeating or paraphrasing what she has said and then asking for more detail. I try not to give advice unless I am directly asked for it, and even then I try to help the person arrive at her own conclusions. If I have a suggestion, I try using her words or ideas to make the point. When I use her words, she knows I have heard what she is saying, and she will be more relaxed and able to hear what I am offering. Usually she has already told me her remedy within the story. She just hasn't put all the pieces of the puzzle together so she can clearly see the solution for herself. Or she may need affirmation of her solution.

Listening to someone tell the story of her dreams is also a way of helping her sort out her life. What lies within includes the unconscious, and the world of dreams is a source of information for us as we live in the conscious world. The ability to draw out a story is important when listening to someone talk about his dreams. If the leader has practiced listening to her own dreams and studied dream work with the guidance of a spiritual director, she can support someone else in listening to his dreams. We are not to interpret another's dreams. This is the work of the dreamer. As a listener, all I can do is listen to his dream, validate that his dream is important, help him sort out his dream, and encourage him to find meaning in his own dream. (Dream work and listening to dreams will be discussed further below.) Being in a constant state of listening requires the attention of the whole person and is hard work.

If both the pastor and other church leaders are always listening, they will be able to hear each other's story, but the leader must create the culture of listening by being a holy listener. Every individual in the group must feel they have an opportunity to be heard. When they feel heard, they will find their voice, believing someone cares about their ideas, and then they will begin to consider themselves a part of the whole. When they feel connected to the group, they will begin to trust the community. A desire to be connected to a community is one of the reasons people attend church and then stay connected in a meaningful way.

One way of being meaningfully connected is involvement in parish leadership. Every year three new members are selected to our vestry to replace three who have served out their terms. The vestry is eager to incorporate these new members into the community and the culture of the twelve-member vestry. To do this we create an opportunity for members of the vestry to share some important characteristics of their leadership style. We accomplish this by using Tom Rath's *StrengthsFinder 2.0.*[12] The vestry has purchased the inexpensive book, which includes a code for each member to complete an online test taking about thirty minutes. The test-taker's results are e-mailed to him, listing his top five leadership strengths. The book gives a detailed description for each of the many possible strengths. At our monthly meeting we set aside the first twenty minutes for two members to share about one or two of their top strengths. This opportunity to talk about our strengths in the group allows each of us to listen and learn a great deal about each member. Every time we participate in the exercise I learn at least one new thing, and usually many more, about members of the church. This has been a very positive exercise in listening that has created a safe environment to begin learning to trust one another during those difficult times of listening, to one another and to the Spirit.

Another way the leader can build trust is to find those people in the congregation who are the keepers of institutional memory, and make friends with them by listening to their stories. A simple question like, "What brought you to St. Augustine's?" usually is all I have to ask, because one story will be followed by many more. Once the congregant is convinced the leader will listen intently to her stories, the leader can learn the history of the person and one perspective on the congregation. By patiently listening over time, the leader can gather a collection of historical stories from many parishioners, giving the leader a better picture of the past. A congregant who has had the experience of a leader genuinely listening to her story about the past will feel heard and trust the leadership. People who are listened to, listen to others in turn, and thus a culture of listening is begun.

John Savage, United Methodist minister and author of *Listening and Caring Skills in Ministry: A Guide for Pastors, Counselors, and Small Groups,*[13] has written a great deal about listening to the past. Savage insists that congregational leaders who seek out opportunities to listen to the stories of congregants who have left the church will have an excellent opportunity to encourage them to return. He reports in his book where as many as 80 percent of those who exited from the congregation return to active membership once the pastor has listened to their story of why they left the church.[14] Listening to stories of the past has many dividends.

As a leader, when I know the history of the church and its people, I can make better decisions about what, if any, changes to suggest. Knowing the history of past leaders, why the furniture is arranged as it is, the past successful and failed programs, what has attracted people to the church and what has caused them to leave will be invaluable information in planning for the future. Ideas often fail because the leader does not take the time to listen, learn, and understand the history of the parish.

Leaders must also listen to the culture in which the parish resides. Karl Barth reportedly once said that sermons should be given with the Bible in one hand and the newspaper in the other.[15] Today he might tell us to preach with our iPad set on split screen, scripture on one side and scrolling news on the other. As church leaders we must know what is happening in our neighborhoods as well as on the global scene. In order to really hear and connect with the people of our congregations, we must know about and have some understanding of the world in which they live.

St. Augustine's Episcopal Parish is located in the southwestern desert of Tempe, Arizona, two short blocks south of the center of the Arizona State University (ASU) campus. St. Augustine's was founded in 1949 on the campus of ASU by university faculty and staff and is still heavily populated with ASU employees and students. Consequently, the membership of the congregation tends to be highly transient. ASU is the second largest public university in the United States. The university is also, largely, a commuter campus. Monday through Friday the population of Tempe swells by over 25 percent due to the number of students, faculty, and staff commuting to the campus. Conversely, the campus and the city feel empty on the weekends. Only recently has the administration of the university begun the difficult work of reinventing the campus life to become more residential. Tempe is a part of the metroplex of Phoenix, the sixth largest city in the country. Tempe and the university are a political island of moderate views within the staunch conservatism of the larger Phoenix area and the State of Arizona. This is the cultural context within which St. Augustine's resides.

Because of the parish's cultural context it has historically been liturgically experimental, open and affirming, and theologically broad minded. These attributes have provided a safe haven for a university community seeking an Episcopal church experience. Over the history of the parish, the one time a clergy leader tried to steer the congregation into an ultra-conservative mode, he nearly caused the demise of the church. It is critical for all church leaders to have a handle on the founding history, social circumstances, political environment, economic past, religious influences, and any other idiosyncrasies of the local culture. The past provides many clues for solutions to current issues and a window into the potential construction of the future.

Congregational leaders must also listen to the wider societal context for clues about what forces might be influencing the parish people. To be in touch with the culture in his community, the leader needs to know what music is popular, what books are at the top of the best-seller list, and which movies are getting the most play. The leader must listen to the music, read the book, and see the movie, especially if the leader intends to critique whatever is in vogue. I cringe when I hear a sermon blasting a particular musical artist when it is obvious the preacher is only taking his cues from an article he read about a song and has not carefully listened to the music himself. There is no quicker way to insult someone, especially young adults, than to offer uninformed criticism about cultural and social preferences.

As Christians we need to know and understand the world in which we live in order to take the gospel into the world. Living insular lives is not what Jesus had in mind when he said, "go into the world." George MacLeod (1895–1991), an influential and yet controversial leader in the Church of Scotland, wrote the following prayer as he was rebuilding the Abbey of Iona during the 1930s, suggesting the church must listen to the culture in order to minister to the love of God.

> Take us "outside the camp", Lord,
> Outside holiness,
> Out to where soldiers gamble, and thieves curse,
> And nations clash at the cross-roads of the world. . . .
> So shall this building continue to be justified.[16]

Even in the midst of restoring a monastery on an island, which might have led the cloister into exclusion, MacLeod heard the Spirit reminding him that the value of rebuilding the ancient facility was only for the sake of sending the message of Christ's hospitality into an inhospitable world. To effectively minister to the world, we must know the world and its needs. Yes, my parish must feed the homeless in Tempe, but we must also know the history behind the reasons that there are no homeless shelters in our city and no interest in building any. Yes, my parish must be involved in interreligious dialogue to develop peaceful responses to hateful language in a divided state, but we must also know why, living in Tempe, we have the best opportunities to be leaders in this most important work. We must listen to the culture in order to know the context and to be prepared to do the work within the community to which the Spirit has fetched us.

LISTENING TO THE INNER SELF

In listening to the Spirit, the other (both as individuals and as a congregation), and the wider community, the leader is beginning to gather essential information needed to guide her congregation. To listen at a truly holy level, she must also be in touch with her own core being. She must learn to listen to herself in order to be prepared to hear her parishioners at the deep level of holy listening.

As the president at Grand Canyon University I was under mounds of stress, as are most college leaders. I was meeting with my spiritual director near the end of one school year and was telling him how exhausted I was and how I desperately needed a vacation. I told him if could just get away, the pressure would ease and things in my life would get better. He replied with what sounded like Irish folk wisdom, "Wherever you go, there you will be." His point was that I needed to get in touch with my inner being, the true source of my exhaustion, the "inner self" that would always be with me. It was obvious to him, but not to me, that I had lost touch with my inner self. I was trying to be someone other people wanted me to be.

I looked in the mirror and I didn't like what I saw. I had cut my hair short to look more conservative. I had put my contacts away and was wearing glasses every day to appear more studious. Every day I wore long-sleeve, white, button-down oxford shirts to maintain that "though I live in the desert, I will not sweat" look. All my suits were dark with a slight pinstripe to portray a fiscally appropriate appearance (the bank executive look). The only color I afforded myself was a little splash of blue or red in my ties. I looked the part of the president of a conservative Southern Baptist college in Phoenix, Arizona. What I saw on the outside was not who I was on the inside however. I had indeed lost touch with who I was. I didn't need a vacation. I needed to reconnect with my true vocation in order to recover my inner being, which was not the president of a university. Worse than feeling like a broken down car that had been recycled, melted, and remolded into someone's lawn ornament was the fact that I felt I had lost touch with God. I couldn't hear God, and I was desperately afraid God wasn't hearing me.

My spiritual director was correct that I needed to rediscover my inner self. His insight shook me enough that I made a decision to re-engage the process of self-reflection. In order to rediscover myself, I had to be willing to look into my inner self. I wanted to see the soul of the real Gil looking back at me in the mirror. I had been hearing my spiritual director; now I was listening to him. Through the effective counsel of my spiritual director, including his willingness to point out that I had lost touch with God and myself, I have, though not without pain, been able to listen to my conscious self as well as my unconscious. Using such tools as journaling, the *Myers-Briggs Type Indicator* (MBTI), and the Enneagram personality test, I have been able to develop an understanding of my conscious self. Then dream analysis has helped me engage my subconscious and discern what it has been trying to communicate to me. The great psychologist of the conscious, the unconscious, and dreams, Carl Jung, wrote, "The unconscious mind of man sees correctly even when conscious reason is blind and impotent."[17] If, standing in front of the mirror, I had been concerned only with my outward appearance, then I would have missed the point of my spiritual director. The outward expression was a symptom of my inner breakdown. I had become blind to who I had become and lost the strength to make any changes in my life. I had to work with all my might to reconnect with my inner self, and to reconnect the unconscious with my consciousness, striving for an integrated self. Somewhere I had lost the desire even to look at myself. I needed to regain my spiritual hunger for self-reflection because the inner desire to be connected to God at the most intimate level is to know God and to know myself. Thomas Merton wrote in *Seeds of Contemplation,* "For me to be a saint means to be myself. Therefore the problem of sanctity and salvation is in fact the problem of finding out who I am and of discovering my true self."[18]

Author and academic Diana Butler Bass writes in *Christianity After Religion: The End of Church and the Birth of a New Spiritual Awakening*[19] that working to uncover who I am in God is the work of the individual and the church as well. She makes a strong case that Jesus's gospel admonition to "love God and love your neighbor as yourself" is the work of knowing oneself, because I cannot love God and my neighbor if I do not know myself. She builds upon Jesus's words, drawing upon the lives of the spiritual giants and saints, Teresa of Avila and John Calvin, who also stressed the importance of inner knowledge as a means of knowing God. Bass suggests that Jesus's question of the disciples, "Who do others say that I am?" which leads to his question, "Who do you say that I am?" will cause the disciples to ask of themselves, "Who am I in light of the I AM?" Bass quotes the non-canonical text *The Book of Thomas the Contender,* "For whoever has not known himself knows nothing, but he who has known himself has already understood the depth of all things."[20] These words resound with encouragement, beckoning us to take the pilgrimage in order find our answer to the question, "Who am I?"

Dietrich Bonhoeffer's poem "Who am I?"[21] was a self-reflective piece he wrote in his journal while in prison. He asked himself the grave questions "Who am I?" and "Why am I doing what I do?" His self-questioning focused on his identity. Was he the person others thought he was? "They often tell me I would step from my cell's confinement calmly, cheerfully, firmly. . . ." Or was he the person he felt himself to be? "Or am I only what I know of myself? Restless and longing and sick, like a bird in a cage . . . ?" Others saw him as strong and self-sacrificing, but he himself felt frightened. To calm the fears of being imprisoned by the Nazis, he busied himself, taking care of others. By processing his feelings on paper, it was easier for him to confront the difficult questions raised by his confinement and his Christian service to others.

I do much of my inner work on the question "Who am I in God?" by writing in my daily journal. Keeping a journal is a spiritual practice. Having a safe and private place to write and express feelings about events in our lives enables us to make observations about ourselves. While we usually think of a journal as a narrative, it could include photos, drawings, poems, or songs. Any creative means of expressing our feelings that allows us to be self-reflective can be an effective form of journaling.

I have kept a journal from the time I was a teenager. One day, sorting through some boxes in the garage, I came across one of my high school journals. As I flipped through the pages, I realized how much I wrote about being depressed. I started going through my journals by the decade and saw depression was a common theme. As an adult, I denied to myself that I was depressed. In my judgment at the time, that would have been a sign of weakness. I blamed my dark moods and feelings on my circumstances, my baseball team having a bad season, donors not giving enough money, the economy being bad. I used my circumstances to explain away my feelings that I was at the bottom of a cold, dark, bottomless well with no hope of finding the light at the top. But after reading my teenage journal and then tracking my adult writing, I was forced to admit that I had been struggling with the problem of depression most of my life. Through the long process of self-reflection in my journals, I began to face the problem and finally sought professional help.

My journal has also been the place where I have worked out a lot of questions and doubts about dealing with leadership problems. Because I have kept a journal for years, I have been able to look back to see how I handled situations similar to those I now encounter. Due to my personality type, I have spent more time journaling about my failures. Using the *Myers-Briggs Type Indicator* and studying the Enneagram have helped me understand why I have focused so much attention on my mistakes. By working with these personality tools, over time, I have been able to shift more of my energy toward processing my successes in the journal. These tools have also built within me a capacity to reflect on why I made certain decisions and how I might make better choices in the future.

In the past twenty years I have taken the Myers-Briggs numerous times, and the results have remained constant. Katharine C. Briggs and her daughter Isabel Briggs Myers developed the MBTI after forty years of research based on Carl Jung's personality types. Myers and Briggs's work posited that there are two pairs of attitudes toward life: Extraversion-Introversion (E-I) and Judging-Perceiving (J-P). (The *Myers Briggs Type Indicator* uses the spellings "extravert" and "extraversion.") There are also two pairs of operating functions: Sensing-Intuition (S-N) and Thinking-Feeling (T-F). People have preferences in their attitudes and functions, leaning toward and operating more from one side of the pairings. While I may be an introvert, there are some traits of extraversion in the shadow side of my personality.

The first pair (E-I) indicates how the person prefers to interact with the world. The extravert depends upon the outer world of people and things to navigate through life and gain energy. The introvert relies more on the inner life of ideas, concepts, and spirit to see the world.

Sensing and Intuition (S-N) are the psychological functions used to perceive data or gather information. The Sensing function uses the five senses of the body to provide information about the outer world. The Intuitive function is the creative and visionary operation that draws upon the inner world of ideas and spirit to bring about a new concept or improve the present situation.

Thinking and Feeling (T-F) are the decision-making functions. The Thinking operation uses the intellect and logic to make a determination. The Feeling function relies upon personal values and experiences to make decisions. Each of us uses both of these functions, but to some degree we will depend more heavily on one side of the spectrum than the other.

The final pair of functions, Judging and Perceiving (J-P), are indications of how a person orders his world. Those operating out of the Judging function are more structured in planning and organization and more decisive in the decision-making process. Those who prefer Perceiving typically take more time to make decisions and gather more data, and are less structured and time-conscious.

Working through the MBTI personality types with a spiritual director can assist the leader in determining how she works best and with whom she might work well in a team. Insights gained from personality typing like the Myers-Briggs is useful but can also be enhanced by working with the Enneagram.

Several years ago, when I was looking for new ways to improve my leadership, a good friend recommended a two-day class on the Enneagram. The Enneagram uses a series of self-reflections that are intended to help us discover and explore our inner self and then determine how we in turn express ourselves to the world. The system is built upon patterns of the way we think, feel, and act. During the workshop we were supposed to explore our type using various narrative descriptors. These are short paragraphs describing personal preferences for handling situations in life. While the Myers-Briggs uses a test of brief questions to determine personality types, the Enneagram relies upon the reader's self-identification in how he handles a situation. (Some Enneagram resources use a lengthy test with a complicated measuring system to help the reader discover his or her Enneagram personality type.) My work revealed a murky picture, with my personality vacillating somewhere among three types. The uncertainty of the Enneagram work left me feeling unsure of myself. Looking back on the experience, I see now that the Enneagram exposed the instability in my life at the time.

I didn't do any more Enneagram work for a few years until I began some spiritual direction training. Once again, I wrestled with the work to determine my personality type through the Enneagram. The training I received broadened my understanding of the Enneagram, and I began to recognize the subtle nuances of personality typing and how time, maturity, and circumstance can cause slight shifting in the typing. (The same can be said of the MBTI.) Working with the Enneagram as a self-reflection tool began to make sense to me. It provided a rich resource to understand my inner life and opened the windows of a new revelation in my work as a spiritual director and a leader.

Richard Rohr, Franciscan monk and director of the Center for Action and Contemplation, working with Lutheran minister Andreas Ebert, wrote *Experiencing the Enneagram*,[22] an excellent tool for determining the personality type and specifically how the type is portrayed in a leadership style. Rohr says the Enneagram is a tool for the "discernment of the spirits . . . to see and discern what's authentic in your life and what's inauthentic, what's honest and what's dishonest."[23]

The leader who listens to his inner being and discovers his personality type can begin to realize what is authentic in his life and start to align his spiritual practices with the preferences God created within him. As a leader, I will be more equipped to listen deeply to the Spirit and to others if I am in sync with God and who God has created me to be. God has given us the freedom to discover and explore a variety of spiritual practices because we are created as individuals. Not everyone is suited to centering prayer. Nor is every person in the congregation comfortable with extemporaneous prayer. A person leans toward a style of prayer because of her personality type. Knowing that my spiritual practices of prayer, study, meditation, and walking are in rhythm with my personality type is comforting. This knowledge also instills confidence in me when I encounter a practice that does not "feel right" or does not seem to fit into my pattern. In these situations, I try to ask questions about the spiritual practice in terms of my personality type. My spiritual director has helped me move into deeper periods of growth and has also saved me from some serious spiritual frustration by guiding me into practices that are in sync with my personality type.

What I have given here is just a glimpse of the MBTI and the Enneagram. The effective use of these tools takes time and work. I have found it best to take a class or retreat in the MBTI or the Enneagram, in addition to using works like Rohr's and working with a spiritual director. A spiritual director who is competent with personality testing, whether MBTI or Enneagram, can assist the leader in the process of listening to his conscious self.

Most spiritual directors will caution us that paying attention only to the conscious self will leave us with an incomplete impression of our inner life. Working with the MBTI and the Enneagram will help describe our personality type, and through this work we can begin to explore the unconscious. However, having a language to explain my personality type does not open the window fully to exploring the world beyond my consciousness. Listening to our unconscious is also necessary, and listening to our dreams is a way of connecting with the unconscious, while working toward a more integrated life and finding our answer to the question, "Who am I?"

Our scriptures teach us that God can speak to us through the unconscious world of dreams, which play an important role in the Hebrew and Christian traditions. In the Old Testament, Jacob's and Joseph's dreams are an important part of the story of the people of Israel. Dreams are an integral part of Daniel's story. The Gospel of Matthew also tells of Joseph's dreams and their role in the life of Jesus. In the scriptures the dream had a meaning intended specifically for the dreamer.

Most likely, receiving a dream message from God would be incredibly rare for us. However, our unconscious does speak to us every night through our dreams. The point of listening to our dream is not necessarily to interpret the symbolism of the dream but instead to learn about our inner self from the dream. Everyone dreams, but not everyone remembers his dreams. But I believe we can train ourselves to remember our dreams, which will then provide us the opportunity to glean valuable information about our unconscious life.

There are three steps to dream work: recounting the dream, writing the dream, and working with the dream. To recount the dream, keep a small notebook by the bedside. If you wake up in the middle of the night and remember a bit of a dream, jot down a few key words and then return to sleep. Before getting out of bed in the morning, look at those words. These few notes will prompt your memory to recount the dream. Lie in bed and allow your mind to review the dream. Next, write about your dream in a journal. Write whatever you have remembered, whether it's a simple image or an elaborate drama. The act of writing may cause other images from the dream to emerge.

Now the work with the dream begins. I find it helpful to write significant dreams I want to work with on my computer. I write the dream in italics. As I write the dream, questions arise, wonderings emerge. I write the questions and musings in standard type. When I have finished writing the dream with my ponderings, I print a copy and carry it with me. I have noticed throughout the day that insights will develop, and I can jot them on the copy of my dream. I keep these notes in my journal and return to them whenever I discover something else within the dream. There have been occasions when the dream has been so significant that I have set aside some time to lie on my bed, quietly and with my eyes closed. When I have reached the space before going to sleep, I have re-entered the dream, allowing my mind to re-play the dream to determine if I can see or hear something new. This method of working with a dream has been revelatory, opening new insights into ministry, relationships, and issues such as depression, stress from fear of failure, and major decisions about vocation.[24]

Dream work is not magic or divination. It is not easy. It takes a significant time commitment, and it requires patience. Just as with the Myers-Briggs and the Enneagram, dream work is best done in consultation with an experienced spiritual director. Listening to our self-reflections is vital for spiritual growth, and this work will produce more reliable results when a trusted spiritual director can ask questions and assist in sorting out what can be learned from the dream. These insights can then be integrated into the consciousness, developing a more complete picture of the conscious and the unconscious—integral for the leader.

More than one institution has suffered or been damaged beyond repair because the leader has not been self-aware and has been unwilling to do the difficult work of listening to his inner world. Introverts can lead as well as extroverts, but not processing personality type and inner life with the help of a trained professional can cause any leader, extrovert or introvert, to be a poor leader at the least, and at the worse, to treat people without dignity.

When the leader looks in the mirror she must recognize her self, conscious and unconscious. The leader must be authentic. Organizations have historically believed that extroverts with the charisma to draw people in the door, and a powerful presence to motivate people into doing what the leader believes is the greatest good, are the best leaders. Religious institutions have been no different in saying they prefer extroverts to introverts.

However, the historical model of the leader as charismatic extrovert is no longer an effective means of leadership. Adam S. McHugh, Presbyterian minister, spiritual director, and author of *Introverts in the Church: Finding Our Place in an Extroverted Culture*, gives us the good news that these stereotypes are breaking down, and new institutional models like learning organizations are emerging, requiring new kinds of leaders. "People who think before they act and listen before they talk can be very effective leaders. The reflective, thoughtful person may be able to learn, and encourage learning, in ways that people who can't stop talking are not able to."[25]

The leader who does not engage in a lifetime of self-reflection cannot hear the people he is leading, and in every situation of leadership, leading without effectively listening is failing to lead. Leadership guru Peter Senge writes in *The Fifth Discipline: The Art and Practice of the Learning Organization,* "Reflective openness starts with the willingness to challenge our own thinking, to recognize that any certainty we ever had is, at best, a hypothesis about the world."[26] He says self-reflection also involves being able to think about what the other person is saying. In other words, our self-reflection, listening to our inner self, prepares us to listen to the other person, allowing to us share a common purpose in building our learning organizations.

LISTENING IS A FULL-TIME JOB

The best way to know you are listening is to ask those to whom you intend to be listening, "Do you feel I am listening to you? Do you feel heard?" Ask those closest to you—spouse, partner, and trusted confidant. Ask employees. Ask leadership teams and key volunteers. "Ask, and it will be given you; search, and you will find; knock, and the door will be opened for you" (Matt. 7:7). Ask those around you if they felt heard—and take to heart what they say. Listening is holy work, a spiritual practice that is worth every ounce of energy that we dedicate to hearing the important matters of another. Holy listening is God work. We pray and God listens to us. We have no greater calling than to listen in turn to those whom God has entrusted us to lead. The sheep know the voice of the Good Shepherd. We must know and listen to the voice of our people. Listening is a full-time vocation, the most important vocation.

FOUR

The Leader as Advocate of Silence

When we have really met and known the world in silence, words
do not separate us from the world nor from other men nor from
God, nor from ourselves, because we no longer trust entirely in
language to contain reality.

—Thomas Merton[1]

Dinah is my only sibling and younger sister by fifteen months. She
has Prader-Willi Syndrome (PWS), a mental and physical handi-
cap caused by the deformity of chromosome 15. Born in 1955, Dinah is one of the oldest people with Prader-Willi. Most who have
the syndrome die in their early thirties from morbid obesity complicated by behavioral characteristics of the syndrome, such as vio-
lent outbursts. These eruptions of violence are often so intense that
along with the other health concerns of those with Prader-Willi, it
can lead to stroke and heart attack. To compound my sister's complex health situation, she contracted pneumonia at nine months.
Her fever rose to over 108 degrees,[2] resulting in brain damage,
eventually affecting her speech. She now has a vocabulary of about
forty-five words and has great difficulty putting more than four
words together to make a sentence. When she is asked a question,
it seems like her neuro-pathways have to warm up before she can
answer. Most of the time, she replies with a "no," "not know," "I not,
not know," or a shrug of the shoulders. Rarely does she respond
quickly with an answer much less an affirmative one. If I ask too
many questions or try to fill in the blanks for her, she becomes an-
noyed or irritated. I have learned to ask a question and then wait in

silence. Admittedly, over the years, my patience and my ability to sit quietly have improved. I have learned that Dinah needs a lot of time to decide if she will answer the question and then how she will communicate what she is going to say. Silence is vital, for without it our communication would be impossible.

Silence is not always the absence of sound. As in the moments when I am sitting with my sister, silence becomes a presence with its own power. Silence can be an entity, like a spirit demanding great respect. The presence of silence can have a thickness like incense hanging heavy in the air. When silence appears as a spirit, a presence, then a great deal can be learned if silence is willingly embraced. In these gifted moments, the presence of silence must be listened to as if it were the greatest sage of holy wisdom, the very voice of God.

In my life, Dinah represents the presence of silence. Without her teaching me that life can be bathed in silence, I could not imagine being able to lead people who desperately want to be heard. A leader, especially in a religious community, who can learn from the presence of silence, will be able to abide in comfort, in the presence of another person. Voices are often muted when someone is suffering grief, illness, and impending death. In times of tragedy, an entire community can be found speechless. A leader who has gained interior power from sitting in the presence of silence will be better equipped to be a container for the silence of the speechless, even the voice of the silent.

When Dinah tries to tell a story, her frustration is visible. She uses her limited vocabulary and poorly formed words along with a variety of unique hand signals and facial expressions. If I can't figure out the story, she will say to me, "You no hear me." At that point, I have to look for another internal reserve tank of patience. I love my sister deeply, so I wait in silence. Sometimes, after what can feel like an interminable period, she finds the strength to string together a different set of words in order to be understood. Sometimes she will have to make several attempts before I can "hear her." The lifelong process of communicating with my sister has taught me to abide in the presence of her silence, praying that I might eventually know what is hidden in her heart, mind, and soul.

Dinah and I had lunch three months after our mother passed away. It was the first time we were able to be alone together. I look forward to our times together because, despite her limited measurable intelligence, she has the wisdom of a crone and the connection with God of a mystical saint. She started the day by asking how my children were doing. She simply names them, and I know she wants to hear what is happening in their lives, especially our grandson Cole. She also loves dogs and wants to know the latest stories of our crazy Jack Russell terrier.

Lunch was finally brought to our table. Primarily due to issues surrounding Prader-Willi, Dinah is very intent on eating, so there is little conversation during the meal. I idly offered a few rambling stories. When the plates were taken away, she resumed her child-like questions about the dog. Somewhere in the little strands of conversation, she told me that she had washed her hair that day.

"Do you wash your hair every day?" I asked.

She nodded an affirmative yes, as if to say, "You idiot brother, don't you?" I smiled a sheepish older-brother grin.

"Do you blow dry and style your own hair? It looks nice." I was trying to make up for my previous stupid-brother question.

"No, Joey," she said, referring to her beloved caregiver.

"You have beautiful silver hair, Dinah," I said in truth.

She said without hesitation, "My momma's hair."

I wanted to cry. At that moment my sister looked like my mother and not like a person with Prader-Willi syndrome. I could see my mother not only in Dinah's hair, but her eyes of love and her voice of tenderness.

Then she said quietly, to no one in particular except herself, "My momma's hair."

After a few minutes in the presence of silence she said, "Momma no more."

I moved my head to acknowledge that our mother was indeed no longer physically present. We sat there for five minutes in pristine silence. It was as if the entire restaurant, the outside world, and God herself had stopped breathing in communal grief waiting to hear what Dinah would say next. Then she shook her head as if to drive the thought of her dead mother out of mind, to rattle the last vision of our mother in the lonely coffin from her memory. She looked at me and changed the subject back to the dog.

I have wondered almost every day since that lunch why she said "Momma no more" instead of "Momma gone" or "Bye-bye momma," which she said at the viewing of our mother's body. I have heard a few people tell her that our mother is with God and in heaven, but she didn't say any of those things. She simply said, "Momma no more."

I have asked myself if she was acknowledging the cold reality of death. Was she making a comment on the absence and loneliness we were experiencing together as sister and brother without our mother? Or does she know something about the afterlife? Can she see the other side, or the lack of it? What I think I heard from Dinah was, "Our mother, who shaped our souls and then set us free into our own identity, is no more. We are now on our own."

Since that day, I have come to realize talking to my sister is like doing dream work. The dream is full of images, strange messages, and unfamiliar characters. As with a dream, I journal my conversations with my sister and then use questions to sort out the experience. "What did that word mean? Did her lifted eyebrow have a hidden meaning? Did the story about her friend at work have a larger meaning?"

I cannot know fully what she is trying to tell me. I can only do the hard work of listening to the words and to the silence. I continue to process our times together, hoping I will uncover some koan. I cannot know what she knows or feel what she feels. I can only know what I feel when I listen to her and can guess at the meaning held in the silence between the words. During our lunch, I was overwhelmed with grief and sadness. Indeed, my mother is no more. Yet, I am also humbly thankful that I can abide in my sister's love and wisdom.

By remaining present to my sister in her silence, I have also learned to abide in God's silence. Silence is not necessarily the lack of noise, nor is it always the sign of absence. My sister is present, though she is silent. God may be silent but also very present. What sustains our human and frail willingness to remain present in the silence of God when a crisis of leadership arises comes from the strength Jesus offers us from his love of the Father God. Jesus said,

> If you abide in me, and my words abide in you, ask for whatever you wish, and it will be done for you. My Father is glorified by this, that you bear much fruit and become my disciples. As the Father has loved me, so I have loved you; abide in my love. If you keep my commandments, you will abide in my love, just as I have kept my Father's commandments and abide in his love. I have said these things to you so that my joy may be in you, and that your joy may be complete. (John 15:7–11)

To abide is to persevere, to stay, and to remain in the presence of another. Jesus is our example, for he was able to abide in God's love while facing the feeling of abandonment. I believe one of our greatest testimonies to God's love, even in the face of the greatest disappointments of life, is to remain in the presence of silence. When I am able to abide in my own silence, the silence of another, and the silence of God, I will intimately know myself, the other, and God much better.

From the Bible we read of God's presence in silence. Elijah came to know and hear God in sheer silence (1 Kings 19:12). The psalmist encourages us to wait in silence to hear God (Ps. 62:5 and Ps. 46:10). Listening to God in silence is a scriptural imperative. "Listen to me in silence, O coastlands; let the peoples renew their strength" (Isa. 41:1). "Be silent, all people, before the Lord; for he has roused himself from his holy dwelling" (Zech. 2:13). "Be silent before the Lord God! For the day of the Lord is at hand; the Lord has prepared a sacrifice, he has consecrated his guests" (Zeph. 1:7). "But the Lord is in his holy temple; let all the earth keep silence before him!" (Hab. 2:20).

To abide in silence is difficult work even when we love someone. I imagine Jesus's love of God to be intense and the Father's love of the Son to be beyond our conception. To say that Jesus and God loved each other may be the greatest understatement. In the test of Jesus's love, he could abide in God's love, even in silent abandonment on the cross. If a leader desires to be in love with

God, in love with God as Jesus was in love with the Father, she will have to accept the uncomfortable idea that this kind of love could take her into the rare place of feeling much like Jesus, abandoned on the cross. As a leader, I never want to feel that God has left me to my own devices, or that God is sitting on the sidelines simply watching me wallow in the muck. I would much rather know that God has my back and is always whispering guidance in my ears. But, unfortunately, I have been in those hard moments of leading a team and an institution when I could not hear God, but I did not believe God had abandoned me, though I felt as if God might have. In the moments of the silence of God, we may though be better able to hear God. In order to hear God in the silence, we must abide with God and stay present in the silence, even when it is painful and we would rather walk away from the challenge or disturb the silence with the sound of our own voice. When the leader can remain with God by abiding in the love of God, we as leaders may hear the voice of God in a new way, one that brings about a resurrection experience for the leader and the congregation. For the sake of the spiritual growth of our congregations, we, as spiritual leaders in the twenty-first century, must advocate that our congregations also abide in the presence of silence, the silence of self, the silence of the other, and the silence of God.

As advocates for silence, leaders must develop space within the community for worship, education, and private encounter, then set aside time for the congregation to abide in the presence of the silence. Leaders must nurture silence in a world working so hard to avoid it. Introverts might crave silence, and they may be more willing to experiment with it. Extroverts will most likely consider silence to be draining instead of energizing. However, a leader who advocates for silence will create moments within worship, the educational experience, or in private counsel when the presence of silence can be nourishing for all members of the congregation. Still, silence cannot be forced on anyone, regardless of personality type. Imposed silence, like the silence of the world my sister is forced to live in, can be oppressive and does nothing to quiet the monkey mind of the individual or the community. Yet when silence is offered gently and treated with care, as if the silence were fragile, silence will become our teacher, mentor, and spiritual guide, like the moments when I abide in the presence of my sister's silence and open my soul to hear her. Leaders who abide in personal silence, the silence of others, and the silence of God will birth healing, creativity, and power within the community and give a new voice to the marginalized, who cry out like my sister, "You no hear me." For when I can sit in the presence of Dinah's silence, I do hear her voice, learn her story, and gain a rich perspective into how to live my own life. Fourteenth-century German mystic Meister Eckhart wrote "Nothing is more like God than silence."[3] While the leader does not have to search out a relationship with a person like my sister to discover the riches of silence, the leader only needs to look within herself and her congregation to discover the powerful lessons silence has to teach us.

Abiding in the Presence of Personal Silence

Before Jesus's first act of ministry, the Spirit drove him into the silence of the wilderness (Mark 1:12). In the desert, the angels of healing nourished Jesus (Matt. 4:11; Mark 1:13). He discovered his voice, expressed in his creative and unique preaching (Matt. 4:1–11; Luke 4:1–13). In the silence of his desert experience, during a forty-day fast in the wilderness, which must have felt interminable, he was given the power of the Holy Spirit (Luke 4:1, 14). In that silence, Jesus knew the fullness of the human experience—loneliness, hunger, uncertainty, and spiritual attack. Because he knew the total range of our earthly life, he intimately knows our experience and thus we can relate to him and have confidence that he indeed has complete empathy with us when we find ourselves in metaphorically similar situations. In these moments in the desert, enduring the vicissitudes of humanity, he was still listening to God, preparing for his battle against the angel of darkness. There in the silence of the barren land, he obtained strength to heal the broken spirit in other people. Jesus gained power to overcome the evil oppressing the marginalized, and discovered the wisdom to preach with a unique creativity. In light of the depth of Jesus's seminal experience, the scriptures surprisingly do not reveal much of his spiritual practice during those forty days. Therefore, we must go to other stories for possible clues about how Jesus practiced his personal silence.

The Gospels repeatedly report of Jesus retreating in the pre-dawn hours to find peace in silence. We read, for example, "But now more than ever the word about Jesus spread abroad; many crowds would gather to hear him and to be cured of their diseases. But he would withdraw to deserted places and pray" (Luke 5:15–16). Alone and in silence, Jesus could listen to the voice of God (Matt. 14:13; Mark 1:35; 6:45–46; Luke 4:42; 6:12; John 6:15). Then, in the hours before his arrest, though he had asked the disciples to pray near him, he sought the solitude of silence to pray. In his agony, and out of the silence, his words of intimacy with the Father erupted within him, beseeching God, "Abba, Father, for you all things are possible; remove this cup from me; yet, not what I want, but what you want" (Mark 14:36). Jesus heard his Abba respond with silence, ending in ultimate *kenosis*.

Jesus was able to demonstrate the power of silence under duress because he had nurtured a lifetime practice of silence. Testimony to his reliance upon silence is found in his final hours. When Jesus was before the high priest (Matt. 26:63) and Pilate (Matt. 27:14), instead of defending himself, he stilled his voice. Through his silence, he was in a position of power over his accusers. Jesus's power of resolve is found in the effect of his silence upon Pilate:

> [Pilate] entered his headquarters again and asked Jesus, "Where are you from?" But Jesus gave him no answer. Pilate therefore said to him, "Do you refuse to speak to me? Do you not know that I have power to release you, and power to crucify you?" Jesus answered him, "You would have no power unless it had been given you from above" (John 19:9–11a).

Under the threat of death by crucifixion, Jesus maintained self-control through the strength of his silence. However, he did not manifest the power of silence instantly on the spot, but instead drew upon the inner reservoir he had built by his sustained practice of silence and constant prayer in the presence of the Father.

We might relegate Jesus's powerful silence to his divinity and thereby dismiss any of our reasons to follow his example of solitude and prayer in the desert. If Jesus, in his humanity, learned from God in the silence, we can learn from Jesus's experience in the desert. We cannot know for sure what happened to Jesus in those mystical moments of silence. But using contemplative imagination, I can evoke a mental portrait of Jesus in solitude. I allow myself to enter into the experience of the scriptural story as if I were a witness to the event. I envision myself waking early in the morning and following Jesus to his secluded place, imagining what I would have seen and heard.

Living in the desert, I can easily picture Jesus sitting on a large stone under a short, low hanging desert scrub that masquerades as a tree. The sun is still pondering its morning arrival. The desert is coldest in the predawn hour. Jesus has wrapped his cloak tightly around his thin body. He shivers, more from the burden of the coming day than from the crisp dry air. He sighs and drops his shoulders, trying to relieve the tightness in his aching muscles. "Bless the Lord, O my soul, and all that is within me, bless his holy name" (Ps. 103:1). He chants the prayer slowly, repeatedly, in an attempt to quiet the voices telling him God's mission is too difficult and misguided. Jesus opens his heart to the love of God he feels surrounding him on the desert floor, the tree giving him a bit of cover, the stone granting him a resting place, the sand, still holding heat, warming his feet. He opens his mind, looking into the starry sky, into the vast majesty of the unseen God. Jesus opens his soul, seeking union with Abba. He holds the silence until, without notice, an image, perhaps the face of the beloved disciple, flashes across his mind. His silence is disturbed. But he returns to his chant: "Bless the Lord, O my soul, and all that is within me, bless his holy name." He repeats his practice of prayer until being interrupted by a disciple who reminds him of the hungry people needing his healing attention.

Silently meditating upon Jesus's contemplative practice has its own healing effect upon my soul. Silence restores our depleted energy. Silence liberates our creativity, releasing those rays of imagination hidden by the black clouds of noise that constantly thunder into our life.

Finding time (even only a few minutes) and space for daily silence is vital to our spiritual journey. Commitment to the same time and place each day allows our mind to relax into the silence with increasing ease. The mental image of Jesus in the desert is a good place for anyone to start with contemplative imagination. Sit with Jesus in the desert. Listen to the silence that exists between Jesus and God. What does it sound like to be in the presence of Jesus's silence? What does it feel like to be with Jesus in the presence of the silence of God? What does this contemplative imagination teach me about my own silence in the presence of God?

From the time of Jesus, silence has been an important part of the Christian practice. The earliest Christian hermits of Egypt and Syria followed Jesus's example of going into the desert in search of the presence of silence. From the second century, we read of men and women who went into the solace of the desert in order to be alone with God. Third century Desert Fathers Anthony of Egypt and Paul of Thebes were probably two of the best-known ascetical monks. When these two men went into the desert seeking solace, others followed, eventually establishing communities nearby, living a simple life, praying constantly, reciting the psalms, memorizing large blocks of scripture, and working in gardens and weaving baskets to support the monastery.[4]

Monasticism and the call of solitary life spread. In the sixth century, Kevin of Glendalough went into the wilds of Ireland seeking solitude and silence. Again, others followed him and a monastery formed. Soon monastic leaders like Benedict of Nursia would write a rule of life in which the study of scripture, prayer, and silence were the central pillars of living a spiritual life together in community. Benedict wrote in his rule, "Monastics should diligently cultivate silence at all times, but especially at night."[5]

While some leaders might find living in solitude like Anthony, Paul, and Kevin attractive, we find ourselves like Benedict, leading a community of faith. Benedict's rule has much to say to leaders about the importance of personal and communal silence. A portion of Benedict's rule for the monastery was his inclusion of the concept of listening to holy readings, which would become the foundation for *lectio divina*. Though it would be extremely difficult to suggest any one person was the first to use *lectio*, Benedict was at least one of the earliest to create a model for the spiritual practice, insisting on daily reading of scripture and inspiring text.

Entering into the scriptural story through *lectio divina* is helpful in moving us as individuals and community into the presence of silence. When the reader allows his imagination to flow into the characters of the story, sitting with the text, and spending time in contemplation of the text, the Spirit can open the listener's mind and soul into new possibilities for understanding the text. Although a variety of methods for *lectio divina* have been developed, the barest outline begins with the instruction to read a small piece of scripture. Set the text aside and allow the mind to contemplate upon the story for a brief time. Return to the scripture and then, taking more time, travel further into the story, looking for something new. Pick up the story a third time. Wander into the narrative, past the words, around the corner to mentally find a place of rest, allowing the story to hold your thoughts and worries.

We do not have to limit *lectio* to scripture. I have found meaning in using *lectio* in reading poems and other texts I hold important in my life. Sitting in silence, using *lectio* while reading the poetry of John O'Donohue, Mary Oliver, George Herbert, R.S. Thomas, T.S. Eliot, Dylan Thomas, and Maya Angelou have helped me sort out some of the struggles in my life. I have also taken passages and lines from novels and non-fiction alike, sitting in *lectio,* listening to what the Spirit has to say to me through the text.

Contemplation, *lectio divina,* as well as centering prayer, yoga, and taking a solitary walk are all ways of entering into silence. But we do not always have to explore our personal silence in isolation. I have found sitting in contemplative silence or centering prayer with others helps me be more disciplined in my practice. Sitting in the presence of silence with a group that meets regularly does two things for me. First, a group can be a container for my silence, a place where silence is expected, honored, even treasured. To not be silent is to disrupt the norm of the group. The expectation of being silent allows me to relax into my own silence and that of the group. Second, when I am part of a group, I am missed when I am absent. My presence adds something to the group, just as each member brings his or her own unique relationship with God to the gathering. A form of accountability enhances my own sense of spiritual discipline.

A deacon in our church offers a weekly centering prayer session. We gather around a table on which sits a single lighted candle. The deacon begins with a simple chant we can easily join. Then she offers a short reading. She rings a bell three times, and we sit in silence for thirty minutes. The deacon brings us out of the silence by quietly chiming the bell. We pray the Lord's Prayer. She allows a brief time for anyone who wants to share a word to do so, and then we depart. Knowing other people are gathering in silence encourages me to join them regularly and gives me assurance that sitting in silence is meaningful not only to me, but to others in my community.

Daily and weekly silence is the foundation of our practice. Living in a world dominated by sound, we must look for opportunities to practice silence for an extended period of time. Silent retreats conducted at a monastery or retreat center can be as brief as a few hours or as long as the forty-day Ignatian time of reflection. Entering and maintaining silence at a monastery or other peaceful setting can be easier than trying to keep silence within our daily routine. A retreat center with a prayer chapel, a labyrinth, paths for walking, and a refectory where those in silence are respected is conducive to a private silent retreat. There are retreats conducted with the distinct purpose of learning about practicing silence. However, if you are going alone to a retreat center, it can be helpful to plan your private retreat as a way of supporting the practice of silence. The plan might include a rhythm of prayer, reading, writing, meditation, and physical activity like walking or yoga, which can create a container for the silence. Without a schedule for the retreat, even someone very comfortable and practiced in solitude and silence may find his thoughts wandering back to the work sitting on his desk at the office. The silence of the retreat is intended to open the leader's soul and prayer life in such a way that when she returns to the office her work can be approached in a different way, built upon the grounding found in silence. Whatever the length of the retreat, it should be concluded with a session of spiritual direction. Participating in such a conversation with an experienced spiritual director before re-entering the world of noise enables us to unpack the effects of silence and prepare our soul for the onslaught of chatter we will soon face.

As leaders, we cannot suggest to our people that they prayerfully read scripture, pray in the presence of silence, engage in centering prayer, or go on a silent retreat if we have not engaged in such practices ourselves. Jesus gave us a good model of leadership, especially in the area of personal spiritual practice. He told his disciples to follow his example in love, service, prayer, and solitude. Leaders must model for their congregations how to grow deeper in relationship and union with God.

A leader who regularly practices personal silence and teaches her congregation how to encounter silence will begin to experience the affects on her life and subsequently upon her leadership. She will find herself capable of entering into deep listening, and she will be less disturbed by anxiety-producing situations, her pastoral care presence will be enriched by her comfort in abiding in the silence of another, and her preaching and speech will take on a spirit-filled power, because from silence comes the wisdom of having been with God. Out of this union with God, a vision for the people is discovered, experienced, and then can be articulated by the leader to the people.

Having been immersed in silence, the leader's voice and the depth of her word when preaching and teaching will intone the holy. Bonhoeffer considers silence indispensable to the leader's ability to be the prophet, priest, and pastor to and for the community. He writes in *Christ the Center* "Teaching about Christ begins in silence. . . . When the church speaks rightly out of a proper silence, then Christ is proclaimed."[6] Out of silence come the words for the community. "One does not exist without the other. Genuine speech comes out of silence and genuine silence comes out of speech."[7] Thomas Merton adds to Bonhoeffer's admonition for the leader, "Life is not to be regarded as an uninterrupted flow of words . . . its rhythm develops in silence, comes to the surface in moments of necessary expression, returns to deeper silence,"[8] for from silence, the leader can find an expression of union and presence before God.

Silence is a power source for leadership. The leader does not run to silence to escape failure. Nor does he run away from it, fearing the experience of being trapped alone with his monkey mind. The leader must embrace silence, for in the presence of silence the leader will discover who she is called to be before God and the congregation. Silence builds the capacity to lead by developing a reservoir of strength within the leader. The power of this strength is acquired by repeatedly going through what psychologist and spiritual writer Morton Kelsey (1917–2001) refers to as the "miniexperience of death and resurrection,"[9] which arises out of silence. As leaders, we spend so much of our time planning, preparing, and doing the work of leadership. However, when we stop and let go of the work for a while, we can reflect upon why we are doing what we do and what we are really trying to accomplish. One day we will die, and at that moment, we lay down all our work, our possessions, and our life, and we will let go. In death we are no longer responsible for the outcomes; we simply are present in death and its silence. By willingly entering into the miniexperience of death through silence, the leader will grow deeper in his relationships with God, self, and others. The letting-go found in silence is liberating for her as a leader. At the same time, she empowers and commissions others, because they are now entrusted to be leaders using their own gifts. When the leader has the courage to risk her authority by letting go of control, the people will be moved to take up their calling and their work.

The congregation gives the leader authority because she in turn provides them with the services of direction, protection, and order. The temptation for her, though, is to fall into the trap of being the charismatic leader who tries to fix problems and keep the people happy. Instead, leadership guru Ronald Heifetz writes in his book *Leadership Without Easy Answers*[10] that he must challenge the people and risk his authority. Leadership is a "razor's edge,"[11] he says, because the leader, instead of giving the people what they want (direction, protection, and order), must instead let the people feel disorientation, threat, and conflict, so that they may adjust their "values and behaviors."[12] The leader, Heifetz says, "Takes the risk of challenging people, directly, or indirectly, slow or fast, soft or hard, guided by his comprehension of and sensitivity to the changes people have to make in their lives as they take account of the questions he raises."[13] This is what Heifetz describes as adaptive leadership. Creating an environment of transformation, adaptive leadership, is dangerous work for any leader. In order to survive as an adaptive leader and be a person who can effectively risk authority without burnout, Heifetz makes seven practical suggestions, two of which require the presence of silence in the leader's life: getting on the balcony and finding sanctuary.[14] Getting on the balcony is the act of stepping away and getting above the fray as the means of evaluating the situation. Finding sanctuary is a matter of the leader finding a mentor and a safe place to do serious self-reflection.

For me, learning to give up control and risk authority has been a lifelong process. Sometimes we have go to great lengths to engage in the "miniexperience of death and resurrection," learning how to let go. In the summer of 2012 I made a walking pilgrimage of almost four hundred miles across Ireland to the city of Glenbeigh. Every day was an experience of death and resurrection through silence. Each day I walked from six to ten hours, through the forests, over the mountains, down the valleys, across streams, sometimes on trails, and other times guided by a rough map, because there was no path to follow. Twenty of the twenty-three days I walked alone, rarely seeing another person. My only companion was the silence. After a day of walking in silence, I would meet my wife. She quickly realized it would take me about an hour or more to "come out of the silence" and be able to tell the story of my daily adventure. In the evening, I would write about my pilgrimage and post the story on my blog. The silence, telling the story, and writing about my journey became the container for the transformational work being done in my life.

Walking in silence began the work of creating a holistic anamorphosis in the substance of my being. Anamorphic process is the slow evolutionary change of a species being morphed into another type. I am using this term as a means of describing the complete transformation of mind, body, and soul into a different person. How I think about God, life, relationships, vocation, and the future has changed dramatically because of my pilgrimage. My words come from a new source within my soul. The sermons I preach vibrate from the experience of walking in silence. The way I once viewed leadership died and has now been resurrected from the burning spiritual fire of silence. Through the anamorphic silence I have undergone, the miniexperience of death and resurrection, affecting change not only in my life, but also in the life of my community, there has emerged a reordering of roles in leadership and vocation within the spiritual community I serve. Residing in the presence of silence solely for my benefit is most likely selfish. However, abiding in the presence of silence for the sake of others means I must practice the spiritual disciplines of silence in order that the community can also feel the transformative anamorphic miniexperience of death and resurrection. If I walk in silence, meditate, engage the scripture in *lectio divina*, or take up any other spiritual practice of silence only for my personal benefit, then I have not experienced the full gift of the silence. If I accept the responsibility of leadership, I will be a better leader because I practice silence and those I lead will also benefit from the silence they can experience vicariously or we encounter together.

I wish I could have understood the spiritual importance of silence earlier in my life. As an introvert, I have a deep desire for solitude and silence. I gain energy from being alone. As a college coach and a university president, I needed to find the time to get away, if only for thirty minutes a day. Solitude and silence did "refuel" my energy tanks. Without time alone, my ability to lead would have been dramatically diminished; I would have burned out sooner. However, during that period of my life, I did not fully understand the palpable power of abiding in the presence of silence. Had I been able to steep myself in the thickness of the silence, to be still in the presence of the healing air of the holy, to breathe deep the fragrance of the silence, I believe my capacity to lead would have expanded. If I had embraced Kelsey's notion of the miniexperience of death and resurrection found in the silence,

I may have been able to reduce my fear of failure (death) and invited others into the anamorphic process of transformation with me.

Coaching college baseball is about mentoring males through young adulthood. If I could have been confident of the work done in me through silence, instead of just intuitively sensing I needed it, I would have been better at letting go and allowing those young men to grow more through their own experience without too much instruction from me. While I was its president, Grand Canyon University was also going through the process of institutional maturation under my leadership. The university would experience its own institutional death and resurrection. If I had been able to saturate myself enough in the transformative work of personal silence, I would have been better equipped to abide in the presence of the silence of the board, faculty, and staff as we waded through the muck of frightening change. Instead of trying to give answers I did not have about the future, I might have been able to allow space for us all to grieve the inevitable loss that I knew was coming. When we as leaders can sit in the silence of the other, we can assist individuals and a community through its own anamorphic process, a worthwhile work and vocation.

ABIDING IN THE PRESENCE OF OTHERS' SILENCE

When a leader and group faithfully practice silence, they will receive the gifts of (1) a deeper empathy and thereby a stronger connection among those participating in the silence, (2) possible new discoveries or solutions to problems, and (3) a better chance to hear what the Spirit is saying to the community, thereby experiencing a union with God.

Catherine de Hueck Doherty (1896–1985) wrote the spiritual classic *Poustinia: Encountering God in Silence, Solitude and Prayer.*[15] She was the founder of Madonna House Apostolate, a community of prayer committed to going into the desert of silence. *Poustinia* is a Russian word meaning "desert." Following Doherty's teaching, the word also refers to a small house or cabin where a person can fast, pray, and read the Bible for twenty-four hours. For Doherty, the desert can be literal, the cabin, or the silence and solitude of the heart. She wrote that the one who goes into the desert of silence does so "not for himself but for others."[16] Doherty's life had her own struggles and trials, and she was sometimes misunderstood. Yet she was the epitome of a servant leader. In the second half of her life, she served the poor and homeless, the voiceless souls of the street. Her tireless strength was very much the result of the significant time she spent in solitude, silence, and prayer. Her time alone with God nourished her soul, so she might empty herself for the sake of others.[17] She wrote, "When you are in love with God you will understand he loved you first. You will enter into a deep and mysterious silence and in that silence will become one with the Absolute. Sobornost! [*unity*] Your oneness with God will overflow to all your brothers and sisters."[18]

Not all leaders serve in the same circumstances as Doherty, but we are all called to serve the silent, the voiceless. Just as Jesus elevated the status of children, women, the poor, the outcast, the sick, and those in prison, by being present to them, leaders must likewise be capable of being present to others in their silence. These times of silence may be caused by grief, pain, loss, loneliness, or frustration. When we are with someone suffering such troubles, all we may have to offer is our presence and our own silence.

We can practice silence in many situations. I do quite a bit of marital counseling. My experience is that the lack of healthy communication skills is the number one cause of a strained relationship. One way I have found to help couples express their feelings without escalating into an argument is to practice being in silence with one another. Being silent with someone is not giving him the silent treatment. Rather, it is practicing silence with the intent of crafting safe space for healthy communication, which can facilitate a better relationship. I ask couples if they can sit together without watching television, listening to music, or reading—if they can sit together without doing anything other than focusing their attention on one another. Typically, they have never tried. I ask them to start by spending one minute a day in silence together, then gradually extending the time to five minutes. I ask them to share after the periods of silence what each experienced. What were they feeling? What were they thinking?

I tell them as they are working on spending time together in silence, they are also practicing for times in their relationship when they might argue. They are rehearsing for timeouts during conversations when they feel the air is "heating up" and they are heading for an argument. When either partner senses the situation is escalating toward conflict, he or she can call for a five-minute timeout. I also encourage them to recognize when five minutes is not enough. At these times, either partner may ask for a longer timeout, as long as he or she promises to reconvene the discussion at the end of the predetermined time period. Having practiced silence in the absence of conflict, they can begin to create an environment for healing when either or both of them have been hurt.

This technique can also be used in church meetings. At times when negative energy and conflict arise, the leader can call for a brief timeout. The timeout could be offered in a subtle way by calling the group into a session of prayer. The leader could start with some silence and then pray with words. Over time, a community can become comfortable or at least tolerant of the idea that the leader will call them into a period of silence, prayer, or contemplation as a means of reducing stress and beckoning the Holy Spirit to be present as the healing agent of conflict.

As president of Grand Canyon University, in board, faculty, and staff meetings, I learned over time to call for short sessions of prayer during periods of stress or heated conversation. These groups were not accustomed to silence in the work setting, but they were comfortable with breaks for prayer, which might include some relatively brief moments of silence. I have often wondered if I had had the courage to call for us to go into our own *poustinia*, we could have averted some of our institutional problems or at least felt more comfortable that we were hearing the Spirit and not trusting our own sense of what was right or wrong. Even having gone through the painful experience of being a university president and having learned much better techniques and strategies for managing conflict, I still have to remind myself today, during times of conflict, that I have to call upon silence as a way to make space for us to hear the Spirit and each other. If we can hold ourselves in the presence of silence during conflict, we may come out on the other side with better solutions and less stress.

I think my best teacher in the realm of silence has been my experience under a wise spiritual guide who relies on silence to offer wisdom, teach, guide, heal, nurture, and at times gently nudge. Now a spiritual director myself, I look for opportunities during spiritual direction sessions to create moments of silence or take advantage of natural lulls in conversation by not filling the space with sound. When I remain silent during my first sessions with a new pilgrim, the person will typically fill the quiet space with words. For me this is an indication he is uncomfortable with the quiet, and I ask him if we can hold silence for two minutes. Afterwards, I ask how the time of quiet felt. If he can begin to talk about the feelings he experienced during the silence, this should be a clue for him to pay attention to the inner self during his own silence. By talking about an experience we often come to our "aha" discoveries, a real moment of success in spiritual direction. Some of my directees have become so comfortable with silence that they will be the ones to look for the opportunities to open time for silence during the session. I have had some of my directees tell me our hour together is the only time during the month that they will have some quiet within it. Once someone experiences the powerful healing energy coming through silence, she will crave it.

Keeping silence is a technique used by other professions who work with healing the psyche. Carl Rogers, developer of the person-centered approach to psychology, wrote about his experience of sitting in long periods of silence with a client in "A Silent Young Man."[19] In Rogers's transcript of sessions with his client, he records periods of silence lasting as long as seventeen minutes.[20] Rogers wrote that the client saw himself as worthless, hopeless, unloved, and unlovable, yet when the client experienced Rogers caring, "in that moment his defensive shell cracks wide open . . . , he becomes a softer person."[21] Rogers admits that he did not know the meaning of the young man's silence. But Rogers also suggests that his willingness to be present in the silence with his young client contributed to the breakthrough. Leaders do not have to be therapists to hold the presence of silence for a person or group.

But the leader's commitment to the healing qualities of silence can facilitate personal and group breakthroughs.

During Clinical Pastoral Education, our director asked us to sit in pairs facing one another, touching knees. Then she instructed us to look into one another's eyes, keeping silence. The first exercise was for five minutes. Then she extended the time. After each of these sessions, she would ask if we were in touch with what the other person was feeling. The experiences, she said, were preparing us to be present to patients who were not in a condition to speak but wanted someone to sit with them. Our director wanted us to practice connecting to the other person's feelings when words were not possible.

The power of sitting in silence and connecting to the feelings of the person in a hospital bed was also extended to engaging with the feelings of the family as well. What I learned from my CPE director about encountering the other's feelings through silence has had tremendous application in my role as pastor and leader in the church. There are times in meetings with leadership groups such as staff or a board when they will express themselves passionately, because they feel deeply invested in an issue. I've been in meetings where two or more people may be talking at the same time—even trying to talk over each other. The outspoken people may be overpowering the introverts or the insecure or those whose cultures have taught them never to act in such a way. In times such as these, the leader must connect with the feelings of each person in the room, recognizing that the silent ones may have important things to say as well. At this point in the meeting, the leader should ask everyone to stop talking for a minute. The leader can recount what he is observing. He can ask the group for a few minutes of silence, so that he and others who have not talked may have time to take in what they have heard and think about how they want to express themselves. Then the leader can begin to invite each person to share his or her thoughts and feelings. After each person has finished speaking, the leader can simply say, "thank you," then allow for a few minutes of silence and again invite another person, not just going around the room, but asking in a random fashion. Episcopal priest and musician Eric Law developed this technique of mutual invitation in his book *The Wolf Shall Dwell with the Lamb: A Spirituality for Leadership in a Multicultural Community*.[22] His method, and my derivation of it, can craft an atmosphere of listening by relying upon periods of silence and reflection. If a group is in conflict, mutual invitation through silence and reflection will allow each member of the group an opportunity to feel included and to express her feelings. Often, new ideas emerge, and those who previously were quiet now feel empowered to contribute to finding solutions to once contentious problems that only generated stress.

Practicing silence has prepared me as a leader to invite others into the healing grace of the presence of silence, but this has only come about because of my experience of others offering the presence of silence to me. Their grace has been influential in my willingness to have the courage to lead through the presence of silence. One of my first encounters with this kind of group silence was when I was on a retreat with twelve people in Glendalough, Ireland. On the third day, our spiritual guide led us through a twenty-four-hour period of silence. We gathered for Morning Prayer and then to begin the silence after prayers, we went on a five-mile walk through Saint Kevin's sixth-century monastery and around two small lakes above the ancient ruins.

At first, walking in silence with a group was awkward. After a mile, the group, without instruction, formed a scattered single file, having found it was easier to keep silence in isolation from the rest of the group. Questions began to arise within my quiet. Should I keep to myself? What if wanted to point to something I saw? Was I alone in my thoughts? Was this my personal experience, the experience of twelve people walking in silence together, or a group experience?

When we reached the lower lake, our guide gathered us at the edge of the water and motioned for each of us to choose a stone from the clear cold lake. Then he held a black flat rock between his hands, folded them in prayer, and breathed on the stone. We mirrored his action, holding our stones in our folded hands and breathing on them. Then he turned and continued to lead us on our silent walk toward the upper Lake of the Angels, the site of

Saint Kevin's private cell. I felt like I had blown the struggles of my soul upon my stone. I began to wonder what the other pilgrims had breathed into their stones—perhaps pain, frustration, troubles, fears, prayers of questioning and doubt, or thanksgiving and praise. As we walked, my small stone began to feel like a big rock, then a bag of rocks, and then a boulder.

When we reached the upper lake, our leader gathered us again at the edge of the water. This time he faced the lake. Reaching out his arm, he dropped the stone in the water. We watched each other as we one by one placed our stone in the lake. One woman flung her rock with all her might into the depths of the glimmering water. A man skipped his stone across the icy lake. My stone was so heavy I barely had the strength to set it at the edge of the water. A close friend put his hand on my shoulder and motioned, silently asking if he could throw my stone in the water for me. I nodded yes. My friend picked up the stone, took a few steps back to get a running start, and with all his might, threw the pain I had breathed into my stone far into the depths of the holy lake. My "boulder" of anguish landed with a splash of relief. When I turned my eyes away from the lake, I saw the group was focused on me, a few smiled, others gave a slight bow of the head. Another gave me a hug. I felt like my fellow pilgrims acknowledged my inner weight and that they were willing to help me carry it.

Our guide blew his breath over his palm. This act was his sign for us to spread ourselves like tiny seeds into the wind for the remainder of the day. I spent most of my time walking around the lake and writing in my journal. I did not see any of the other people who were on the retreat until we gathered late in the afternoon at the house where we were staying. We ate our evening meal in communal silence. The air seemed pregnant with stories we wanted to share, but the telling would have to wait until morning. That night I dreamt I was lying in the silent, cold, hard darkness of Saint Kevin's cell.

In the morning silence before breakfast, we gathered in the tiny chapel. Our leader handed out sheets on which were printed a few ancient Celtic prayers and some contemporary poetry. He twirled a wand around a singing bowl, and in silence we prayed the common prayers. I could feel the emotions swelling in my heart, and when he circled the bell to end our silence, I began to weep and then sob. The community held my silence, while I released the pain and emotions. They sat close and waited in the presence of silence until the wave of my emotion finally gave out. My weeping was from the feeling of finally being able to let go of four years of trying to fit into the mold of being a college president, a role for which I was unprepared and unable to fulfill in the way others expected. In the retreat group, a few knew me well, and the rest I had met just days prior to our time of silence. Together, though, in silence, they carried the weight of my pain. They did not have to know my troubles, but in silence they were willing to pray for my release from the heaviness I was experiencing. Collectively they were willing to abide in the presence of my silence. Having personally experienced a group inviting me into the presence of silence as a healing act of grace, I now, as a leader, intimately know the depth to which the presence of silence within a small supportive community can lead as a means of releasing buried pain. I have tried, with some success, to replicate this experience for others on weekend retreats and at a silent retreat day at our parish.

Without practice, when moments of accidental or incidental silence arise, the individual and the group are rarely prepared to receive the benefits of the silence. While a retreat is an excellent opportunity to share in communal silence, learning to abide in others' spiritual silence does not totally require that we participate in an organized exercise. Other settings can work as well. As I said in a previous story, creating regular opportunities for group centering prayer and silent contemplation opens space for the community to "listen" in silence to one another. Communal silence can be the occasion we "hear" one another's pain without having to discuss our troubles. I may not be able to explain the depth of my pain or display my emotions, but if you can sense my weight through the silence then I may be able to lay the weight down, if only for a few minutes.

In communal silence, we can also find rest, hear what the Spirit is saying, and enter into individual and communal discernment. Silence, the absence of sound and the presence of the spirit, can be refreshing, allowing us to think and breathe. When we are exhausted, we know a good night's sleep can renew. On more than a few Sunday mornings, I have looked out onto a congregation that looked tired from the demands of their lives and have thought the best thing we could do was take a collective nap. People need rest, and silence in worship can be God's way of providing us all relief from a weary life. I find nothing wrong if someone would fall asleep during the silence in worship; maybe he needed the nap. Sleep reinvigorates our ability to think clearly and enhances our creativity, and the benefits of silence can be as life giving and generative as a good night's sleep or a great afternoon nap.

A rested congregation most likely will be in a better place to hear what the Spirit is saying and to be in union with God, especially when faced with critical decisions. A discernment group or committee is a wonderful channel for someone who is searching for God's word in making an important decision in life. This type of committee is typically used when a person is discerning a vocational call to ministry. However, I have found these groups to be extremely helpful for people in our congregation who are considering a career change, a geographical move, and many other exciting possibilities. I will discuss discernment committees at length in chapter six. However, in this chapter the germane consideration is that serving on a discernment committee can be a privilege for a group of people who are collectively listening to the Spirit in silence while someone is considering a decision. Not only will the discerning person hear the Spirit, but my experience has been that the people on the committee typically do some discernment in their own lives as well. On more than one occasion, during the process of discernment, a committee member has come to me as their pastor telling me they have been wrestling with a decision in their life and serving on the committee helped them come to a decision.

We have an average Sunday attendance of 140. Over the course of six years, nearly sixty people have served on at least one discernment committee. Because so many of our congregational members have experienced the power of residing in the silence of discernment, I believe we have witnessed a climate change in our listening ability across the breadth of the community. We have become a group of people who are especially sensitive to those who are seeking answers to life decisions, and if the person desires, we are prepared to enter into the discernment process with her. We know how to keep silence and not overwhelm her with advice. Instead, we listen in silence to what the Spirit is saying. Likewise, when our parish is considering a substantive change, we know how to practice long periods of discernment and collective silence. While we may not be as accomplished as our sisters and brothers at the Friends House down the street, we do emulate them in many ways.

In addition to implementing discernment committees as a means of creating openings for communal silence, it is important to infuse silence into the education of the parish. When silence permeates every aspect of our life together, we become more at ease with one another in silence and with the Spirit of God in her silence as well. (I will say more about this later in the chapter.) *Godly Play*, developed by Jerome Berryman, is a beautiful method and curriculum for children's education that encourages silence in a child's spiritual development (Berryman considers *Godly Play* a particular method, like Montessori). *The Art of Engaging Holy Scripture* is an excellent spiritual formation curriculum that its creator, Jim Clark, refers to as *Godly Play* for adults. In Clark's teacher preparation courses and materials, as well as the student literature, he has included periods of silence for reflection as a regular part of each class and individual work to be done during the week.

Leaders can also teach a congregation the power of being together in silence by creating moments of intentional, as opposed to accidental, quiet as a part of the worship experience. By capturing natural moments of transition between readings, after the sermon, between prayer petitions, or any other appropriate times that fit with the style of the congregation, the leader can assist worshipers in becoming more accustomed to ever increasing times of silence. Explaining the purpose of silence can help set the congregation at ease. I have frequently preached sermons about the energy gained from incorporating silence into one's personal life. When silence becomes a part of the liturgy, the unspoken message of the Spirit will hopefully emerge in the soul of those individuals prepared to hear with their ears and their heart. Prayerfully, I can hope the same preparation is happening in the collective unconscious soul of the congregation.

With practice, we will learn that sometimes the voice of the Spirit is subtle, other times gentle, and as some have experienced, at times confronting, prophetic, and calling us to confession. When we listen to the Spirit in our silence and in the presence of the silence of others, it requires the various ways each member of the community can hear the different tones of the Spirit's voice, both in the conscious and unconscious. The Spirit may speak to us in the quiet smile of a child, the wordless kiss of a lover, a dream, the breathless moments after the death of a loved one, the speechless effort of a Prader-Willi sister, the air we breathe when walking for hours alone, the deafening sound of loneliness, and the crushing weight of making a life-changing decision.

In these moments, the sounds of silence, we will indeed know a deeper empathy and connection among those in the silence, we can discover solutions to problems, and we can discern what the Spirit is saying. By opening our hearts in silence we can, individually and communally, experience a union with God. Here in these moments of silence, we are resting our head on the Spirit's chest. *Amen!*

As I hold my sleeping grandson, I know he hears my heartbeat, and I pray he is hearing my love. He cannot understand the words of love I whisper, but he feels my gentle kisses on his cheeks. He may not comprehend why my tears of joy make my face shine in smiles, but he smiles back, and then I am swept away into the paradise of eternal love. I crave to hear God in this way, and I know I must be hearing God each precious minute I am with my holy grandchild. I believe when we as leaders steep ourselves in the presence of silence, listening to the heartbeat of God, swept away in our craving to hear God, we can trust the voice of God's Spirit to speak to us in our own silence and in the silence of others. The leader who is permeated with silence in the very core of her being will lead humbly, focusing on the needs of others with wisdom, a wisdom which comes from abiding in the presence of God's silence.

ABIDING IN THE PRESENCE OF GOD'S SILENCE

I have written about silence, about holding silence, and even about leading a congregation from the context of silence, which I know may seem impossible. But to suggest now that we sit in the presence of God's silence as a way of leading may be frightening, because the notion of God's silence is often perceived as God's absence, or worse, God's disappointment, disapproval, or anger with us. I want to consider the idea that the silence of God may at times, instead, be an indication of God's suffering—and we may be asked to sit with God in the suffering of the Spirit. By sitting with God in this suffering, we can discover a new kinship and a deeper love of God radiating towards us in our suffering, even to the point that we may hear God anew in a prophetic revelation for us in our leadership. We cannot know Easter without the three-day journey of Good Friday, into Saturday's tomb of cold death and even to the depths of hades. Having traveled the three days of silence, we are then able to share the unbelievable message of God's love in the face of possible disaster or perceived defeat—and most leaders have spent plenty of time in the not-so-Good Friday and the un-Holy Saturday of leadership. We as leaders know suffering, so if we can find strength in being present to God's suffering, we will be better leaders for the experience.

Mother Teresa's story inspires us, stirring our soul. She was a saint of mercy and service to the poorest of the poor in Calcutta. Teresa was also a woman with a spiritually broken heart. In 1947, traveling on a train toward a much overdue rest after seventeen years of teaching in Calcutta, she heard Jesus's voice calling her into fifty years of ministry to the most broken children of India. According to letters she wrote to her spiritual director near the end of her life, she was forlorn and sick of heart, because she never heard Jesus's gentle and sweet voice again after that train ride. It is hard to fathom Mother Teresa having to abide for fifty years in the presence of God's silence. Yet she did so, faithfully responding to the calling she heard on that train. But maybe in that silence God was not absent, but suffering with Mother Teresa and those to whom she ministered.

Dietrich Bonhoeffer may also have understood the pain of that haunting absence of sound, the silence of God he experienced in prison. In those days of threat and interrogation, and nights of bombings, while ministering to the death cries of fellow inmates, Bonhoeffer felt such intense grief that he identified it with God's grief. For Bonhoeffer, God's pain was in hearing Jesus cry out from the cross, the moment of his crucifixion as a leader, "My God, my God, why have you forsaken me?" Apparently Bonhoeffer must have wondered what God's suffering felt like in the moment Jesus died. Bonhoeffer asked what it was like for God to sit in the silence of the three days of Jesus's muted death. I wonder if abiding in the silence of God's suffering gave Bonhoeffer the inner courage to go to God, in God's grieving, thereby strengthening the pastor's resolve to lead so faithfully in the face of his own execution? We may get a glimpse of Bonhoeffer's experience of being in the presence of God's silence in the poem he wrote from his prison cell, *Christians and Pagans*.[23] Bonhoeffer knew he went to God with his suffering, but then Bonhoeffer wrote, "Men go to God when he is sore bestead. . . . Christians stand by God in his hour of grieving."[24] A later translation of the poem provides some modern clarity stating that some will go to God "in God's need and dread" when God is "distressed" and "oppressed."[25] Bonhoeffer is opening the door for the leader to go to God in God's grief, recognizing these times not as God's absence but as God's presence in silence. Bonhoeffer seems to be suggesting that God seeks our presence as a means of saying, "I am God and I identify with your pain. Come and see."

In grief we can find our words muted, buried under waves of emotion, for in the pain of grief, the agony of losing a loved one, the words of others can mean nothing. So, we retreat to silence, looking for comfort. If, indeed, we believe God was incarnate in Jesus Christ, we can find solace in God's knowing and identifying with us in the experience of every persecution endured by the Savior. In God's experience through the Christ, God understands our being nailed to the cross of our brokenness. God suffers in silence, in pain. We then can go to God, "when he is sore bestead," and reside in God's quiet silence of grief. Together, bonded, we can be comforted like two mourners clutching one another in the silence of their mutual grief. I believe the experience of being present to God in God's grief will shift our expectation from a God who is constantly on call to medicate us when we are licking our wounds as suffering leaders, to a position of gaining healing strength from the God who knows our suffering and appreciates our presence in God's times of pain. These brief instances of exchanged grief create within us a larger capacity for a spiritual leadership that is both mystical and political. Mystical in that we can approach, if for just a moment, a Jesus-like intimacy with Abba, a union with God, and political in that we recognize that in order to lead we must be willing to risk at the highest level.

God suffers when the earth is disregarded, as if it only exists in order to feed our unquenchable desire for natural resources. God is deeply grieved when children and women are sold into sexual slavery. God sobs when humans butcher one another in the name of the Holy Divine One. Can we not be present in God's silence, in God's grief? How then do we console God in God's grief? Doing something to redirect the forces destroying the earth and one another is critical. Being committed to change and to leading others to make a difference is of vital importance. We cannot know God's grief any more than you can know my grief, nor can I know the reality of yours. Still, I can sit with you in your silent grief, and you can reside in mine, and we can both be present to God in God's grief. Going to God when God is sore bestead, being in the presence of God's silent grieving, will change my perspective on the work to be done on God's behalf while I am living on this earth.

As a leader of a church community, I no longer feel I must give in to the immense pressure being heaped upon me to grow the church numerically and financially. Indeed, the trap of being a CEO pastor and an entrepreneur who attracts the unchurched masses must be avoided. Instead, as faith leaders we are called to be like Jesus, to be in the midst of those of who suffer, willing to risk our authority, willing to let go, willing to die a leader's death. Jesus, facing death, which was perceived by his disciples as failed leadership, tells them, "Unless a grain of wheat falls into the earth and dies, it remains just a single grain; but if it dies, it bears much fruit" (John 12:24). Whether the church survives another day is not the leader's responsibility; the future of the church lies in the hands of God. Our job as leaders is to be present to those in our community, especially in times of loss. Having been present to God in God's suffering, we as leaders are better equipped to be present to those in our community who are suffering. And through this mutually shared experience, we may be better able to lead.

When I am willing to abide in the presence of God's silence, I continue to lead in the steadfastness of Mother Teresa as she heard the call of God and then toiled for fifty years in the presence of God's silence. Abiding in this part of the love relationship with God can be arduous and at the same time inspiring, as it moves us to take courageous actions and instills in us a strength previously unknown to us and the community. Even though the work is challenging, God is still fetching us, calling us, beckoning us forward to abide in God's love, in God's silence, in order to hear most clearly what the Spirit is saying, even when it seems there are no words from God. Silence may be teaching us to be steadfast leaders.

Leading in the face of God's silence can be the most challenging lesson we learn from the wisdom of the spiritual director, for many leaders and many in our congregations will not understand this abidance in silence as a positive component of service. God's silence has been perceived mostly in negative terms. But maybe God's silence is calling us into a deeper relationship with the Divine. Perhaps God's silence is a secret working in the soul of the leader and the community. What if God's silence is calling us to travel into another level of trust of God and one another? I earnestly believe that God's silence is an opportunity for us as leaders and community to be still before the Lord, humble ourselves, be ever more present to the heartbeat of God, and expose ourselves to the sensitivities of God—in other words, to feel what God is feeling. The palpability of God's silence, the thickness of abiding in the presence of the silence of God, will call the leader to lead with the vulnerable recklessness of Jesus and with the passion of the post-resurrection disciples. Who knows? Maybe the church and its leaders who are willing to abide in the silence of God are being called to such a time as this. The decline of the institutional church in a post-Christian world requires extra-ordinary leaders who are willing to be intimately connected to the suffering and the silent in order to know and hear the Spirit, who will be instructing us how to lead in this new and challenging era.

LEADERS AS ADVOCATES OF SILENCE

Silence is a powerful tool in the hand of a creative leader. The comfort level of the leader who enters into the presence of silence is not dependent upon introversion or extroversion. The one necessary ingredient is the willingness of the leader to enter into the holy, silent space, the presence of silence with pure openness to possibility. Leaders are called to place themselves in the presence of the silence and allow the wind of the Spirit to form us like stone.

Near Prescott, Arizona, there is an outcropping of red rock, rounded and made smooth by millions of years of wind. While the wind itself makes no sound, its movement across the rock creates a noise we can hear. The wind sculpts the stones into artistic monuments in testimony to the wind's presence. Just as the wind shapes the rocks, silence will shape the people if the spiritual leader and the congregation have the courage to stay present in the silence. By advocating for silence in his or her personal life, in corporate worship, in meetings, in personal encounters with those seeking counsel and discernment, and in teaching opportunities, the leader can create an environment where the spiritual power of silence can be experienced in every aspect of parish life. Silence will prepare the hearts of the people to hear what the Spirit is saying. In silence the people can discover a stillness allowing the formative hand of the Spirit to mold the soul of the community. Silence, over time, will become the evidence of the Spirit's power of presence among the people. Indeed, the advocacy of silence is a challenging endeavor, because the leader will be asking the congregation to fully embrace silence in worship and spiritual formation, placing themselves in the windy element of the formative Spirit. Yet if the challenge is taken up, the results for the leader and the community will be a lasting work, a monument.

FIVE

The Leader as Wisdom Teacher

> Wisdom, after all, is not a station you arrive at, but a manner of traveling. . . . To know exactly where you're headed may be the best way to go astray. Not all who loiter are lost.
>
> —Anthony de Mello[1]

Noah Seabern Young ("Seab"), my grandfather, died in January 1990. Though he physically left this earthly realm years ago, all I have to do is close my eyes, and I can see him standing next to me, ready to tell another story. His father, Ulysses Eular Young, was half-Cherokee; his mother, Jennie Thompson Reddick, was Irish. She died from the flu during an epidemic when Seab was nine months old. After Jennie's funeral, Eular took the trunk containing all her worldly possessions into the field behind the house, where he sat with them for hours. Then overpowered by his immense grief and wrapped in the darkness of the night, he torched the trunk. The only vestiges of his beloved wife were a few family photos someone else kept and Eular's tortured memories. For some reason, maybe because Jennie had wanted Seab to be a girl, Eular didn't cut his hair until he was nine. I have a picture of him with a ponytail.

I remember my grandfather as a short, stocky, barrel-chested man with thick hairy forearms. His face and hands were dark and lined from years of hard work in the sun. My grandfather had a round face and flat nose, reflecting his Cherokee heritage. He smelled lightly of Old Spice aftershave, sweat, and cigarette smoke. His pleasant aroma enhanced his attractive, manly features. He always wore pressed khakis, a long-sleeved cowboy shirt over a white t-shirt, brown roper boots, and a cowboy hat. In the summer, we often sat under the tree in front of his small, whitewashed frame house in the country. On those warm, western Oklahoma evenings, he took off his cowboy shirt, revealing his strength, even for an older man. He would ease himself down onto a turned-over metal bucket and, leaning back against a tree, light a perpetual stream of Camel cigarettes.

My grandfather told the same dozen or so stories over and over again, and to this day I can recite most of them nearly verbatim. His stories fell into three categories. First there were tales about his father's Cherokee ways and memories of his mother. He also told stories about his wife, Allie Pauline, who died when she was in her mid-thirties. And he told countless stories about his children, especially his son, Eular (named after his grandfather Ulysses Eular), who was killed in Fort Hood, Texas, when his Army helicopter was struck by lightning. Every story was constructed with subtle nuggets of wisdom. Every account of his son was intended to give me some guidance about how to be a young man and eventually how to be a father. What he told me about his daughters always seemed laced with instructions on how to treat young women.

I never met my grandmother. She died much too young, years before I was born. But through my grandfather's stories, I've always known my grandmother. He told me things about my grandmother that even my mother, her oldest child, didn't know. My grandfather's love for his wife was still intense thirty years after she had died from an insidious cancer. He loved to tell stories about how her shocking red hair and lightening blue eyes would fetch his soul from across the field where they picked cotton. She wasn't any bigger than a broom handle, he would tell me, but no man ever dared mess with her. According to my grandfather's stories—a mix of metaphor, parable, and fact—my grandmother always covered his back in any fight where he was outnumbered. Evidently she was not afraid to use a broken bottle or whatever else was handy as a weapon. As a nine-year-old boy, I fell deeply in love with those images. As a teenager, I would marry the vision of my grandmother, in the woman I have been with for over forty years. My grandfather's stories were about the binding strength of love found within the family circle told in such a way that as a nine-year-old boy I could learn from them and continue to glean from his wisdom twenty years later. His wisdom stories still whisper in my ear and resonate in every part of my being, continuing to shape how I live my life.

Wisdom offers great gifts, speaking across time from generation to generation. Wisdom is one of the powers of life gained from the positive energy of love. Wisdom is a compassionate spirit constantly teaching in gentle ways. Wisdom grows in the life of the hearer like a garden that is lovingly tended every day, becoming evident in the conscious awareness of the learner like a plant breaking newly through the soil. Wisdom has been working like tiny seeds deep in the fertile soil of the unconscious, roots driving deep for water and stems pushing high toward the sun of the consciousness. Such work produces wisdom, humble and supple, constantly open to learning new truths of eternal value. Wisdom is a path that must be steadily walked. The pilgrim walking the way of wisdom shares what she has learned along the way with others because she loves the journey. There is no single way of wisdom, just some roads easier to travel. The way of wisdom is a gift, like a good map, shared through the art of storytelling, enjoyed like the taste of cool water at the end of a long journey.

My grandfather did not share his stories to ensure I would live my life exactly like his. Rather, he intended to give me grounding, so I might live life in my own unique way. His stories were his blessing of wisdom into my life. Every leader needs at least one wise soul in his or her life who will be that sage who communicates best through storytelling. Valuable life stories and wisdom go hand in hand, teaching us how to live and lead. While every person who has a leadership position may not be wise, every leader should be maturing in wisdom, one of the most important characteristics of a leader.

The late Irish poet John O'Donohue wrote in *Anam Cara*, "Wisdom, then, is the art of balancing the known with the unknown, the suffering with the joy; it is a way of linking the whole of life together in a new and deeper unity." He goes on to say what

I believe is most critical for the leader in understanding wisdom: "Ultimately, wisdom and vision are sisters; the creativity, critique and prophecy of vision issues from the fount of wisdom."[2]

We must seek the teaching of sister wisdom through sages in our life—listening and learning from her about how to make sense of the journey we have traveled. Sister wisdom will show us how to recognize useful insights found within the stories of life. She will teach us how to effectively discern meaning from the archetypal myths. Wisdom, through her guides, will build within us the desire to balance the confidence coming from what we know in life with the humility we gain by recognizing what we do not know. She will help the leader to discover the means to manage the suffering and joys of leadership. Wisdom prevents the leader from sinking too low in times of struggle, nor rising too high in moments of success. From the wisdom that has flowed into our life through our relationship with sister wisdom, the leader will gain the inner resources needed to be the wisdom guide for other people, while at the same time, the leader will be able to cast a vision the people can see, understand, and are willing to follow.

The vision arising out of the fount of wisdom is not a strategic plan, a mission statement, or a big hairy audacious goal. While these business-driven planning mechanisms are not necessarily bad methods for managing an organization, they are not the vision birthed out of wisdom. They are simply tools to be used in assisting the congregation to move the vision forward. The leader's vision will reflect wisdom and shine with God's promises, inspiring us. The vision will provide us with a possibility of a better way of life, encouraging us. And the vision will create an enthusiasm among the people about the work to be done. As a people we are inspired by the promise of the vision, encouraged by the hope, enthused by the expectation created by vision, and moved to work in fulfilling the vision. The leader who is a wisdom guide will see a vision that liberates the congregation to become the people God is calling them to be.

In order to serve as a wisdom guide, the leader will need to be a storyteller weaving parables, myths, and teaching in such a way as to guide the pilgrimage of the congregation. Not every leader has evolved to become a wisdom guide. But by learning the ways of wisdom, he can begin to walk the path of the wise. Her life of prayer and nurturing from her wisdom guides will bring about wisdom in her life. The wise leader will seek wisdom from a variety of sources, tell engaging and meaningful stories as a way of communicating wisdom, and preach sermons as a wisdom guide and spiritual director for the congregation.

PEOPLE AS SOURCES OF WISDOM

If the leader is going to be a wisdom guide, she needs teachers, guides, spiritual directors, and mentors in her life who will share their wisdom with her. I feel blessed to have had some wonderful guides. Those who teach us wisdom will be our models, like my Clinical Pastoral Education (CPE) director was for me. On the first day of my CPE program, the director, who is Sikh, looked me straight in eye and told me, "You are not the Lone Ranger." Indeed not. She saw straight through my natural tendency to go it alone. The director spent the remaining twenty-four weeks teaching and mentoring me in the ways of being a hospital team member in which all the staff, from maintenance workers to the chief resident, worked together toward the health of the patients. She mentored me in ways of wisdom by taking me with her as she made her rounds through the hospital, meeting with patients, staff, and administration. She taught me that my role, as a part of the team, was to be available as a spiritual presence for everyone in the hospital. My work with the patients, if done well, she said, could open the door for the staff to see me as someone whom they could trust with personal matters. The director taught me how to carefully listen to the staff amidst the constant demands being placed upon them in the hospital. She reminded me that in order to share wisdom, I had to be available, I needed to listen deeply, and, she said, I had to listen with thoughtful open-ended questions. The director then went with me on my early rounds, listening, asking questions, and sharing with me her experienced wisdom.

A wise teacher, spiritual director, or mentor will be someone who has an abundance of life experience. According to Richard Rohr, author of *Falling Upward: A Spirituality for the Two Halves of Life*,[3] it is someone in the second half of life, asking the important and often unanswerable questions of life. Rohr says, "The first half of life is discovering the script, and the second half is actually writing it and owning it."[4]

A second mentor in my life, my spiritual director, is in his second half of life. He had over forty years of experience, leading large parishes. He understood the rigors and trials of being the leader of a large religious organization. His years of faithful spiritual practice while being a prominent leader in the community provided a deep well of wisdom. His consistent presence and wise guidance has shaped my life immeasurably and has been a reliable resource for me. Meeting regularly with someone I trust has been comforting, because I've known my wisdom guide would be ready to listen and help me sort out life. He has walked with me through difficult struggles, times of spiritual dryness and other times when I was flying a bit too high, but mostly through the mundaneness of life. He has helped me gain new insights and guided me in reflecting on my leadership style. In my leadership experience there have been times when I felt overwhelmed or confused and I needed someone to talk to about the variables and options of leading. I have wondered how I would have made it through my transition from coach, to president, to priest without him.

Finding a wisdom teacher who is the best fit for our personality type, our spiritual needs, and our occupational concern is not easy. We may need relationships with several people we rely on to offer us their gifts of wisdom, because one person may not hold all the keys to our leadership development. The leader of any organization may have a business mentor, a spiritual director, a therapist, and a trusted pastor. While too many voices could be difficult to manage, and expensive, being in relationship with a wise spiritual director and a mentor or coach also prevents us from being a disciple of one person and developing a myopic view of leadership. Building such a network of wisdom guides will take patience on our part and prayer that God will lead these needed mentors into our life.

STUDYING AS A SOURCE OF WISDOM

Our wisdom guides will encourage us to follow their example of life-long study. Continuing education is an excellent avenue for networking with potential mentors and wisdom guides, and for staying current in our field and learning new skills. Some church judicatories mandate that clergy earn a certain number of continuing education units each year, which I commend. But even without such requirements, finding programs challenging us to learn and push us in our leadership development is vitally important. Obviously, not all leadership programs address developing the leader as a wisdom guide. But workshops on adaptive leadership, spiritual direction, becoming a mentor or coach, determining a *Myers-Briggs Type Indicator* as it relates to leadership, and the Enneagram will give us the opportunity to learn more about wisdom. Lack of money, time, and energy can be barriers for overtaxed faith leaders but ultimately should not deter us in our professional growth, especially in light of the need to lead in this radically changing era.

Our personal study should include reading about the wisdom way. Scripture and other writings on spiritual practice, the world of the seen and the unseen, and the realm of the conscious and unconscious can be excellent resources for our continuing journey toward wise leadership. Great wisdom can be found in books written about, and by, the saints of our faith. The mystics Teresa of Avila and John of the Cross, two staples from the spiritual director's library, were transformed by their travels through the dark night of the soul. We may discover that their rare wisdom provides a map in our journey down similarly rough and rocky roads.

Of course, books are important to spiritual leaders. In a 2012 survey, the Barna Group, a leading research organization focused on the intersection of faith and culture, reported that 92 percent of all pastors buy at least one book a month and some as many forty-six books a year.[5] Anne Lamott, in *Bird by Bird: Some Instructions on Writing and Life*, voices the viewpoint of those who are constantly reading: "For some of us, books are as important as almost anything else on earth. . . . Books help us understand who we are and how we are to behave. They show us what community and friendship mean; they show us how to live and die."[6]

Unfortunately, most of us have precious little time to read. Therefore, we must be selective. We can read reviews before taking on a book. If a book doesn't have my interest and imagination at fifty pages, I give myself permission to set it aside, maybe to read later. Because I love books, parishioners often give me their favorite read, which goes on my stack of "next to read," and when it comes to the top of the pile, I'll browse it carefully enough, though I may not read every word. While I am a discriminating reader, I'm not afraid to venture out, trying new topics, checking out a variety of authors, even reading something that strikes me as disagreeable, strange, or bizarre, always looking for one valuable nugget.

By reading wisdom stories, sacred texts, history, and biographies, we can learn about vast differences in religions, cultures, ethnicities, gender roles, and sexuality, hopefully gaining some insight as we move forward in our ever-shrinking, multi-ethnic, broadly diverse, post-Christian world. I can never know what it feels like to be of another religion, culture, race, gender, or sexuality, but I can read, listen, and observe others. I have a common ground of understanding with my Jewish sisters and brothers because I have read their holy scripture. In order to have a similar baseline with my Muslim brothers and sisters, I must read the Koran. Reading, conversation, and experiencing religious practices of other faiths can deepen the leader's understanding and enrich his source of wisdom. As a leader, I must make every effort to not only be sensitive to others, but to be well informed. Innocently, we can make terrible cultural and social missteps. But there is little excuse for being uninformed.

One of the most important things I have learned from authors whom I have enjoyed reading is to give them permission to mature, move on, and change their views. Early in my career at

Grand Canyon University, one of the departments invited a well-known author and speaker to the campus for a lecture. During the question-and-answer period, someone asked the author about something he had written a few years ago. He didn't answer the question, saying he had evolved since writing the book and that the question was no longer relevant. It was a good lesson for me. It's been fun watching the spiritual and theological progression of Christian writers like Brian McLaren (*A New Kind of Christianity: Ten Questions that Are Transforming the Faith*[7]) and Rob Bell (*Love Wins: A Book about Heaven, Hell, and the Fate of Every Person Who Ever Lived*[8]). I doubt if McLaren and Bell have enjoyed the criticism they've received from many members of the evangelical community. Some of their readers have not appreciated the evolution of their theology. But McLaren and Bell are not alone. Other progressive writers have suffered similar criticism from their readers. Readers' opinions of the theologian Dietrich Bonhoeffer vary, depending on whether they have read *Cost of Discipleship* or the later *Letters and Papers from Prison*. Typically, those who have read and loved *Cost of Discipleship* are shocked to hear Bonhoeffer write in *Letters and Papers from Prison* that he could "see the dangers of that book."[9] The author had matured beyond the point of thinking that faith could be acquired through holy living. We learn to be wise leaders by going on pilgrimage with authors, gaining from their wisdom as they evolve.

We also need to read fiction as a resource for fueling our life with creative stories and parables. A friend suggested I not take a book to study to bed, and I admit, after writing too many crib notes late at night, I have trouble going to sleep. Better to read fiction before sleep; besides, a good novel can stir up some interesting dreams. Reading good fiction can expand our imagination and prompt our creativity. Fiction can be both fun and sobering; it can take us on adventures and open our minds to ancient truths as well as new ways of thinking. Novels can provide spiritual directors with stories they can use as examples, such as Susan Howatch's *Starbridge Series*,[10] which some spiritual direction programs require participants to read. Reading fiction has also enhanced my preaching. Alyce McKenzie's *Novel Preaching: Tips from Top Writers on Crafting Creative Sermons* is an excellent resource for exploring the connection between writing fiction and preaching.[11]

While reading Cynthia Bourgeault's non-fiction book *The Meaning of Mary Magdalene: Discovering the Woman at the Heart of Christianity,* I discovered the mid-twentieth-century novelist Charles Williams.[12] C. S. Lewis writes that Williams, his fellow Inkling, "was a novelist, a poet, a dramatist, a biographer, a critic, and a theologian: a 'romantic theologian' in the technical sense . . . one who considers the theological implications of those experiences which are called romantic."[13] Williams's seven novels, including *The Greater Trumps*[14] and *Many Dimensions,*[15] have given me a language for thinking theologically about my supernatural and paranormal experiences.

Author Paul Elie—in *The Life You Save May Be Your Own: An American Pilgrimage,* where he mines the lives of Flannery O'Connor, Thomas Merton, Walker Percy, and Dorothy Day—dares suggest that the wisdom found in books, both nonfiction and fiction, can even bring about a transformation that can be salvific. "Certain books, certain writers, reach us at the center of ourselves, and we come to them in fear and trembling, in hope and expectation—reading so as to change, and perhaps to save, our lives."[16] Indeed, the wisdom gained from reading can powerfully alter our worldview and how we approach our relationships with God and with others. Being faithful readers of wisdom literature gives us a better chance of not repeating the mistakes of history and of maybe saving lives.

Of course, reading about any topic can only go so far in teaching us what we want to learn. At some point we have to experience the world in which we live.

Nature as a Source of Wisdom

My experience in nature has been a deep well of wisdom for me. On my pilgrimage across Ireland, walking alone in nature for hours and days in silence was an incredible adventure. Spending a month being swallowed up in the glorious majesty and

overwhelming power of Ireland's mountains was in itself quite
the wisdom teacher. Because of the remoteness of some of the
paths I walked, at times I felt as if I had traveled back in time
into an ancient world where I could more easily hear what nature had to say to me. Alone, walking where few travel, seeing
land untouched for centuries and stones and trees covered with
ages of moss, walking on bog, I found many times the fog and
forest were so thick I could barely see the path on which I was
walking. In those moments alone, I had to stop, breathe in the
sights, sounds, and smells—allowing my imagination to freely
roam, opening every pore of my being so that nature could be
my teacher.

On my pilgrimage, I encountered a wild ram, a red deer, an
Irish hare, and countless ravens. All had guidance and wisdom to
give me. I had the opportunity to hear and learn the lesson from
each creature of nature. I knew I could learn from these blessed
and gifted creatures for these four specific reasons. First, I was
walking in nature. I was present to their environment and very
respectful of their home. Second, I am a vegetarian. While this
is not the place to make a theological case for vegetarianism, just
maybe herbivores can sense who are not carnivores or omnivores
and are thus no threat to them. Third, I was in a near fasting state,
eating only one 300-calorie protein bar during an eight-hour hike.
Fasting heightens our spiritual sensitivities. Fourth, I was open
to hearing what each creature and nature herself had to say. I
stopped, remained quiet, listened, and opened my soul.

Nature infuses us with wisdom through our willingness to be
vulnerable in her presence. When we place our lives in the hands
of Father Sky and Mother Earth, we learn humility. Before embarking on my pilgrimage, I knew I wanted to achieve my goal
of walking almost four hundred miles across Ireland. I trained,
bought good equipment, and studied the trails. However, Ireland's
nature humbled me, and at points when I thought I could not or
would not finish the journey, I fell into despair, feeling I was going to fail. At those moments of humility and weakness, however,
Father Sky and Mother Earth would encourage me with messages
from the raven, the deer, the hare, or the ram.

The messages seemed to arrive when I needed them most. One day I got way off the trail and felt very lost. I stumbled across a farmhouse and was fortunate to find someone at home who was willing to give me directions. She told me to backtrack about a mile and a half, and at that point I would come to the path I had missed. When I got back to where I thought she had directed me, I was faced with two gated trails. By my compass and map and according to the woman's directions, each seemed plausible. I stood there studying, wondering, and ready to flip a coin. As I was staring over one of the gates, I saw a solitary raven hopping down the path. I dropped my backpack over the gate and climbed to the other side. When I resituated my backpack and started walking toward the raven, he held his ground for a minute and then opened his wings and flew down the path until I couldn't see him any longer. Coincidence? You may believe whatever you like. But I had such experiences more than once over twenty-three days. What wisdom did I learn from nature through this experience? Be open to the possibility, and you might find a new wisdom guide who happens to be covered with black feathers.

Whether you think animals may ever speak to you or not, God's creation can be a place where we obtain spiritual wisdom. Watching an amazing sunrise, a gorgeous sunset, beautiful clouds, a hauntingly colorful sky can inspire us to open ourselves to new possibilities before God. Walking along a mountain's ridge, or across the magical desert floor, or fording a gentle stream, being in nature and taking in her grandeur can deepen our wisdom and enrich the stories of our life.

At the end of my pilgrimage, I was able to spend ten days in Ireland with my spiritual director of fifteen years. Over the years, I have been extremely open with my spiritual director, sharing even unusual experiences with him. However, I had not encountered and communicated with nature and her creatures like I had in Ireland. I processed what happened, talked about my feelings, and explored what I thought I was learning. He listened patiently and was engaged in my stories. Then, as he has always done, without judgment, not intending to "teach me a lesson," he told me his own story of growing up in the open expanses of nature in

Ireland. After his story, he handed me a copy of John O'Donohue's *Benedictus: A Book of Blessings.*[17] "You might find this interesting," he said. Then we went on a walk to the cemetery to give some perspective on the pilgrimage of life and death. As my spiritual director, he was able to listen to my story, validate my experience with his own, and add perspective to my journey by giving me O'Donohue's book. He was a wisdom guide using the alchemy of spiritual direction to make gold out of the earthy materials of my pilgrimage. We can gain wisdom from the experiences of life, especially those discovered in the mystery of nature, if we have a spiritual guide to assist us in deciphering the signs of our journey in nature.

THE WISDOM TEACHER AS STORYTELLER

My pilgrimage across Ireland gave me plenty of stories. Many of them I have written on my blog and used in sermons. A few of these tales qualify as a wisdom story. Telling such a story is a craft that can be learned through listening to good storytellers and then by practicing our own storytelling. Wisdom stories, sources of inspiration and guidance, are told for the purpose of sharing the wisdom we have gained through experience, like my pilgrimage. Carl Jung says in his memoir *Memories, Dreams, Reflections* that the wisdom story is the vessel of spiritual transformation, like the alchemist's vas in which the substance of renewal and rebirth are mixed.[18] Ethicist Stanley Hauerwas wrote in the article "Theology and Story" that "a story is to help you deal with the world by changing it through changing yourself."[19] A wisdom story creates a vessel for the transformation within the storyteller, the listener, and the community.

A wisdom story can be a biblical tale, an ancient myth, a parable, or a personal experience. After telling a story, I am sometimes asked if it was a "true story." Good wisdom stories contain truth though maybe not fact. Biblical scholar Bruce Chilton argues in *Rabbi Jesus: An Intimate Biography,* that Jesus's parables were most likely personal stories told from his experiences.[20] I find it fascinating and humorous to think of Jesus planting a garden with his mother, casting seed, and watching where it landed. Maybe his mother was the one who pointed out to Jesus, by way of correction, that he was casting the seed too far afield, so some seed landed on the hard path, some on the rock, some among the thorns, and too little on fertile ground. Just as with Jesus's parables, wisdom stories bear being retold many times. His stories were simple enough to be remembered, yet complex enough that people have been revisiting them and discovering new truths hidden in them for two millennia, and we still have not fully unveiled every marvel of them.

I believe people enjoy and connect best to personal stories. However, when I tell a story that is not my experience, I tell listeners where I heard or read the story. If the story is from my imagination, I let my listeners know. I am also very careful to site exegetical or historical sources I use in sermons, such as one of my favorites, the commentary series *Feasting on the Word: Preaching the Revised Common Lectionary* by editors David L. Bartlett and Barbara Brown Taylor.[21] I also like to look for story material in unique resources like *The Jewish Annotated New Testament* by editors Amy-Jill Levine and Marc Z. Brettler,[22] and *Three Testaments: Torah, Gospel, and Quran* by editor Brian Arthur Brown.[23]

Every time we tell a story, we are inviting the hearer to travel with us to a far away land, the territory of imagination and dreams. Author John Gardner, in his excellent though caustic book *The Art of Fiction: Notes on Craft for Young Writers,* tells us that, as writers and storytellers, we are creating a dream world in the reader's mind.[24] Our stories must paint a picture, filled with enough detail to draw the hearer deep within the story so she feels as if she can touch, taste, and smell the story.

Most of my stories come from personal experience. I keep a journal and notebook to record memories, conversations, sights, sounds, and ideas, and to track my spiritual progress, keep notes about creative ideas, record dreams, let my imagination roam, and talk to God. The journal is a way of having a conversation with the inner-self about what might be emerging in leadership. A journal is also an excellent tool when we meet with our spiritual director, mentor, coach, priest, counselor, or wisdom guide.

Before I start writing a particular story, I usually process through the ideas with my wife, spiritual director, therapist, and a few good friends. Each of these people will listen to the story with my best interest in mind. They will help me process conscious as well as hidden meaning in the story by asking open-ended questions, so I can hear myself discover the answers. Without working through a story with a trusted mentor, we may find ourselves telling a story we are not ready for others to hear. The story may be too raw and our emotions might overwhelm us. A storyteller never wants to intentionally or unwittingly use the congregation or listeners of the story as a "group therapy session."

After processing my feelings, I write the story—a practice preferred by most introverts. (Most extroverts prefer telling the story extemporaneously.) I believe it is very important to write the story first and then practice telling it before going public with the story, because once a story is told in an open forum, it cannot be retracted. I would not want the general public to read the first drafts of the story I have written, and in the same manner, I don't want someone to hear a story I haven't thought completely through. Therefore, I write several drafts. When I am comfortable with the story, I read it out loud. Listening to the story leads to another series of revisions. Then I let others read it. My wife is my first reader. If the story involves someone whom the hearers will know, then that person is the next reader. Depending on my emotional attachment to the story, I will look for other readers. When I feel the story is ready to be heard, I practice telling the story until I can do so without notes. I don't want my audience to think I have simply memorized the story. Instead, I want to tell it so they know the story is engrained in the fiber of my being, not just my mind. Once I own the story, I am ready to tell it in public.

My wife, an educator for thirty-four years, has helped me improve my storytelling. One of her crafted skills is reading children's books aloud. Years ago she started reading to her elementary classes. Then, of course, she read to our children. She taught at the university for some time and read children's books, with great success, to college students. As a school superintendent, she would read to teachers and administrators, always praised for her exuberant presence. Even in retirement, she has been invited back to the annual school district Christmas gathering to read a children's story. During Advent she would read stories to the children as part of our Sunday morning church service. The adults were as mesmerized as the children. Watching and listening to her read aloud over these years, I came to realize she knows these stories so well that she is actually telling the story instead of reading it. I have watched her "read" a story to a group without looking at the book. Her gift comes from her infatuation with children's literature, her joy of sharing something she dearly loves with others, and the gratification she experiences in "reading" in a way that conveys the story's profound meanings for all ages. Her delivery, a vital component of excellent storytelling, has been stimulated and nurtured throughout her life by the simple reality that stories change lives. I have learned from listening to my wife's reading of children's stories to adults that my stories need to be as captivating, taking the listener back to those wonderful days of being a child, listening to a beautifully read story.

A well-told story should be as artistic as theater or movie making. The artistic delivery should enhance the story, altering the life of the hearer, whether listeners hear them as part of a large congregation or one on one. My passion for the story and its execution should be the same if I am telling it to one person who stopped by to chat or a hundred people who are listening from the pews, for stories will impart more enduring influence on the hearer than the best exegesis and most vigorous exhortation of a brilliant sermon. Countless times congregants tell me they have made the connection between my story and their lives. Rarely do they engage me about some theological comment I have offered in the sermon. Indeed, as church leaders and pastors, we are called to preach the good news of the Gospel and bring theology alive, and like Jesus, we can do this best through stories in our sermons.

The Wisdom Teacher as Preacher

Storytelling and preaching are two different skills. Obviously, there are many good storytellers who do not proclaim the Gospel, and being a fine exegetical preacher does not automatically translate into being a good storyteller. But being a good storyteller will make any preacher better. And being a good storytelling preacher will afford the pastor and leader of the congregation the best opportunity to use preaching as a platform for congregational spiritual direction and wisdom teaching, for the best way to offer spiritual direction is through the narrative of life—the story.

Pastor and seminary professor Kay Northcutt, in her book *Kindling Desire for God: Preaching as Spiritual Direction*, writes, "Preaching as spiritual direction relies upon pastors who understand their religious authority to be grounded by prayer, intimacy with God, and an explicit knowledge—as well as felt experience—of being the 'God-person' and the spiritual guide for their congregation."[25] The pastor who accepts the role as spiritual guide for the community must be steeped in the wisdom tradition and skilled in the art of storytelling in order to effectively deliver her knowledge and felt experience to the congregation. Northcutt goes on to say that preaching as the wisdom guide "is not about fixing problems—life is ultimately insoluble, after all—but about ongoing guidance and orientation to God, self, and others."[26] Indeed, the idea of leader as spiritual guide has been the entire focus of this book. The congregation's leader must be very aware that her sermon is the time when most of her spiritual guidance will be given to the majority of her congregation. Corporate and church consultants and *Myers-Briggs Type Indicator* experts Roy Oswald and Otto Kroeger, authors of *Personality Type and Religious Leadership*,[27] write, "It is from the pulpit that clergy communicate to the majority of their lay people on an ongoing basis. Less than 15% of congregational members see their clergy at least once throughout the week."[28] Because we have so little time with our congregations, we must carefully craft our preaching and teaching if we are going to provide them meaningful spiritual guidance.

Kay Northcutt once asked me which of the preachers I have heard I thought best used preaching as spiritual direction. In the Episcopal tradition, the best two I have been privileged to hear are Barbara Brown Taylor, author of several books, including *God in Pain: Teaching Sermons on Suffering;*[29] and John Claypool

(1930–2005), author of twelve books, including *The Preaching Event*.[30] These two outstanding preachers are powerful storytellers who use their sermons as means of being, in Northcutt's words, "the God person who is the spiritual guide" to congregations. They have "enfleshed"[31] the Gospel for the congregation through preaching as spiritual direction. The very words and experience of the preacher will bring God as close to the people as the person Jesus called "daddy." In the best of circumstances, preaching through good storytelling brings to life words that otherwise flounder, lifeless, on a printed page.

John Claypool was a Southern Baptist pastor who became an Episcopal priest. Claypool played a profound role in my own journey from the Baptist to the Episcopal world. Two people separately encouraged me to contact Claypool while I was president of Grand Canyon University, and I treasure his personal letter encouraging me to follow my heart and the calling of God. He died not long after I left GCU and had begun the process toward priesthood in the Episcopal Church, but because of his influence on my life, I have spent hours studying his preaching style. Claypool was able to successfully transfer the best of his extemporaneous Baptist preaching style into the script-friendly Episcopal Church. To do so, he effectively used storytelling as the vehicle to carry the sermon. In his book *The Preaching Event*, he writes, "When one's motives are generous and not acquisitive, and when one's purpose is to make healing contact with the depths of another, I still believe experiences drawn from the reservoir of one's living can be a powerful resource."[32] He offers us these words as a man who found a way to tell a healing story about the death of his young child. Few marriages survive such tragedy and neither did Claypool's. He was honest about his pain and found a way to communicate his suffering of loss to his congregations. Claypool's preaching became enfleshed speech in the community, because he became personally vulnerable by practicing confessional preaching, telling authentic stories with faith implications and faithfully proclaiming the gospel. Such incarnational preaching is a priestly craft and the heart of spiritual direction through preaching.

Of course, God is always the central character of the sermonic story. Incarnational preaching implies that the preacher, to the best of his or her ability, is constantly showing, not telling, how God is the center of his or her life and how the hearer might likewise gain from the experience of this incarnational union with God. Incarnational preaching is heard, at its best, when the hearer is witness to the communication going on between the preacher and God.

Yale theology professor Miroslav Volf suggests in *Against the Tide: Love in a Time of Petty Dreams and Persisting Enmities*[33] that the preacher should deliver his sermon as if God is anxiously waiting to hear what he has to say. My best preaching happens when I can, with integrity and enthusiasm and without engaging in group therapy, express to God what is happening in my life. I am talking to God as if I am talking to my spiritual director and I am waiting to hear what God's response is to me. If I have a conversation with God in front of my congregation and they witness this dialogue, maybe they will hear God speaking wisdom to me, and just maybe, they will gain some direction from God while prayerfully listening in. You might counter that God already knows what is transpiring in my life. I believe, though, a good story always bears repeating, even to God. Indeed, if God is the heavenly Father, surely he enjoys my simple and childlike stories. At least, I pray, God is as patient with me as I was with my son, who by the age of five loved to tell a good story, over and over again. This is not to grant the preacher permission to frequently retell stories or repeat sermons. But again, if the sermon story is good enough and well delivered, it could become as popular as a favorite hymn or a beloved poem.

The point of telling a good story as the heart of a sermon is not necessarily to entertain the congregation, though it will, but for the sermon to be a means of offering group spiritual direction for the congregation. Preaching as spiritual direction is only effective when God is a meaningful partner in the conversation going on between the preacher and the congregation.

In April 2000 I had the privilege of witnessing such a conversation between John O'Donohue and God. Listening to O'Donohue was like eavesdropping on an intimate conversation with the Divine. He was the quintessential voice of Celtic spirituality and focused on the development of the soul, the seat of wisdom, which in turn, he believed, produced a commitment to social justice. Tragically and unexpectedly, O'Donohue died in 2008 at age 52. Through the opportunity of hearing O'Donohue speak to God, I was able to experience incarnational wisdom enacted. O'Donohue, unknown to him, had provided spiritual direction for me in the midst of a crowded meeting hall. I was transformed. I was inspired to begin trying to let those who heard my preaching listen in on my conversations with God, those palpable chats where God in the flesh was sitting across the table from me sipping a cup of coffee.

Twelve years later, the experience of listening to O'Donohue was still resonating with my soul. When my wife and I were preparing our trip to Ireland in the summer of 2012, her spiritual director suggested, as part of our pilgrimage, that we visit O'Donohue's grave. When we arrived at the home of my spiritual director in Kildysart, County Clare, he too suggested we visit O'Donohue's final resting place. When two out of two spiritual directors thought we should make a pilgrimage to the saint's grave, we felt like God was telling us something. The visit to his gravesite turned out to be an experience of the Divine. Even from the grave, O'Donohue was still speaking to me, letting me in on his eternal conversation with the Divine, providing me spiritual direction and continuing motivation to let others in on my personal conversations with the Holy One.

Our visit to O'Donohue's grave took us to the Creggagh, on the western coast of Ireland, a region where the landscape is the opposite of what you might envision on the island known for its forty shades of green. This area is the largest karst in Europe, a virtual desert due to the vast exposed layers of limestone, the steady and severe ocean winds, and the absence of surface water. The contrast between the romantic images of Ireland and the actual landscape in this region perfectly parallels the juxtaposition of O'Donohue's beautiful poetry against his intense commitment to social justice.

The Creggagh cemetery is like many others in Ireland. Ancient graves as well as the tombstones of those who died last week surround medieval ruins of a church burned by the controversial English Puritan Oliver Cromwell. O'Donohue's grave was easy to spot among the stone markers. Fittingly, his burial place is set apart with a four-foot high piece of petrified oak bog found under centuries of compressed black peat. Like the oak marker, wisdom comes from being pressed down under the weight of the ages and then resurrected as a testimony to a prophet. I wrote about this incredible trip to his gravesite in a narrative poem I would later use in a sermon in order to create an image for the congregation. The poem was a way of providing spiritual direction to the congregation about death and resurrection. I offer this as an example of what you might do in a sermon.

Pilgrimage of tearful softened heart lures us three to this lonely seaside graveyard. Bog's oak standing guard over the Bard's tomb, his soul's currack floating on bowl bent clouds hovering the blue still sea of Fanore Burren. Ravens in the rookery give announcement. Cows in abandonment moan in mourner's wailing. Indeed this grave here rests Ireland's too young lost voice—of spirituality he mystically found birthed in the Connemara primordial landscape eons steeped into the life of the rustic Gaelic being. Ancient church torched of Cromwell's hell still in defiance sings spectral Mass from choirs of plots marked only by heaven's rough stones, lying near the artist of the soul weaver of words, who offers his blessing to the sweet liturgy. Harp need pulled to hear not this day, for wispy breeze through sun shocked fields of glistening limestone give angelic muse to the Bard's lusciousness. He who is nestled in the bosom of Mother Earth's deepened green bed, he of the virgin soul of gods knew first favored love, did know of visions verse we can only ached to glimpse. Our grief is burdened from his silent voice—we too stare death's fetching . . . reminding us all we are mere dust; save for the song filled day our heart leapt in hope filled rhythm fluttered by the Bard's dream, for that day we too would feel the veil thin in which we sojourn.

Standing at the foot of the grave of the gifted Irish poet-prophet, I could not help but feel a holy shudder from the realization that he had been a wisdom sage to millions of readers, and I had the humble experience of being in his presence while he was having a conversation with God. His prose is deeply profound and a guide for our age. O'Donohue's words are so psalm-like in their poetry and timeless in meaning that his books could be an appendix to the wisdom texts of our scripture. At his gravesite, against the backdrop of the Connemara, with the sound of the ocean only a hundred yards away, his voice and poetry from twelve years earlier were echoing in my mind. His life and story were embedded in my memory; he had become incarnate within me.

We use words like "influenced," "touched," "moved," or "inspired" to convey the meaning of our unique experiences like my visit to O'Donohue's grave. However, incarnation is at times the best descriptor of the moments when God becomes fully present with us through wisdom guides and their teaching. As we provide spiritual direction through preaching, we are offering incarnational wisdom to the congregation. When we preach, we are talking to God, in union with God, and this conversation has the potential to become embedded, incarnate in our listeners. O'Donohue, for me, was the embodiment of what it may have been like listening to Jesus preach and teach. Listening to O'Donohue, reading his work, and visiting his grave together changed how I went about preparing and delivering sermons.

My purpose in preaching as spiritual direction is to ask my listeners to consider their experience with God by letting them in on my experience. As with spiritual direction, the congregation has come to church to hear what the God-person has to say about living a life in union with God. The preacher as spiritual director is simply offering a map with subtle guidance as to how they too may enter this holy experience. Spiritual direction preaching is about showing our congregants the way to travel, not telling them how to get there.

The purpose here is not to tell you how to prepare a sermon. There are countless numbers of books on preaching, and I have already mentioned some excellent works in this chapter. Besides, according to Oswald and Kroeger, some of our preferences in preaching preparation may be tied to our personality type. However, preaching a sermon as spiritual direction becomes a mind-set and an approach, more than a matter of how the sermon is written.

While your congregation may never know the ins and outs of your sermon preparation, the people will be able to see the evidence of your work. A significant portion of "showing" the congregation the pilgrimage path instead of simply "telling" them about what lies ahead can be found in the way the preacher prepares her sermon. A physical education teacher who is in great shape can model for his students the benefits of exercise. The same can be said about the preacher preparing a sermon. If the preacher uses the techniques of spiritual direction in putting the sermon together, I believe the congregation will become aware of the benefits of spiritual direction. Here is one method of writing a sermon with congregational spiritual direction in mind.

Beginning Monday, sit with the text using *lectio divina.* After praying the text through the three cycles, reflect by writing in your journal what you are hearing from the Spirit. There is no need to ask, "How am I going to preach this sermon to offer spiritual direction to the congregation?" Leave that to the Spirit. Tuesday, follow the same pattern of reading. During your time of journaling, again ask, "What is the Spirit saying to me in this text?" Sit with your reflections for a while, giving yourself some time to hear the Spirit. Carry your journal with you through the day, and jot down words, phrases, and ideas as they emerge in the course of the day. Using this model, I have found the Spirit will pique my curiosity about at least one thing in the text—if not send a resounding text message to my soul saying, "This is it!" By Wednesday, I am reading my commentaries and doing research. Thursday I begin to make some serious notes and outlines. I work at shaping the sermon around the spiritual direction maxim, "This is how to be," not "This is what to do." By Friday I am writing my sermon. Saturday evening I read my sermon through a few times and make any edits necessary. Sunday morning I am up very early and go through my sermon a few more times. My intent is to deliver my sermon while only glancing at my notes; sometimes I never look at my text.

A story is the crucible of most of my sermons. The stories come from personal experience, novels, the news, and whatever else I observe and read. Not every sermon is a parable, though most are. I rely on a poetic cadence to deliver my stories. Listening to poets like O'Donohue and preachers like Claypool has influenced my sermonic cadence. The story influences the flow, energy, and rhythm of the telling of it. Every voice inflection has a purpose. Listen to the sermons of those preachers you admire. Listen to your sermons not to mimic their style, but instead to improve the quality of your sermon voice.

Our voice speaks the sermon and our body delivers a message as well. Whether standing behind a pulpit or sitting in a chair, I try to let my entire body feel the story, be in the story, be absorbed by the story, lost in the story—but not as a distraction. The storyteller must be present to the listeners. For me to tell a story about my walk across Ireland, I must be able, in mind, body, and soul, to feel as if I am still in Ireland and must bring the story to life so that the congregation can feel as if they are walking with me. Every movement in my story has a specific significance. If I point with my finger while telling the story, it is because I actually pointed out something I saw for the sake of a person walking with me. I might act out the taking of a picture or stepping around something. The point of the sermon is not the preacher's performance—but delivery does matter. Good storytelling uses the body to bring the story to life.

Those who engage in incarnational preaching and wisdom storytelling look for the actions of God in every morsel of life, from the mundane to the exotic, and seek to make visible to the congregation the actions of God in the preacher's life. Of course, incarnational preaching and wisdom storytelling, as with sermons in general, must rely on the Spirit to enflesh the sermon, to breathe the word into the hearer's ears.

Even though the sermon has been preached on Sunday, we are not done telling the story. By Tuesday of the following week, I post the sermon on my blog. The significant number of people reading the post is always a surprise to me, reminding me there are several folks connected to our community from a distance. Our church communities include more than just the people who attend on Sunday morning and live in our neighborhoods. Our sermons are read (and sometimes heard) by visitors checking out the church before attending, former members who have moved away, people in our parish sharing the sermon with a relative or friend, and by people we may never meet. Sermons have a lasting as well as a long reaching impact. When the sermon is enfleshed in the story of a human encounter with the Divine, the value of the sermon is enriched and many of our listeners will experience the holy conversation between the Spirit of God, the person delivering the sermon, and the listeners (or readers).

The pastor can dramatically improve her ability to lead through the work of preaching as spiritual direction if she will hone the craft of enfleshed storytelling. Leaders who are good storytellers can motivate and inspire their communities at the most critical juncture in the congregation's life, because storytelling can draw the entire community into the presence of God through a common understanding of life as a narrative. The Bible is the scriptural story of the relationship between God and God's creation. Jesus told stories to deliver his message, teach his disciples, and prepare them for his absence. Stories are the power of life. Good stories feed us with creative energy. Great stories provoke our imagination. Fantastic stories transform us. No other form of leadership will be as effective in mobilizing the people to see the leader's vision as a well-told and gripping story. Leadership through beautifully told stories in preaching as spiritual direction provides the people with a picture of God's desire to be in relationship with the congregation on a personal and communal level. The leader needs to preach as if the future of his personal story and the congregation depends upon the spiritual guidance he delivers in his weekly encounter with parishioners, because it does. If every member of our congregation attended weekly, at the most they would be receiving between 13 and 26 hours (if the sermon takes between 15 and 30 minutes) of spiritual guidance from the pastor annually. Pollsters often consider "regular church attendance" to be three out of eight Sundays.[34] Therefore, a "regular attendee" by these standards would attend church twenty times a year, reducing the amount of preaching heard to between five and ten hours annually. These are sobering numbers for the regular attendees. How much more concerning for those attending less often? With so little time available with our parishioners, I believe we need to concentrate the majority of our time showing them through storytelling how to practice spiritual disciplines and how to live spiritual lives. Our congregants have the best chance of remembering what we want to teach them from a good story.

In her book *The Practicing Congregation: Imagining a New Old Church,* Diana Butler Bass writes, "Pilgrims . . . who have journeyed into the place of imagination and risk, must be able to come home and relate the tale. . . . They must be able to help others see what they have seen . . . and authentically embody the story. . . . They must show how the story transformed them."[35]

As you know, I coached college baseball for twenty years, ending my career in 2000. In 2011 Grand Canyon University inducted me into their Sports Hall of Fame. I was pleased so many of my players attended the ceremony. I was also humbled many of those players said what they remembered was not what I taught them about baseball, but what I taught them about life through the stories I had told. Listening to them repeat stories I told years before made me laugh, because they added their impersonations. At the same time, tears came to my eyes. As a coach, I hoped I had made a positive impression on their young adult lives, but seeing them as men and listening to them recount those stories deeply moved me. Of course, I know not every player would say they had a good experience under my coaching. Not every one of them would remember even one of my stories. But given the years I coached and the number of players who went through our system, the fact that so many remembered the stories felt affirming to me. I think the storytelling may have been my best coaching technique.

As pastors and spiritual leaders of our communities, we are coaches to many of those who attend our churches. Over the course of time, if they remember at least one story, we have touched their lives in a lasting way. I believe Jesus knew storytelling was the best way to teach his disciples and those who followed him in The Way. Many of those people whom Jesus taught only heard him speak once. His story had an obvious lasting effect because we are still retelling them today. As Christian leaders, I believe we must lead like Jesus and to be like him we must be wisdom storytellers, wisdom preachers, and wisdom leaders.

Six

Leadership in the Discerning Community

Discernment does not simply confirm our hunches or intuitions. Instead it is a perilous practice that involves self-criticism, questions, and risk—and it often redirects our lives.

—Diana Butler Bass[1]

In November 1996, my wife and I celebrated our twenty-fifth wedding anniversary by taking our two young-adult children with us on a two-week holiday to England, Scotland, and Ireland—our first trip to the Celtic islands. We spent three days in Ireland, and I knew I had to go back. In the summer of 2004, I had the opportunity to return to Ireland for a two-week pilgrimage with a group of twelve people who stayed at a retreat house in Glendalough. Nearby was an international hostel close to the site of an ancient monastery, and many of the people who stayed at the hostel were walking the Wicklow Way, an 80-mile trail from Dublin to Clonegal. Because of their enthusiasm, I became fascinated with the idea of a walking pilgrimage. In 2006, I walked 120 miles across a portion of the Wicklow Way and a neighboring trail, St. Kevin's Way. However, the ten-day walk didn't satisfy my desire for a transformational experience; it felt like a precursor to something grander. Something was missing. I knew in my soul I had to walk Ireland coast-to-coast. When I returned home in 2006 I began planning the pilgrimage. By the summer of 2011, I felt the time was right, so I started an intense preparation. My daily routine is to walk three miles, but I knew from my 2006 walk this wasn't enough, so I increased my physical regime. My ten-day walk in Ireland had also taught me that I needed to prepare my soul for the long, challenging pilgrimage. As my physical preparations increased, I intensified my spiritual disciplines. Even with all this preparation I couldn't fully imagine what I was getting myself into. I expected the experience would change me, but I had no idea the deep level of transformation that would take place in my life.

Now that I am on the other side of my pilgrimage, I am coming to understand, even if I wanted to, I cannot undo the intense change I have experienced. Even still, the transformation continues to emerge. I am now negotiating with myself how I will "live, move, and have my being" in God and in this world. I have changed, and the way I perceive life has changed. I have come to recognize that a pilgrimage is not about the destination, but about the journey traveled. I was not walking to Glenbeigh just to see the city. The experience was rather about the four-hundred-mile walk on the way to the western coast of Ireland. What was revealed to me in my journey has substantially made a difference in how I am now living my life. Because of the pilgrimage, I spend more time pondering what I see. I listen more carefully to what I am hearing. I savor more what I taste. Every touch is more sensitive.

As heightened as my outward senses have become through the pilgrimage, my inner life has grown richer, the result of my uncovering a new way of listening to the unconscious. The pilgrimage experience has expanded my interior imagination, adding to the pool of symbols and images I have known from earliest memories. I am coming to better understand the old and the new archetypes, which are seen in my interior imagination, though they may seem to me only a tiny light glowing in the darkness. Though still in the shadows, these newly discovered spiritual markers are now moving from the unconscious into my conscious awareness. As my interior world reveals itself more and more, I am hearing the whispers of God more regularly and less muffled. Though many months away from the pilgrimage, I feel as if I am still walking in Ireland, all the while I am here, engaging with nature, people, the stuff of life, and the responsibility of my many roles in parish leadership.

Like making a pilgrimage, leading a community as a spiritual director is not an enterprise you decide to adopt today, embark on tomorrow, and then have up and running in a month. To lead as a spiritual director is to live your life like a wisdom guide who is walking on a long pilgrimage. You will not necessarily "arrive" anywhere, because there is no goal to achieve, but only a way to be. The leader must commit to a lifetime of pilgrimage, a lifetime of being transformed. The walk across Ireland is an encapsulation of what has been happening to me over a lifetime of learning about leading as a spiritual director. When I started my leadership journey almost forty years ago as a young high school teacher and baseball coach, I had never heard the words "spiritual direction," but I wanted to learn how to be the best leader possible. And when I started walking out of Dublin on the Wicklow Way, I had no idea what would transpire over the next twenty-four days, but I had a passionate desire for the experience of pilgrimage. My journey of leadership continues to shape me into who I am today and will be tomorrow—the same way my pilgrimage continues to transform the way I see the world and encounter God. Leading as a spiritual director and wisdom guide is the art of pilgrimage, to be learned, honed, and shared throughout the leader's life.

THE DREAMS OF A LEADER ON PILGRIMAGE

One of the ways I have been able to trace my pilgrimage as a leader has been to pay attention to my dream life. When I was a college baseball coach, I often had nightmares about arriving at my beautifully manicured field only to find it had been destroyed by some natural disaster, and being left with the impossible task of trying to repair it in time for the most important game of the season. When I was president, I had nightmarish dreams of standing naked before the faculty while trying to present my vision for the university. Now, as a priest, I have dreams about the struggles of leading a spiritual community.

Early on as a parish pastor I had a very revealing dream about my work in the church. Because the dream felt so profound, I have spent significant time over the years journaling and processing the dream with my spiritual director and mentor in order to learn what my unconscious and God have been trying to tell me about my leadership.

> I was alone in the parish hall. The tables were fully set, and all the plates had uneaten food on them. I went to each table and took every plate to the kitchen, where I carefully scraped the food into a large bin. I became exhausted going to all the tables and carrying full plates to the kitchen. I filled several large bins with uneaten food. I stood back and looked at all the food, piled high in the bins. Then I heard a voice, "Why haven't the people eaten the food?"

Through my work with this dream I have indeed discovered quite a bit about how I lead. The voice in my dream could have been God's, but more likely the question came from my unconscious, wondering why no one was eating what I served. I thought I was working hard, doing the "good stuff" of parish ministry. But I had to ask myself if I had been working on the meaningful things that affect people's lives in spiritual ways. Was my work providing space for the Spirit of God to do transformational work? I began to evaluate my relationship with God, my inner self, and others, while continuing to work on the dream. The things I learned have in many ways affirmed what I have written about in this book. My work with the dream led me to understand that leadership in the parish, like coaching and being a university president, is about relationships.

Through my work experiences I have been afforded the privilege of meeting hundreds of other leaders, many of whom have been extremely successful in their field. I have had conversations about leadership with some of the best in sports, education, and religion, as well as people from business, government, the legal profession, and medicine. The consistent theme I have taken away from these encounters has been that leadership, above all, is about relationships. And what I have come to discover is that leadership relationships are best built through the approach used in spiritual direction.

Franciscan friar, Catholic priest, and spiritual director Richard Rohr writes, "Good leaders must have a certain capacity for non-polarity thinking and full-access knowing (prayer), a tolerance for ambiguity (faith), an ability to hold creative tensions (hope), and an ability to care (love) beyond their personal advantage."[2] Here, Rohr is describing what it means to lead by spiritual direction. The lynch pin, the heart of this way of leading, is the ability of the leader to be in a meaningful, significant, give-give relationship with the people she is leading.

Just as in spiritual direction, leaders develop relationships with parishioners one at a time. In time, the relationships between the leader and the individual congregants are spread like a web. The leader has a relationship with individuals, families, and small groups within the congregation. Through these connections, a congregational relationship emerges between the leader and the community as a whole. The web-like interconnectedness creates a dynamic of social and spiritual interaction between the people, forming a congregational energy, a way of life together. The people worship together, play together, work together, and make decisions together. The leader who is attentive to the web of spiritual energy, especially by leading the congregation through spiritual direction, will foster a community of discerning individuals and hopefully, a discerning community. This type of community will have these features:

- The leader is a wisdom guide who nurtures the community through the ideals of spiritual direction.
- Some members of the community will have an appreciation for and be involved in the practice of spiritual direction.
- Members, individually, in small groups, and as a congregation, will practice discernment as a means of making decisions and often are willing to try other ancient methods of listening to the Spirit.

- Members are steeped in prayer, with specific sub-groups taking up the practice of daily prayer on behalf of the community.

A discerning community does not happen by accident. The leader and the congregation must walk and work together toward developing trusting relationships, relying on what each person, in community, hears from the Spirit. Pilgrims need maps, and I had two to guide me in walking from Dublin to Glenbeigh. The following are a few markers that I hope will be helpful in pointing the way.

Leading a Discerning Community

Before embarking on the leadership pilgrimage as a wisdom guide, the leader must first discern whether she or he is being fetched by God to lead in this manner. I would recommend to anyone planning a walk across Ireland to make serious preparations, and I would give the same recommendation before beginning to lead through spiritual direction. If you discern that leading through spiritual direction is a good path for you to follow, or if you simply want to experiment with or adopt a few techniques, go slowly and be specific with yourself about what parts of this way of leadership you want to add into your leadership. Find a spiritual director so you will have a constant conversation partner on this journey. Add centering prayer, *lectio divina*, journaling, or dream work into your daily spiritual practice. Then begin to use your developing spiritual direction practices during pastoral counseling, office conversations, sidewalk chats, phone conversations, and e-mails. Use examples in sermons about spiritual practices you have incorporated into your own spiritual journey. Maybe include a story about your relationship with your spiritual director. Work to deepen your listening skills. Incorporate silence into meetings and worship. Preach about the benefits of spiritual direction and discernment and then begin to preach sermons as moments of spiritual direction for your congregation. Think about yourself as a spiritual director and wisdom guide in every possible situation so the people can hear what the Spirit is saying in their lives.

There are challenges in deciding to lead by spiritual direction. Leading this way may not fit your personality type, or you may discern it is not for you, or this may not be what your community needs or is willing to follow. There isn't a perfect model. Honestly, following someone who leads through spiritual direction can be frustrating for those in the congregation who are looking for a CEO pastor. Also, from my experience this model can be more time-consuming for the leader than other models. Because, while the leader spends time in her own spiritual direction and discernment, she will also be committing a significant amount of time in providing spiritual direction to others, as well as considerable time guiding the congregation through decision-making via the discernment process.

Given the challenges of this way of leading, I am convinced the leader must first discern that God has called her into this practice and then commit to the path. The leader must work throughout her career in developing the way of leadership best suited to her. She will face many opportunities and challenges, causing her to continually reevaluate her leadership style. The question spiritual leaders must always keep before them is, "Is God calling me to lead in this way?" When we hear God asking the question, "Will you lead through spiritual direction?" we have a choice as to an answer. For me, the response has been the words in the Baptismal Covenant, "I will, with God's help." Only with God's help have I been able to engage the congregation as a spiritual director leading a discerning community.

Two of my spiritual mentors have repeatedly offered me the following words of advice. First, remember: wherever you go, there you will be. Leadership through spiritual direction is a long path, which takes patience to nurture. For a significant period of time as you develop these new leadership skills, under stress, you will most likely revert to old leadership habits. Be patient with yourself. Be good to yourself. Give yourself time. Second, you are not the Lone Ranger. You will need spiritual and wisdom guides to travel the journey of leadership alongside you.

Guiding a parish toward become a discerning congregation will take a long time, years maybe, and will include teaching about spiritual direction and prayer as listening, as well as practicing discernment in personal decisions. But all this can start only with a leader who is willing to guide the congregation through corporate spiritual direction. Without that foundational piece, I believe the community will have little or no understanding of what is happening, and they will most likely become confused or frustrated by the process.

The goal is not for you to be the spiritual director for the entire congregation, but to lead through the mindset and methods of a spiritual director. Although you might be the spiritual director for a few people in your congregation, you are not everyone's spiritual director. Nor is the goal for everyone in your congregation to have a spiritual director. There might be people in our congregations who faithfully pray for us every day, who may have never heard of spiritual direction, nor ever want a spiritual director, and that is okay. Hopefully, though, key leaders on your staff, your board, your lay leadership team, and some in the congregation will seek out spiritual directors, mentors, or wisdom guides. If a handful of our leaders are meeting regularly with their spiritual directors, I know they are praying and practicing the spiritual disciplines, which will bring them closer to God. I have found in my community that leaders with spiritual directors talk to their wisdom guides about our congregational issues—and I rely upon the fruit of those conversations. Not that their spiritual director is going to tell our leaders what to do or how to think, but instead, he or she will help our leaders sort out what they are hearing from the Spirit. Leading by spiritual direction depends upon more than one person in the community being involved in the practice of spiritual direction. I am convinced the pastoral leader can hear the Spirit with greater ease, thereby discerning God's fetching, when at least a few members of the congregation have committed themselves to listening to what the Spirit is saying through their own personal practice of spiritual direction and discernment.

Once the leader has made a commitment to lead through spiritual direction, then she is ready to take the second step in developing this type of community. She must begin teaching the congregation about discernment and providing opportunities for them to engage in the process. The greater the number of people who have participated in discernment in their daily lives, the more likely the community will become comfortable using the process in making congregational decisions.

JOURNALING AND INTEGRATION MAPPING

Spiritual direction is a lifelong process, and leading a community by means of spiritual direction requires the same amount of patience. Discernment itself requires preparation, time, and patience, and the leader will take whatever time is necessary to teach the community the ways of discernment, for individuals, small groups, and congregational decisions.

The benefits of investing valuable time in developing a discerning community will be that the congregation will have the knowledge of how to discern when considering important matters individually and in small groups. Then with this knowledge and practice of discernment, many members of the congregations will have the capacity to assist in developing discernment processes for the entire congregation, which take into account the complexity of the various issues. As in spiritual direction and individual discernment, these processes for the congregation will include seasons of prayer, fasting, and silence.

The first lesson the congregation must learn is how to discern by listening to the fetching of God. Typically, we talk about trying to figure out what God is calling us to do. We think in terms of this: "Is God calling me to be a pastor, deacon, or teach a Sunday school class?" Or, for the congregation, we talk about this: "Is God calling us to start this or that ministry?" However, I don't like the implications or the baggage many people have attached to the word "calling." First, it implies we are doing something as opposed to being a particular way. True, a discerning community is doing many things, but more importantly they have chosen a way to be, which then helps them decide what to do. Second, the word "calling" suggests we are to receive a direct message from

God, like skywriting. If I believe God has one specific path for me to follow, then if I unfortunately don't see the writing in the sky or misinterpret the message, I will somehow miss out on God's will for my life. Instead, I think the image of being "fetched," as in "drawn or allured by one's lover," better conveys that the Spirit of God is whispering in the ear of our soul, not creating a "spiritual to-do list" for us to complete before the end of the day. I believe God is fetching us, like a lover, to walk hand in hand with God on the journey of life. There is no one best way to walk across Ireland. Nor is there one best way to live your life. But by walking with God the Lover, we will see the world much differently both in the interior and the exterior life, which will assist us in the discernment process.

Individuals and the congregation listen to God in many ways. One way to hear God is through journaling. Offering classes on how to journal is a means of sparking conversations about listening to God and discerning how God is fetching us to live. We can consider journaling as a form of prayer, writing to God, asking questions. "God, what kind of life are you fetching us into?" This question is open-ended enough to be asked at the beginning of any discernment process, be it individual, small group, or congregational discernment. We must be as clear as we possibly can about what we are discerning. Our journal entries can include what we are hearing from the Spirit. Then we can ask ourselves, "How do we feel when we think about the possibility of living our lives in the way we hear God fetching us?" We can hold the idea we are discerning lightly for some time, carry it around with us, sit with it and see if this is something we really want to embark upon. We can fast (individually or as a community), give up something dear for a brief time, and contemplate if our desire to follow God's fetching stays strong during the time of sacrifice. Listening to what the Spirit is saying requires steadfast work.

Another form of journaling that can be taught for use in individual, small group, and congregational discernment is a technique I call "Integration Mapping." The name comes from an information systems technique sometimes referred to as "Interface

Mapping," which is used to diagram how one information system will "speak" to another. Integration Mapping is designed to creatively identify and illustrate all the "players" (speakers) and all the factors involved in the decision. Having the information in front of me and not swirling in my head, I will be better able to listen to God and discern more clearly.

I like to start creating my map with a large piece of paper (24" x 36"), using colored pencils to do my writing and drawing. I would use a larger size paper or a white board for small group and congregational discernment. The piece of paper represents the "terrain of the decision," not necessarily a path to be followed. I start with contemplating a few questions. First, what is the idea or issue that I (or we) are considering, and where do I place it on the map? In other words, what are we discerning about? I need to name the issue in order to know what I am working with. Am I trying to decide to start a new career? Am I deciding what college to attend? Is the congregation trying to decide whether to add a new style of worship service? We must be able to articulate what we are trying to discern before we can actually do the work of discernment. Second, where am I (or we) on the map? I need distance between my self and what I am discerning in order to better see all the issues and players at hand. Physician and Harvard professor Ronald Heifetz writes in *Leadership Without Easy Answers* that we must "get on the balcony, and distinguish self from the role."[3] I am concerned when I find myself too close, or too intertwined, with the issue. I need to objectify what I am discerning and not confuse the self with the issue.

For example, when a person is discerning how to respond to God's fetching him into the priesthood, he and the discernment committee are trying to hear the Spirit. If the committee members say they are not hearing the Spirit beckoning this person, he might think, "The committee doesn't like me." The discernment is not about whether the committee likes the person or even believes the person will be a good or bad priest. The process is about hearing the Spirit. If what he is discerning, being a priest, is too intertwined with his identity, in other words, if he can only see himself as a priest and not in some other servant role, he may find it almost impossible to be objective about what the committee is telling him. He might block out any possibility of learning from the process. Through using the Integration Map, the discerner's unconscious may reveal a struggle with personal differentiation. Non-differentiation can reveal itself on the map when he draws his "self" and the issue too close together, even identifying both with the same color. However, if he can objectify the issue on the map, "get on the balcony," I believe discernment will be much clearer.

In the same way, when the community is discerning a decision, they also need to be able to separate their congregational identity from the issue at hand. The inability to make this kind of congregational differentiation is often reflected in the words, "That's not the way we've ever done it; therefore, we are opposed to even considering change." The fear of change is the signal that the community is suffering from a collective fear of loss. The congregation fears change, because they perceive the new idea as a threat to their congregational identity. The congregation is afraid if they accept some change, they will become something other than what they have been. In the Episcopal Church this fear of the loss of identity caused by change often manifests itself in any discussion concerning the use of a musical instrument other than the organ in worship. Many congregations have a "sacred cow" that has nothing to do with its service to the ministry of God's people. If the congregation has invested too much of its identity in something other than its core beliefs, the community will never be able to discern potential change for the good. In congregational work with the map, lack of differentiation may be more difficult to recognize. But when I've worked with groups and asked them what colors to use, I have seen them use the same, or similar colors, to identify themselves and the issue. Such behavior may indicate the inability to differentiate the collective personality from the issue they are discerning. Whether working with an individual or a congregation, having a diagram they can visualize will assist people in recognizing the need to differentiate from the issue and "get on the balcony" in order to get a better view of the discernment process.

The next step with the Integration Map is to write on the map the names of the people and institutions involved in making the decision. Include those who might be interested in or affected by the decision. I place the issues, other people and institutions, and myself on the map closer or further apart to indicate how much each influences the other. The closer they are to me on the map, the more influence they have on me. The closer they are to the issue, the more they have at stake in the decision. When I am working with Integration Mapping in a personal decision, my wife is somewhere fairly close to me on the map. There are few decisions I would take the time to map out that do not involve her in some significant way. I use a different color for my wife because she is clearly her own person. I encircle her name with a spiral of words describing her opinions and feeling about what I am discerning, leaving room for opinions and feelings I discover during the process of discernment. I repeat the same process with the names of the other people and institutions I think are factors. I keep the map for the duration of the discernment, allowing me to add new people or institutions that I may not have thought about in my first day of working with the map.

As I add people and institutions to the map, I begin to draw lines between the different players and the issue as a way of further illustrating their influence on my discernment or their concern with the outcome of what I decide. For example, when I was discerning whether God was fetching me into ministry in the Episcopal Church, my mother had little influence on my decision. But she did have serious concerns tied to the fact that I had left the Southern Baptist church I had grown up in. My entering the Episcopal Church compounded her concern. She was unfamiliar with my new church, one that some of her friends told her was not Christian. I had to decide thickness and what colors to use for the line between my mother and me on this issue. Some lines are thick and dark, representing strong connections and influences. A thinner line means the influence is less significant. Dotted lines are for even less pronounced relationships or influences. The colors used for the lines reflect the connections between those on the map. Most of the time the line between my wife and me is thick with intense color. However, if she is ambivalent about what I decide on this particular issue, then the line between us might not be as thick or intensely colored. I connect all the players as they relate to the decision, each other, and to me.

Next, I add those to the map who may have an influence but are not in the room, such as those who have died. The dead often have significant influence on decisions we make. My deceased grandfather is typically on my map when I make personal decisions. Some founding parishioners who have passed away still influence how I, and many others in our congregation, think about our institutional issues. Different ethnic and cultural perspectives may need to have a place on the map. The generational distinctiveness of the Tweens, Generation X, and Generation Y may also need to be noted on the map. Leadership groups within the church should be identified if they have a stake in the decision. The more complicated the decision, the messier the map may look. Of course, seeing a visual of the complexity of the issue staring back at me and the congregation might initially intensify the knot in all our stomachs. However, by getting all the messiness out of our heads and onto a piece of paper, giving us a balcony perspective, we are getting a clearer picture of the situation.

Guiding the congregation in the ways of spiritual direction will bear the fruit of the Spirit. Constantly encouraging them to hear what the Spirit is saying will open their spiritual ears to words they may not have heard before. Showing them the wisdom of becoming a discerning congregation will help them to see a new way of being community together. At the start of teaching a congregation about becoming a discerning community, parishioners will begin to ask you to help them discern—regarding the possibility that they are being fetched into ministry, a decision to lead a ministry, whether to take a major leadership role in the church, or some other major life decision, such as taking a new job or relocating. Help them construct an Integration Map, journal, and pray. After a season of doing this interior work, encourage them to consider engaging with a discernment committee.

DISCERNMENT COMMITTEES

During the first six years of my ministry at St. Augustine's, we established multiple discernment committees for individuals to make decisions about vocation, mid-life career change, and which college to attend, among other decisions. These committees have involved over sixty people in the congregation. I strongly recommend against using a "standing discernment committee," because this practice prevents many within the congregation from having this powerful spiritual experience. I have found that those who serve on a discernment committee find the experience to be spiritually stimulating. They often report back to their friends in the congregation how the discernment committee caused them to pray and reflect much more often about how God was speaking into their lives.

The leader of a discerning community will have to teach the congregation about the value and processes of a discernment committee. These committees can be used to discern both individual and congregational matters. Discernment committees work best with five to seven members. Fewer than five, and the circle will be too small to hear the Spirit from enough different points of view. More than seven and the meetings will take too long.

Choose people to serve whom you imagine have a discerning heart, are good listeners, or want to learn. The group members do not need any experience in being a part of a discernment committee, just openness to the process. Not every member of the committee needs to know each other. For individuals who are discerning a decision, invite one or two people who are acquaintances or colleagues and a few others the individual does not know. For some decisions where a truly objective perspective is needed, inviting a person from outside the community may be helpful.

Once you have commitments from the group, before calling the first meeting, ask someone to serve as the chair and another person to be the scribe. The role of the chairperson is to set the times for the meeting, open and close the meetings in prayer, be the timekeeper, and facilitate the meeting. The facilitator ensures the integrity of the discernment process by encouraging the committee members to ask open-ended questions, listening to the Spirit and not talking more than they are listening. The scribe takes simple notes for reference in future meetings. The notes need not be verbatim or overly detailed, just enough to be quickly reviewed at the start of each meeting to prompt the committee's memory as to what has been discussed.

From my research about discernment and my experience of conducting over fifty such committees (and offering training for numerous congregational discernment groups within our diocese), I have learned that committee meetings organized in the following manner will produce the best results.

The committee should plan to have four to seven one-hour meetings within a period of eight to fourteen weeks. Meetings longer than one hour are too draining on the participants. The meetings work best if they are held one or two weeks apart. If they are any farther apart, the continuity of the conversation gets lost.

Before the first meeting, suggest that the members read either Elizabeth Liebert's *The Way of Discernment: Spiritual Practices for Decision Making*[4] or *Practicing Discernment Together: Finding God's Way Forward in Decision Making*[5] by Lon Fendall, Jan Wood, and Bruce Bishop. Both are excellent primers about discernment. There are other well-written books and articles to prepare the committee for discernment work. In addition, a spiritual director or consultant with experience in the process could be invited to the first meeting to give the committee guidance in discernment.

Either you or a consultant should facilitate the first meeting, which focuses on organizing and learning about discernment. Explain why you have gathered this discernment committee. If group members read a book, review the book briefly. Or if no reading was assigned, discuss what discernment is about and outline the process. Prepare a schedule for the discernment process. Make the assignment for the second meeting, when each member of the group will take up to eight minutes to share a time when he or she made an important decision and how that decision was made. This helps everyone to get to know each other and sets the stage for the person discerning to tell her story at the next meeting. If the discernment committee was established to work on a congregation matter, the pastor or congregational leader proposing the idea, or who knows the most about the issue, will be the one to tell the story about the concern at hand.

At the third meeting, the discerning person (or the person speaking on behalf of an idea) will have the floor. Let her tell her story and what she thinks God is fetching her to do. She might take up to thirty minutes. For the remainder of this meeting and at all subsequent meetings, the hearers will ask open-ended questions, allowing the discerner, in her answers, to hear what she is thinking and feeling about the potential decision. Questions that elicit deeper reflection can be as simple as, "Tell me more about that," or "How did you arrive at that conclusion?" or "Why do you think or feel that way?" The worst question to ask is "Don't you think that . . . ?" because this is not really a question but an attempt to guide someone into agreeing with the questioner's conclusion. Open-ended questions suggest the person asking the question really wants to hear the answer. Such a question is also intended to be a way for the person answering the question to delve deeper into an area that she may not have thought about or an idea not fully developed. When a question is answered thus: "I need to think about that for a minute," the discernment process is operating at its best. Reflecting upon and talking about something deeply important can clarify our thoughts and help us consider the strengths and weaknesses of what we are trying to decide. Listening to one another by asking open-ended questions is also important when the committee is discerning a congregational issue.

Before the final session the committee should meet in order to write what they have heard. The scribe should condense these notes into bullet points. Having a single written synopsis allows members to speak with anonymity, if necessary. At the final meeting, the chair can present what the committee is hearing from the Spirit. The discerner can ask the committee follow-up questions and should have an opportunity to share what she has heard from the Spirit as well. The chair and the church pastor should be available for a follow-up meeting with the discerner, especially if she was upset, or strongly disagreed with the report of the committee. If the discernment was about a fetching into ministry, for example, and the committee did not offer an affirmation, the person could be very disappointed. The purpose of the discernment committee is for the discerner to hear the Spirit while in the midst of a group who has committed to listen to the Spirit, even if it is not what she wanted to hear.

If the committee is considering a matter that affects the entire congregation, the facilitator and scribe will both need to take notes about what committee members have discerned in listening to the Spirit. Some people will not have heard anything from the Spirit, or will be ambivalent, and this should be recorded as well. The committee then should draft a document reflecting what the group has heard, including all voices (though not the names of the people). This document will then be shared with the pastor or congregational leaders in order to make a decision about next steps, including the possibility of not moving forward.

Discernment is a multi-layered process and is not easy work. I can hear the Spirit speaking while I am alone in my prayer, while reflecting in my journal, and working on my Integration Map. But, I believe I need a discernment committee to ask the difficult questions I may not ask myself. I pray the committee will see things in me that I may not see myself or am afraid to face. And I depend on them to help affirm, or not, that I am listening to the Spirit and not having a self-convincing conversation with myself. Indeed, the discernment process is an intimate experience conducted in public. The process is one of vulnerability for the discerner, but also for the hearers, because often members of the committee will find themselves processing their own discernment questions during the time together.

The discernment process is a way to move beyond our personal opinions in order to hear and trust the Spirit. To that end, the outcome of discernment is never someone saying, "I think you should do this or that." The committee's response is, "I am hearing you say . . . and it sounds to me like the Spirit might be saying . . ." What emerges out of discernment is sometimes, "Yes, I am ready to take this step," or sometimes, "No, I am not being fetched by God into church ministry." More often than not, what is heard from the Spirit is "wait" or "not now." The person discerning might say, "I need to spend some more time processing," or "I need more information," or "I thought I was discerning about this issue, but really, this other question emerged while I was listening to the Spirit." Working with a discernment committee can help us sort out what God is saying. When we have heard God in the midst of the discernment committee, we can feel a sense of courage instilled in our soul that will bolster us in following the path onto which we are being fetched, especially if the path is one we did not anticipate. As difficult as discernment might be—because it exacts the price of time, causes us to be honest with ourselves and with others, and sometimes even leads us into suffering when we do not hear what is pleasing—the discernment committee process is still reliable because when we stay steady with the process we will witness our community moving closer to God, we will discover answers to the God questions, and we will experience the fruit of the Spirit.

Once group discernment has been established as a practice among the people, those who have participated will become comfortable with this model in congregational matters. Those who have served on discernment committees can share their experiences with others in the congregation.

Remember, this is a long, slow pilgrimage. Most congregations are used to voting on congregational decisions based on the personal opinions of individuals (or what the individuals believe they have heard from the Spirit). Usually decisions are reached after long business meetings of discussion and debate. However, even though a church may continue to make decisions by the democratic process, a discerning community will only do so after they have done the hard work of hearing collectively what the Spirit is saying. Most discerning congregations will find at least one identifiable process, which includes discernment committees. They will learn to make decisions through seasons of prayer and silence, where the Spirit will guide them without having to vote on the issue.

THE WORK OF THE DISCERNING COMMUNITY

When the Spirit broods over the community like a hen over her chicks, the work of discernment becomes ripe with possibility. The work of the discerning community is twofold: to hear the Spirit's fetching and then to respond. In order to hear the Spirit, the church must be in constant discernment, sometimes considering new paths. In church life it often seems the congregation is traveling down a path laid out for them by those who founded the church years ago or by their denominational leaders. English poet, zoologist, and organizational consultant David Whyte wrote in *The Heart Aroused: Poetry and the Preservation of the Soul in Corporate America,* "In effect, if we can see the path ahead laid out for us, there is a good chance it is not our path; it is probably someone else's we have substituted for our own."[6]

The identity of the church and path of the church should not be confused. While the location of the church and denominational affiliation may never change, the path of the church could alter if the congregation is paying attention to God's guidance through regular discernment. A church founded in a vibrant downtown community fifty years ago should take a different path as it becomes an inner-city parish. The work of the now inner-city church, surrounded by a community totally different from the one that existed when it was founded, must be about the hard work of discerning what new path God is fetching them to walk.

A discerning community must desire to see the vision God has in store for them, a path unique to their generation, location, and resources. Only they can discern the path intended for them by the Spirit. I don't think visions are transferable. In other words, what our community is supposed to be doing in our neighborhood may not be what your congregation will discern is their ministry. My experience of leading out of this model is that if the community seeks to see the vision of the Spirit, they will see that vision because they work at discernment.

Discerning communities must be more interested in spiritual development than in the orchestration of numerical growth, though these concerns are not mutually exclusive. A leader who is a spiritual director will walk alongside the people, listening to their heart and to the voice of the Spirit. Together, the leader and the congregation will hear the Spirit and see the vision. Through prayer and discernment a vision will arise, uniquely suited for the spiritual growth of the congregation.

The vision may emerge as one word. Maybe three words will appear. Sometimes a phrase, rarely a full sentence will come to mind, but a meaningful word will make itself very prominent in the thinking of the leader and the community. The word or words may be "heard" while the leader and community are deep in prayer or *lectio divina*. The vision may be "seen" while the leader journals or the people are studying the Bible together. The visionary experience could be "tasted" during a season of fasting. Those who yearn to see the vision and know the heart of God's loving desire for the people will begin to collectively see the Spirit's vision for them. The pastor must have the courage to turn the vision over to the people and trust it is the work of God. If so, then the people will discern the vision for themselves and make it their own. The triune partnership of God, leader, and people will imagine God's vision for the congregation and together do the work required to live into the vision.

Shortly after arriving at St. Augustine's, I conducted a retreat for our leadership team and vestry. The congregation was at its lowest ebb in sixty years. We needed to discern how God was going to move us from a survivalist mode to one of hope. We used Diana Butler Bass's book *Christianity for the Rest of Us: How the Neighborhood Church Is Transforming the Faith*[7] as the basis for our time to study together. She writes, "discernment points the way, guides the way, and becomes the way—the way that begins with God-questions, that winds through wisdom, and ends in the healing of the world."[8] Our God-questions were simple: "Who have we been?" and "Who is God calling us to be?" One of the members of that vestry was a founding parishioner. All but two of the twelve had been at the church over twenty years. Our vestry relished having been founded as a university parish and hoped this would be their future. They took pride in having been a place where people gathered to celebrate and party. They also were a humble people who had been faithful to the Episcopal prayer traditions. We worked with their sense of the past as a way toward seeing a new vision.

The vestry could have said, "Yes, we want young people but we want them to do church the way we used to do church." These courageous leaders saw a new way ahead, knowing they might not live long enough to see the fruit of their sacrifices. Indeed, three of those vestry members have since died. But part of their legacy was to see how the past had been a foundation for a future that would look vastly different from what they could imagine. Leading through spiritual direction is a holistic process, encompassing the total life of the organization, involving as many people as possible, encouraging those who are current members to remember the stories of the past, while they work together, listening to the Spirit, in order to cast a vision of hope for the way things can be in the future. What emerged as the vision for our parish was three words: prayer, discernment, and hospitality. These three words are now the lens through which every idea, suggestion, and proposal are to be seen.

A discerning community with someone leading by spiritual direction can use the discernment process when considering any range of possibilities for the church: beginning new ministries, a building project, buying or selling property, significantly changing the church by-laws, starting or closing a school, creating a homeless ministry, or hiring a new pastor. Every congregation, with its leaders, will have to determine what constitutes a "major" decision in their context. When the idea, issue, or project emerges, however complicated, the congregation must rely on the Spirit to guide them in discerning whether it fits within the fabric of parish life, who they have been and who they are becoming. The key players involved might change from idea to idea. The resources needed to complete a project vary. The congregational politics underlying certain issues are sometimes murky. The theological implications can be hard to identify. If what we are working with is serious enough to engage in discernment, then we must take the time to sort it out. Some of the steps I will outline may be omitted because the idea seems fairly straightforward and not too complicated. However, the more complex the issue, the more involved the discernment, which may require additional committee work or town hall meetings. After using this model the leader and community could discover a different technique or step of discernment that best fits their community. Whatever steps are used, though, the leader should initiate his process first.

To do so, use the Integration Map to get a visual concept of the intricacies of the idea. The design of the discernment process must be based upon the complexity of the issue, who is or will be involved, how many people are affected, and the level and intensity the potential change may cause. The leader should meet with her spiritual director and mentors to discuss the matter and review her Integration Map. Her personal discernment may be about whether she is capable, or willing, to lead the parish through the discernment process and the start up of the project, especially if the new idea includes capital fund-raising, a major building project, or making a dramatic change in the way the community worships. Likewise, the person proposing a new ministry or idea should also engage in personal discernment. After individual discernment, at least one discernment committee within the congregation should focus on the decision. At least one town hall meeting should be designed for the church members to listen to one another and their leaders. There should also be a season of prayer and fasting for the congregation. Sometimes congregational discernment may involve a limited number of people and take only a few weeks. On the other hand, some issues may involve the entire congregation and take a year to process.

For example, let's say I am considering whether it would be hospitable to include one of the youth on our board (vestry). On the surface, this idea may seem simple enough, not needing a complicated or lengthy discernment process. However, after drawing my Integration Map for our congregation, and discussing the issue with my spiritual director and mentor, I can see many complexities in the community. (The concerns I point out might not be the same for your congregation, in which case you would not use all the steps I am going to offer in this example. But there could be a matter under consideration in your congregation that would indeed demand full-blown discernment.) In order to add a youth to our board we would have to change the by-laws. The congregation has never had someone under twenty-one on the board. We don't have a lot of youth, so the pool to draw from would be limited. And what if we go through the entire discernment process and in the end the board (the ultimate authority in our congregation) votes against idea? Whose feelings are going to get hurt and how angry will they be?

There are many ways to "make" this very commendable idea a reality. However, as the leader of a discerning community, and an adaptive leader (as discussed earlier in this book), I must take the risk of handing the vision I have discerned over to the people by allowing the idea to make its way through the discernment process. In a discerning community, good ideas, like having youth on the church board, may never come to a vote because what is heard in the discernment process may be "no" or "not now." This does not mean the idea is not a good one; it means the community may not be ready for the idea. In a purely democratic polity, I could promote the idea and most likely get it approved, using my leverage and charisma as the leader. (Of course, even in a democracy good ideas are voted down every day.) However, this is not the way of a discerning community, nor of a leader using spiritual direction. There is risk in relying on discernment. Sometimes good ideas will be jettisoned. The point of discernment, however, is not to promote the idea, but to enter into the process. Practically, then, how do I as a leader nurture the community through the discernment process after I have done my own discernment?

After using my Integration Map, I start with informal conversations with those in our community, with staff, other clergy, and lay leaders. These conversations are a way of testing the water for receptivity to the idea of adding a youth to our board. I ask a few of our leaders to be in prayer with me for a season, with the specific purpose of listening to the Spirit and discerning if they sense the idea of a young person being on our board should move forward.

The congregational process begins when I put together a discernment committee to listen to the Spirit and determine if the vision is indeed good for our community. In this way I am handing the idea over to others, trusting that if they cannot see the vision, then the community is not ready, at least not now or maybe ever. If the committee does not discern that this idea fits within the matrix of our community's vision of prayer, discernment, and hospitality, the idea needs to be dropped. If they have discerned now is not the time to present the idea, I can wait until another season when the timing could be better. However, if those to whom I have entrusted the vision see this idea as the way the Spirit is guiding us, then we begin to think about when and how to share the concept with the wider community.

There is always a best time to present an idea and I believe in trusting the natural rhythms of life. The liturgical year has beginnings and endings to teach us to be sensitive to the natural flow of time, and wise leaders move in concert with those. For example, if the discernment committee has been positive about adding a youth member to our board, we might consider offering the idea to the wider congregation at the beginning of the school year, when the congregation's focus is already on youth and children. When my leadership team and I, with the assistance of our discernment committee, feel the timing is best, I call the congregation and the board into a season of prayer and discernment. This could be for a month or six months, maybe longer depending on our sense of how much deep listening is needed by the congregation. The more serious the issue, or the more divided the congregation, the more time we will take in listening. People cannot feel rushed. They must be given time to discern what the Spirit is saying. I arrange for a series of town hall meetings. (Once again, some issues may not need every step I am describing. Depending on the complexity of the idea under discernment, town halls may not be necessary.)

An explanation about how these town hall meetings will be different from political town halls is given at the beginning of the meeting. Town hall meetings in a discerning community are like the second and third meeting of an individual discernment committee. This is a time when the congregational members can tell their own story and make their opinions heard. The people are also encouraged to ask open-ended questions of the leaders and one another. Granted, not every question will be open-ended, but a skilled leader can help shape questions as they are asked, so deeper listening can take place. I also set aside times for small group discussions, either at the town hall meetings or at subsequent gatherings.

During these meetings I use Eric Law's method of mutual invitation (discussed in chapter four), so everyone in the community has an opportunity to be heard. These conversation groups will give those who desire to participate a chance to hear what the community is hearing from the Spirit. The greater the number of people involved in the discernment process, the more likely there will be community buy-in, and the better chance for the sustainability of the work of having a youth on our board. (I recognize some congregations will make final decisions with a congregational vote. In such cases, the process leading up the congregational vote can be the same as I have described above.)

When we have reached the end of our season of discernment about whether to add a young person to our board, I place the item on the board agenda, because in our church polity, the board is the deciding group in changing by-laws. Because I develop the agenda, I can arrange the board meeting to allow ample time for each person on the board to be heard. Again, I use mutual invitation to give everyone an opportunity to share what he or she is thinking and feeling about the proposal. Then when the decision is to be made, several options are available. Admittedly, some decisions, such as changing a by-law, might demand a vote. Personally, I think voting lends itself to peer pressure and manipulation. (I discuss voting further below.) Therefore, in a situation like this I encourage the board to consider using secret ballots. Still, I have to ask, where is the voice of the Spirit in an "up" or "down" vote? Does voting in a faith community mean fifty-one percent of the people heard the Spirit and forty-nine percent did not? Indeed, the Spirit can work through voting or any other method; the Spirit can obviously do all things. However, the question is this: are we as a deciding body willing to take the final decision out of our hands and place the choice in the hands of God?

Another option is consensus building. Of course, this model can lead board members to think they need to set their personal feelings aside in order to "go along with the group." Peer pressure and manipulation might be even more significant factors in this method, because decision makers don't have the privacy of a ballot. Instead, the group might place two pieces of paper in a hat, one with "yes" and one with "no" written on it, then pray for the Spirit to decide, and draw out one slip of paper. Another method would be to ask each person to place his or her "yes" or "no" vote into the hat, pray for the Spirit to be present, and then draw.

While we might feel more comfortable with traditional decision-making methods, like voting, such methods might prevent our being stretched as much by the Spirit as we would be by drawing the answer out of a hat. Taking a chance at a new method moves individuals and groups out of their comfort zone and pushes them into a deeper listening of the Spirit, causing a richer and more complete discernment. The leader can pose different decision-making possibilities, but the group must wrestle with what is best and choose the technique. The decision-making technique is important to the group because they have to own the process while at the same time exhibiting they are vulnerable enough to allow the Spirit to fully participate in the decision. I believe we must find some way for us to demonstrate we are taking the risk of relying on the Spirit and not completely on our human intellect and opinion. Over time, I think it would be best if the group could arrive at some level of comfort about not voting on every issue. In a democratic society, we have become so accustomed to a majority-rule mentality that as people of faith, we potentially could confuse what we are hearing from the Spirit with our confidence in our opinions. We want God to be present and participate in our lives. We have trouble listening to one another. How can we listen to God if we cannot let go of our control in voting? We have free will. God will not control our minds in how we vote. God will only speak. Our job is to listen. Ironically, I have found that some groups feel the need to vote about the idea of not voting. By using unique and unfamiliar methods of decision-making about less critical issues the group can ease into the idea of making more complex decisions without voting.

I realize some groups may never be willing to draw the decision out of the hat and voting may be the only way to make a decision. But because I have spent a great deal of my life in professional and college sports, I believe situations creating winners and losers in churches only cause future problems. Often the losers in a contentious vote are constantly looking for another chance to win back what they feel they have lost. My experience has been that there is no such thing as a win-win scenario. Processes like discernment create an environment where each person will be able to accept the final decision, even if they disagree, and move on, rather than leaving the congregation or figuring out how to get the decision overturned. Words matter. If we use words like "win," then, indeed, there must be winners. When there are winners, then there are losers. Only the winners suggest there is such a thing as win-win. The winners achieved their goal and feel confident that they must be right, because they won. The losers, on the other hand, are waiting for a better day. There might be a final circumstance that is best for everyone, but my experience is that everyone will want his or her own definition of "best." Words are how we communicate, and some words, phrases, and terms should not be in the Christian lexicon. I believe "win-win" is one of those phrases.

Christians follow the path of Christ, who emptied and humbled himself. We are fetched to do the same. Leaders must move the people into thinking about decision-making as "give-give," where we put the needs of others first. We must use methods of discernment and decision-making that include an opportunity for everyone to be heard so that collectively the community can hear what the Spirit is saying. Discernment keeps the church focused on its vision, not allowing the congregation to be pushed by the winds of the latest successful program, or as one of our leaders likes to say, "the latest shining object" intended to grow the church.

A discerning community uses its practiced process to hear the Spirit when considering new programs and suggestions. If the community has discerned wisely before making the decision, then most likely the vast majority of the members will move forward after the decision has been made. We fervently pray that fewer congregants will have hurt feelings, because the decision has rested in the hands of the collective and the Spirit, not the ballot box. A discerning community will be willing to wait upon the Spirit and trust the process. If one more person feels included and one less person is hurt by a decision, then the process, while more complicated, is worth the time spent.

Decision-making is risky business, no matter how it is conducted. Even members of a discerning community guided by wisdom and vision will at times find themselves vehemently disagreeing with one another. When a decision has emotion attached to it, like my example of adding a youth member to the board, no matter what the outcome, some people could be upset or even angry. Families might leave the church. Pledges might be withdrawn. The leader could lose his job if numbers and money decline. In the face of conflict, the leader must continually hold a space for prayer and discernment in his own life, while inviting others to pray, discern, hear and trust the Spirit of God after the decision has been made.

When there is disagreement and even hurt, the community has a better chance of remaining intact if the leader as spiritual director has fostered a discerning community, one in which every voice, including the Spirit of God, has been heard. In times of harsh conflict, the congregation will find ways through prayer to stay in communion with one another. They can do so if they have made decisions for the sake of the community, which owns the vision, rather than individual agendas. Bringing those who are hurt and angry together with those who feel the best decision has been made is not easy work, but the strain is worth the effort. A spiritual director and leader will spend the necessary time with each party, separately, then together, in an effort to help the two groups find ways of listening with deep empathy to one another's stories. This could take months. Healing is possible when the two groups, or individuals, can take on a give-give attitude, reaching across the divide in the hope of being a servant to the other party.

We should not shy away from conflict, because if we can find ways to stay in communion, the community's capacity for discernment will deepen. When those in conflict have learned how to listen to someone they strongly disagree with in the presence of God, their hearts will soften and they will be better able to yield to the fetching of the Spirit. When God is fetching the entire community, we will be living out the Spirit's best vision for our life together.

Listening to the Spirit and to one another takes tremendous patience and precious time. A discerning community will take the necessary time—painstaking time—to listen to all the concerns of the congregation and then contemplate together in prayer, waiting upon the Spirit. Doing these things together—listening, contemplating, praying, and working through conflicts—the congregation will experience the Spirit speaking into the open space created within the congregation because they have spent sacred time together.

THE DISCERNING COMMUNITY IS LIFTED UP IN PRAYER

A discerning community must include members who are committed to pray daily for the leadership and the members. Congregations are full of small groups who meet for a variety of reasons, and most of these groups include prayer as an important part of their gathering. However, the church that is becoming a discerning community will have at least one small group whose sole reason for meeting is prayer.

Anglican theologian Martin Thornton wrote extensively about the ascetical remnant within the church. He was writing in the mid-twentieth century to pastors faced with apathetic and declining membership. He encouraged spiritual leaders to find those faithful ones among the dwindling community who would commit to practice spiritual disciplines and become the "spearhead" of the Spirit. He wrote in *The Heart of the Parish: A Theology of the Remnant*[9] that the remnant is not a "clique detached from the whole," but instead is the "palpitating heart" pumping "the blood of life to all the body." Thornton's vision for the church was that it would become a healthy organism "pervaded by the power of the Remnant's Prayer."[10] He built his theology of the remnant on the work of Jesus as the "director of souls"[11] for the disciples. Thornton saw the parish pastor as the spiritual director of the remnant, even one or two souls, who would be the heart, pumping the life of prayer into the church.

Thornton could easily have been writing to the mainline church in America today. The remnant is those members, no matter how few, who are on their own spiritual pilgrimage and who take seriously the practice of daily intercessory prayer for the church and their personal practice of spiritual disciplines, which often includes spiritual direction. The leader may know these folks are on a spiritual path similar to hers through conversations about prayer for the community or spiritual direction. This group is not the pastor's "inner circle." These people may not even know each other or know that others have a spiritual director. The remnant doesn't meet as "the remnant" or "pastor's discerning group." The remnant, however, is those faithful souls who are the salt for the community, flavoring and sustaining the community with the power of their prayer.

Leading through spiritual direction is not about appointing a particular small group to make those "special decisions" or to "whisper in the ear of the pastor." Rather, the purpose of leading through spiritual direction is to be the "director of souls" for those in the congregation who are willing to better listen to what the Spirit is saying to them individually and collectively. The hope is that the church will continue to mature in its understanding and practice as a discerning community and that the number of those who are a part of the fabric of the remnant will grow. These individuals might be attracted to one another by their similar spiritual interests and practices. Some of them might form small groups with the purpose of praying for the church members individually and as a community.

At St. Augustine's, we have two such groups. One is a local chapter of the ecumenical organization known as the Daughters of the King, whose members vow to pray for one another and the community they serve. Whenever they gather, it is for the sole purpose of praying for the congregation and those who request prayer. Before every service one to three of the Daughters gather with the liturgical party to pray for the worship service and all in attendance. Within the first month of being at St. Augustine's, our bishop made a parish visit. He and I were standing in the hallway with the other members of the worship team waiting for the start of the first service. He recognized two of the women standing with us as Daughters by the unique cross they wear. He turned to me and said, "You will always know you are being prayed for when you have Daughters in your congregation." We host another group known as the Canon Community of St. Mary of the Annunciation. This is an Episcopal neo-monastic, non-cloistered group of men and women whose primary spiritual practice is to be a praying community. As monks, they gather daily to offer prayers for our community and the world. St. Mary's is an ancient monastic model of a tiny group of people praying for the church and the world. These two groups are examples of the scriptural admonition that when two or three are gathered to pray daily for the community, the congregation will feel the presence and power of the Spirit. When we pray for one another, calling those in need by name, we are mindful of one another. The prayers of these two small (remnant) groups have changed our congregation. Moreover, these prayer groups have been spiritually shaped by God through their faithfulness to prayer, which is a reciprocally transformational power used by the Spirit in the discerning community.

Time to Start Walking Your Own Pilgrimage

I want to encourage you as a leader. In truth, no matter how you lead, there will always be risks. However, being a midwife to the spiritual development of a congregation, no matter the size, can bring the spiritual fruit of the Spirit that Paul writes about to the church in Galatia: "love, joy, peace, patience, kindness, generosity, faithfulness, gentleness, and self-control" (Gal. 5:22–23a). This fruit is born in the heart of the leader and those whom she guides.

Some of my greatest thrills as a leader have been watching others learn how to effectively lead while under the guidance of the Spirit.

Leadership is about our relationships with God, our self, and others. Spiritual direction is about these same relationships. When you lead as a spiritual director you will be developing your relationships with God and yourself and assisting others to enrich their own relationships with God, self, and others. These relationships are not built upon the expectations that God or my spiritual director will give me the right answers. Spiritual directors rarely give answers; my experience has been that God does so even less often. Instead, both the Spirit and the director have guided me to find the answers already existing within my soul. Leading through spiritual direction has the same purpose. The people must find their own answers. You are fetched to be the wisdom guide and spiritual director who will help them discover those answers. The pilgrimage will be a long, slow walk for everyone involved. The journey is not about the destination. Rather, it is about the transformation that will take place along the path. God be with you. Time to start walking.

Notes

INTRODUCTION

1. Jonathan Sacks, *The Dignity of Difference: How to Avoid the Clash of Civilizations* (London: Continuum, 2002), 12.
2. Huffington Post United Kingdom, "Scientists Find DNA Sequence Associated with Leadership Qualities," http://www.huffingtonpost.co.uk/2013/01/15/health-leadership-gene-dna-sequence_n_2479658.html
3. Bennett J. Sims, *Servanthood: Leadership for the Third Millennium* (Cambridge, MA: Cowley Publications, 1997).
4. Angela H. Reed, *Quest for Spiritual Community: Reclaiming Spiritual Guidance for Contemporary Congregations* (New York: T&T Clark International, 2011).
5. Sue Monk Kidd, "The Story-Shaped Life," *Weavings* 4, no. 1 (Spring 1989): 21.

CHAPTER 1

1. Francis Kelly Nemeck and Marie Theresa Coombs, *The Spiritual Journey: Critical Thresholds and Stages of Adult Spiritual Genesis* (Collegeville, MN: Liturgical Press, 1990), 69.
2. From a lecture presented for the Clergy Leadership Project, a program of Trinity Wall Street, May 4, 2011.
3. Martin Thornton, *Feed My Lambs: Essays in Pastoral Reconstruction* (Greenwich, CT: Seabury Press, 1960).
4. ——, *Spiritual Direction* (Cambridge, MA: Cowley, 1984).

5. ———, *The Heart of the Parish: A Theology of the Remnant* (Cambridge, MA: Cowley, 1989).

6. ———, *Feed My Lambs*, 21.

7. ———, *Heart of the Parish*, 192.

8. ———, *Prayer: A New Encounter* (Cambridge, MA: Cowley, 1988), 61.

9. Thomas Merton, *Spiritual Direction and Meditation* (Collegeville, MN: Liturgical Press, 1960).

10. Thomas Dubay, *Seeking Spiritual Direction: How to Grow the Divine Life Within* (Ann Arbor, MI: Servant Publications, 1993), 32–33.

11. Richard J. Foster, *Celebration of Discipline: The Path to Spiritual Growth* (San Francisco: HarperSan Francisco, 1988), 186.

12. To "respect the dignity of every human being" is taken from The Baptismal Covenant found in *The Book of Common Prayer*; it is the expectation of every baptized believer.

13. Dom Augustine Baker, seventeenth-century Benedictine monk, quoted in Merton, *Spiritual Direction* (Collegeville, MN: Liturgical Press, 1960), 20–21.

14. Dubay, *Seeking Spiritual Direction*, 77.

15. Morton Kelsey, *The Other Side of Silence: Meditation for the Twenty-First Century* (New York: Paulist Press, 1997), 261.

16. Thornton, *Spiritual Direction*, 25.

17. Ibid., 125–26.

18. Joyce C. Mills and Richard J. Crowley, *Therapeutic Metaphors for Children and the Child Within* (New York: Brunner/Mazel Publishers, 1986).

19. John O'Donohue, *Anam Cara: A Book of Celtic Wisdom* (New York: HarperCollins, 1997).

20. O'Donohue, *Eternal Echoes: Celtic Reflections on Our Yearning to Belong* (New York: HarperCollins, 1999).

Chapter 2

1. Margaret Guenther, *Holy Listening: The Art of Spiritual Direction* (Cambridge, MA: Cowley, 1992), 14.

2. Dietrich Bonhoeffer, *Creation and Fall: A Theological Interpretation of Genesis 1–3*. Trans. John C. Fletcher. (New York: The MacMillan Company, 1959), 35.

3. Ibid.

4. Henricus Renckens, *Israel's Concept of the Beginning: The Theology of Genesis 1–3*. (New York: Herder and Herder, 1964), 116. Quoted in Ray S. Anderson, *On Being Human: Essays in Theological Anthropology* (Grand Rapids, MI: William B. Eerdmans Publishing Company, 1982), 226.
5. Anderson, *On Being Human*, 71–72.
6. Carlton Stowers, "In the Line of Fire: When a Gunman Terrorized Worshipers at Wedgwood Baptist Church, One Unlikely Hero Summoned the Courage and Faith to Challenge a Killer," *Dallas Observer News*, October 7, 1999, www.dallasobserver.com/1999–10–7/news/in-the-line-of-fire/
7. Christian Smith with Patricia Snell, *Souls in Transition: The Religious and Spiritual Lives of Emerging Adults* (New York: Oxford University Press, 2009).
8. Ibid., 142.
9. Robert C. Fuller, *Spiritual, But Not Religious: Understanding Unchurched America* (New York: Oxford University Press, 2001).
10. Ibid., 76.
11. Katarina M. Schuth, "A Change in Formation: How the Sexual Abuse Crisis Has Reshaped Priestly Training," *America* 206, no. 1 (January 2, 2012): 17–20.
12. This is my own interpretation of Merton's words in his preface to *Mystics and Zen Masters* (New York: Noonday Press, 1966).
13. Karl Rahner, *The Mystical Way in Everyday Life: Sermons, Prayers, and Essays*. Ed. and trans. by Annemarie S. Kidder (Maryknoll, NY: Orbis Books, 2010), xv.

Chapter 3

1. Elizabeth Liebert, *The Way of Discernment: Spiritual Practices for Decision Making*, (Louisville, KY: Westminster John Knox Press, 2008), xix.
2. Martin Thornton, *Spiritual Direction*, 125.
3. Pierette Stokes, "Healing the Postmodern Soul," *Presence: An International Journal of Spiritual Direction* 17, no. 4 (December 2011), 33.
4. E. Glenn Hinson, *Spiritual Preparation for Christian Leadership* (Nashville: Upper Room Books, 1999).
5. Dietrich Bonhoeffer, *Life Together*. Ed. by Geffrey B. Kelly and trans. by Daniel W. Bloesch and James H. Burtness (Minneapolis: Fortress, 1996), 98–99.

6. Ibid., 98.

7. Miguel A. De La Torre, *Reading the Bible from the Margins* (Maryknoll, NY: Orbis Books, 2002), 35.

8. Geffrey B. Kelly and F. Burton Nelson, *The Cost of Moral Leadership: The Spirituality of Dietrich Bonhoeffer* (Grand Rapids, MI: W.B. Eerdmans, 2003), 58.

9. Ibid., 1.

10. Ibid., 17.

11. Ibid., 85.

12. Tom Rath, *StrengthsFinder 2.0* (New York: Gallup Press, 2007).

13. John S. Savage, *Listening and Caring Skills in Ministry: A Guide for Pastors, Counselors, and Small Groups* (Nashville: Abingdon Press, 1996).

14. Ibid., 7.

15. There is no authoritative source for this familiar quotation. But in an article in *Time* magazine, dated May 31, 1963, Barth recalled that "40 years ago he advised young theologians 'to take your Bible and take your newspaper, and read both. But interpret newspapers from the Bible.'" See http://ptsem.edu/Library/index.aspx?menu1_id=6907&menu2_id=6904&id=8450

16. George F. MacLeod, ed. Ronald Ferguson, *The Whole Earth Shall Cry Glory: Iona Prayers* (Glasgow, UK: Wild Goose Publications, 1985), p. 45. Quoted in J. Philip Newell, *Listening for the Heartbeat of God: A Celtic Spirituality* (New York: Paulist Press, 1997), 82–83.

17. Carl G. Jung, *Answer to Job* (Princeton, NJ: Princeton University Press/ Bollingen Paperback Edition, 1991), 24.

18. Thomas Merton, *Seeds of Contemplation* (Norfolk, CT: New Directions Books, 1949), 10.

19. Diana Butler Bass, *Christianity after Religion: The End of Church and the Birth of a New Spiritual Awakening* (New York: HarperOne, 2012), 186.

20. John D. Turner, trans. *The Book of Thomas the Contender, from Codex II of the Cairo Gnostic Library from Nag Hammadi*, www.gnosis.org/nag-hamm/bookt.html. From James McConkey Robinson, *The Nag Hammadi Library in English* (San Francisco, Harper Row, 1977). The following quote is translated in *The Other Bible*, ed. Willis Barnstone (New York: HarperCollins, 1984), 300. "Rather, the Kingdom is inside of you, and it is outside of you. When you come to know yourselves, then you will become known, and you will realize that it is you who are the sons of the

living Father. But if you will not know yourselves, you dwell in poverty and it is you who are that poverty."

21. Dietrich Bonhoeffer, ed. by Eberhard Bethge, trans. by Reginald Fuller. *Letters and Papers from Prison* (New York: MacMillan Publishing, 1967), 197.

22. Andreas Ebert and Marion Kustenmacher, eds. Trans. by Peter Heinegg. *Experiencing the Enneagram* (New York: Crossroad Publishing, 1992).

23. Ibid., 4–5.

24. The author has derived some of his dreamwork from Robert Bosnak's *Tracks in the Wilderness of Dreaming: Exploring Interior Landscape through Practical Dreamwork* (New York: Delacorte Press, 1996).

25. Adam S. McHugh, *Introverts in the Church: Finding Our Place in an Extroverted Culture* (Downers Grove, IL: Intervarsity Press, 2009), 124.

26. Peter M. Senge, *The Fifth Discipline: The Art and Practice of the Learning Organization* (New York: Doubleday/Currency, 1994), 277.

CHAPTER 4

1. Thomas Merton, *Thoughts in Solitude* (New York: Farrar, Straus and Cudahy, 1958), 86.

2. Loretta Stafford, *Dinah's Story: A Child with Prader-Willi Syndrome* (Fairfax, VA: Xulon Press, 2002), 48.

3. Albert Nolan, *Jesus Today: A Spirituality of Radical Freedom* (Maryknoll, NY: Orbis Books, 2006), 96.

4. Justo L. González, *The Story of Christianity: The Early Church to the Present Day* (Peabody, MA: Prince Press, 2004), 138–43.

5. Joan D. Chittister, *The Rule of Benedict: Insights for The Ages* (New York: Crossroad, 1992), 124.

6. Dietrich Bonhoeffer, *A Testament to Freedom: The Essential Writings of Dietrich Bonhoeffer.* Ed. by Geffrey B. Kelly and F. Burton Nelson (San Francisco: HarperOne San Francisco, 1995), 113.

7. ———, *Life Together*, 83.

8. Thomas Merton, *No Man Is an Island* (New York: Harcourt Brace, 1955), 261.

9. Morton Kelsey, *The Other Side of Silence*, 128.

10. Heifetz, *Leadership Without Easy Answers*, 2001.

11. Ibid., 127.

12. Ibid., 126.

13. Ibid., 243.

14. Ibid., 257.

15. Catherine Doherty, *Poustinia: Encountering God in Silence, Solitude and Prayer* (Combermere, ON: Madonna House Publications, 2000).

16. Ibid., 26.

17. Ibid., 111.

18. Catherine de Hueck Doherty, *Fragments of My Life* (Combermere, ON: Madonna House Publications, 2007), 200.

19. In Carl R. Rogers, ed., with Eugene T. Gendlin, Donald J. Kiesler, and Charles B. Truax, *The Therapeutic Relationship and Its Impact: A Study of Psychotherapy with Schizophrenics* (Madison, WI: University of Wisconsin Press, 1967).

20. Ibid., 9.

21. Ibid., 9.

22. Eric H. F. Law, *The Wolf Shall Dwell with the Lamb: A Spirituality for Leadership in a Multicultural Community* (St. Louis, MO: Chalice Press, 1993).

23. Dietrich Bonhoeffer, *Letters and Papers from Prison* (New York: MacMillan Publishing, 1953), 200.

24. Ibid.

25. Dietrich Bonhoeffer, *A Testament to Freedom*, 515.

CHAPTER 5

1. Anthony de Mello, *Heart of the Enlightened: A Book of Story Meditations.* Ed. by Stephen Mitchell (New York: Doubleday, 1989), 38.

2. John O'Donohue, *Anam Cara: A Book of Celtic Wisdom* (New York: Cliff Street Books, 1997), 195.

3. Richard Rohr, *Falling Upward: A Spirituality for the Two Halves of Life* (San Francisco: Jossey-Bass, 2011).

4. Ibid., xi.

5. David Kinnaman, "Pastors Love Books!," July 31, 2012, http://www.ecpa. org/news/98978/Barna-presents-research-on-Pastor-reading-habits.htm

6. Anne Lamott, *Bird by Bird: Some Instructions on Writing and Life* (New York: Pantheon Books, 1994). 15.

7. Brian D. McLaren, *A New Kind of Christianity: Ten Questions That Are*

Transforming the Faith (New York: HarperOne, 2010).

8. Rob Bell, *Love Wins: A Book about Heaven, Hell, and the Fate of Every Person Who Ever Lived* (New York: HarperOne, 2011).

9. Dietrich Bonhoeffer, *Letters and Papers from Prison* (New York: MacMillan, 1971), 369.

10. Susan Howatch, *Glittering Images* (New York: Knopf, 1987). There are six books in the series, which describes the history of the Church of England.

11. Alyce M. McKenzie, *Novel Preaching: Tips from Top Writers on Crafting Creative Sermons* (Louisville, KY: Westminster John Knox, 2010).

12. Cynthia Bourgeault, *The Meaning of Mary Magdalene: Discovering the Woman at the Heart of Christianity* (Boston: Shambhala, 2010), 148.

13. C.S. Lewis, ed., *Essays Presented to Charles Williams* (Grand Rapids, MI: Eerdmans, 1968), vi.

14. Charles Williams, *The Greater Trumps* (Grand Rapids, MI: Eerdmans, 1987).

15. Charles Williams, *Many Dimensions* (Grand Rapids, MI: Eerdmans, 2001).

16. Paul Elie, *The Life You Save May Be Your Own: An American Pilgrimage* (New York: Farrar, Straus, and Giroux, 2003), xiii.

17. John O'Donohue, *Benedictus: A Book of Blessings* (London: Random House, 2007).

18. C. G. Jung, *Memories, Dreams, Reflections* (New York: Vantage Books, 1989), 201.

19. Stanley Hauerwas, "Theology and Story," in *Truthfulness and Tragedy: Further Investigations in Christian Ethics* (Notre Dame, IN: University of Notre Dame Press, 1977), 73. Cited in Brad J. Kallenburg, *Ethics as Grammar: Changing the Postmodern Subject* (Notre Dame, IN: University of Notre Dame, 2001), 75.

20. Bruce Chilton, *Rabbi Jesus: An Intimate Biography* (New York: Double Day, 2000), 175.

21. David L. Bartlett and Barbara Brown Taylor, eds., *Feasting on the Word: Preaching the Revised Common Lectionary* (Louisville: Westminster John Knox Press, 2008).

22. Amy-Jill Levine and Marc Zvi Brettler, eds., *The Jewish Annotated New Testament: New Revised Standard Version Bible Translation* (New York: Oxford University Press, 2011).

23. Brian A. Brown, *Three Testaments: Torah, Gospel, and Quran* (Lanham,

MD: Rowman & Littlefield Publishing, 2012).

24. John Gardner, *The Art of Fiction: Notes on Craft for Young Writers* (New York: Vintage Books, 1983).

25. Kay L. Northcutt, *Kindling Desire for God: Preaching as Spiritual Direction* (Minneapolis: Fortress Press, 2009), 58.

26. Northcutt, 58.

27. Roy M. Oswald and Otto Kroeger, *Personality Type and Religious Leadership* (Herndon, VA: Alban Institute, 1998).

28. Oswald and Kroeger, 43.

29. Barbara Brown Taylor, *God in Pain: Teaching Sermons on Suffering.* (Nashville: Abingdon Press, 1998).

30. John R. Claypool IV, *The Preaching Event* (New Orleans: Insight Press, 2000).

31. Richard F. Ward, *Speaking of the Holy: The Art of Communication in Preaching* (St. Louis: Chalice Press, 2001), 19.

32. Claypool, *The Preaching Event,* 1.

33. Miroslav Volf, *Against the Tide: Love in a Time of Petty Dreams and Persisting Enmities* (Grand Rapids, MI: Eerdmans, 2010), 19.

34. Rebecca Barnes and Lindy Lowry, "7 Startling Facts: An Up Close Look at Church Attendance in America," http://www.churchleaders.com/pastors/pastor-articles/139575-7-startling-facts-an-up-close-look-at-church-attendance-in-america.html

35. Diana Butler Bass, *The Practicing Congregation: Imagining a New Old Church* (Herndon, VA: Alban Institute, 2004), 99.

CHAPTER 6

1. Diana Butler Bass, *Christianity for the Rest of Us: How the Neighborhood Church is Transforming the Faith* (San Francisco: HarperSanFrancisco, 2006), 95.

2. Richard Rohr, *The Naked Now: Learning to See as the Mystics See* (New York: Crossword Publishing, 2009), 158.

3. Ronald A. Heifetz, *Leadership Without Easy Answers,* 252.

4. See chapter 3, note 1.

5. Lon Fendall, Jan Wood, and Bruce Bishop, *Practicing Discernment Together: Finding God's Way Forward in Decision Making* (Newberg, OR: Barclay Press, 2007).

6. David Whyte, *The Heart Aroused: Poetry and the Preservation of the Soul in Corporate America* (New York: Currency Books, 2002), 89.

7. Butler Bass, *Christianity for the Rest of Us.*

8. Ibid., 97.

9. Thornton, *The Heart of the Parish,* 23.

10. Ibid., 24.

11. Ibid., 38.

CPSIA information can be obtained at www.ICGtesting.com
Printed in the USA
BVOW05s1154050614

355438BV00002B/3/P